CREATIVE
DEFENSE

CREATIVE DEFENSE

EVIDENCE AGAINST EVOLUTION

NICHOLAS COMNINELLIS, M.D.

Master
Books

First printing: September 2001

ISBN: 0-89051-357-0
Library of Congress Catalog Number: 01-91163

Unless otherwise noted, all Scripture is from the New International Version of the Bible.

Printed in the United States of America

Please visit our website for other great titles:
www.masterbooks.net

For information regarding publicity for author
interviews contact Dianna Fletcher at (870) 438-5288.

CONTENTS

Evolution is a process which has produced life from non-life, which has brought forth man from an animal, and which may conceivably continue doing remarkable things in the future. In giving rise to man, the evolutionary process has, apparently for the first and only time in the history of the Cosmos, become conscious of itself.

— Theodosius Dobzhansky

All flesh is not the same flesh: but there is one kind of flesh of men, another flesh of beasts, another of fishes, and another of birds (1 Cor. 15:39; KJV).

CHAPTER ONE

STRATEGIC INSTRUCTION

A heated battle is being fought throughout the world today. Unlike military combat fought with the armament of guns and missiles, this battle is waged using powerful ideas as weapons. Unlike civil unrest demonstrated in public, this conflict is played out in classrooms, churches, and universities. And unlike soldiers who train via marksmanship and physical exercise, troops in this war must be prepared through prayer, patience, and remarkable wisdom.

The battle is over the truth of the origin of life and the universe. It's a battle about beginnings — about identifying the birthplace of everything that exists.

Yet this all occurred some time ago. So why is it important today to understand how it all began? In short, knowing the truth about our origin is essential because of how it affects our understanding of human nature. Our attitudes toward ourselves and toward other people, and the way we treat them, are profoundly influenced by where we believe we came from. If people are actually just the end result of billions of years of chance biochemical reactions, as evolution proposes, then the inherent value of human life is very low. People can justifiably view themselves and others as no different or better than any other animal.

But the truth is that people were specifically designed by an intelligent Creator, with care and attention to each cell, organ system, and individual person. Human beings possess far more inherent value and complexity than any other object that could possibly be designed or built.

The truth about our origin also has a great impact on our concept of God and on our interaction with Him. If humans are, as evolution says, an accidental by-product of biological mutations, it's a strong argument against the existence of any superhuman power or intelligence.

But in truth we are actually the craftsmanship of an astounding God who planned the universe, humans, and all other creatures. This is a person whom everyone simply must learn about and get to know.

We are in a war — evolution's war against the truth about creation. The stakes are extremely high, and virtually every person on the planet is at risk. It's a war which touches on people's most inner convictions. It's a war where passions flare. It's a war over life — physical life, spiritual life, and even eternity.

WHY ANOTHER BOOK?

The war against evolution is being fought by people from all walks of life: students, professors, scientists, teachers, writers, parents, and pastors. The most important soldiers in this war are people like you and me — individual Christians who take advantage of opportunities to speak up and explain the truth about creation.

Yet, mounting an effective defense and answering people's legitimate questions can be very challenging. The issues are complex, and often demand that we draw upon information from the fields of cosmology (study of the universe), geology, relativity, chemistry, physics, statistics, biology, genetics, paleontology, and archaeology — information that few Christians have readily available. Too often we neglect to speak up or to take a stand because we feel inadequate to defend the truth. But this need not continue!

The objective of this book is to give Christians easy access to the most useful resources to defend the reality about creation. Used in conversations, presentations, and research papers, this book will help make the explanation of the truth more complete, compelling, and convincing. It will also help to greatly reduce the necessary preparation time.

ORGANIZED RESOURCES

A great wealth of information has been written on the vast subject of creation and evolution. My intention has been to survey the information, identify the major concepts, and provide the best supporting evidence available. *Creative Defense* organizes information on several levels:

- **Chapters.** Each chapter contains a group of related concepts.
- **Concepts.** The major themes of the creation/evolution debate.

- **Rationale.** An intentionally brief discussion of the reasoning and explanation behind the concepts.
- **Evidence.** Quotes from recognized authorities that lend credibility to the concepts and rationale.

Please note the following information with regard to the selection and use of quotes and references:

- Every effort has been made to include evidence from the most recognized leaders in their fields, published in the most widely respected scientific journals.
- Some quotes and references are older than those commonly used on other topics. This is intentional. First, they help to provide an important historical perspective on the subjects. They also represent conclusions of some of the best thinkers and researchers of all time. And in some cases, they present the only evidence available on certain themes.
- Most quotes contained herein could be included under more than one concept heading, although in most cases I have limited them to the single one most useful. However, a few quotes are so beneficial that they are included under more than one heading.
- When an asterisk precedes the quotation, the information enclosed is a direct quote from the publication. If there is no asterisk, the information listed is a summary of the publication.
- Care has been taken to assure accuracy of the quotes and references. Any corrections or additional resource recommendations would be gladly received.

CREATING YOUR PRESENTATION

Through excellent preparation you can take full advantage of your opportunities to speak out. The general principles for planning a written or spoken presentation should always be followed, including these:

- Start well in advance.
- Thoroughly research your subject and select the concepts to present.
- Create an outline for your presentation.
- Have others edit your writing or critique your speech.

In addition, a paper or lecture on creation will be more successful if the following special guidelines are also used:

1. Be appropriate for your audience.

Become familiar with the people you are going to address. Your presentation must be appropriate to their level of understanding and to their felt needs. Otherwise, they may not clearly comprehend your message, or they may disregard your address as irrelevant. It is especially important in advance to know your audience's understanding of:

- *Creation.* If your audience is chiefly made up of people who already trust in the biblical account of creation, then your aim will likely be to increase their understanding, answer specific doubts, and enhance their own ability to communicate the truth. But if they are uncertain about creation, or are committed to evolution, then your approach must be quite different. You'll likely need to first describe the concept of creation, explain its evidence, and show the flaws in evolution.

- *God.* If your audience already has faith in Jesus, or at least in the concept of a personal God, then you can more readily quote the Bible as evidence, for they already recognize its authority. But if your audience does not have this foundation, then you will likely need to back up and first explain a rationale for faith. Then you can more effectively refer to the Bible as reliable evidence.

- *Science.* Discussions surrounding creation and evolution regularly involve reference to some concepts in science. Be certain to tailor your presentation to the scientific understanding of your audience. They may, for example, already know how to use exponential numbers or how to calculate probability. But if they don't, you'll likely need to first explain these concepts if you're going to use them as evidence in your presentation.

By understanding the makeup of your audience, you can select and present the most appropriate concepts, and do so in a way they will best understand.

2. Be aware of bias.

A major obstacle to accepting the truth about creation comes from each person's bias. *Bias* means our tendency to find what we first decided we want to find, rather than what's actually present. It means our inclination to see what we really desire to see, rather than observing the trust about what actually exists.

Bias is everywhere. For example, many people still erroneously believe that whites make better students, and blacks make better athletes, or that men should be pilots and women should be flight attendants. Bias keeps people from seeing the truth.

Investigating ideas of creation and evolution tends to magnify people's bias even more sharply. Some individuals don't want to be confronted with a truth that may force them to rethink their entire perspective on God, history, science, and the value of human life. They find it easier to just dig in their heels, hanging onto ideas that have little support, rather than to look at the facts and reconsider.

Help your audience overcome the obstacle of bias. In your presentation, it is important to:

- Point out that each person has an individual bias.
- Ask them to identify their bias regarding creation versus evolution.
- Challenge them to disregard their bias and reconsider the evidence.
- Ask them to be willing, if necessary, to change their views about creation.

Denying reality has its costs. We may dispute the existence of gravity or electricity on the grounds that we cannot see them. But they will nevertheless make us fall or give us a jolt. Similarly, clinging to false ideas about origins causes people to totally miss some of the most remarkable aspects of life. Be certain to help your audience to recognize and overcome the power of individual bias.

3. Work within the allocated space and time.

Your presentation will almost always need to fit within a certain number of minutes or pages. Know in advance what is your allotment. This way, you can adjust the length of your discussion so that you cover the material successfully. Creation is an extremely broad subject. If you do not have much time or space to work with, it is usually better to focus a presentation on a small component, such as one or two key concepts, rather than attempt to address the entire subject.

4. Use visual aids.

In our media-driven culture, your ability to convince an audience may depend more upon the quality of your presentation than on the quality of your arguments. Employ creative visual aids such as photos, illustrations, and charts to draw attention, add vividness, and make your presentation easier to understand and remember. Make full use of the innumerable ready-to-use visual aids then can be downloaded via the Internet. The extra time invested will likely lead to a greater impact upon your audience.

Watch Your Attitude

Be very clear about what you wish to accomplish. Certainly we intend to help people understand the truth about creation. We want them to be convinced of the facts, and to pass on these truths to others. But there is much more at heart. We want them to also understand and personally trust in the Creator.

Attitude is essential. Our objective is to ultimately point people toward Jesus — not simply to win an argument. An audience has a keen way of knowing whether or not the speaker or writer is really concerned about them, or is just trying to dominate the discussion. If they believe it's the latter, they will often dismiss the speaker, in spite of his or her skill. For this reason, Peter reminds us:

> But sanctify Christ as Lord in your hearts, always being ready to make a defense to everyone who asks you to give an account for the hope that is in you, yet with gentleness and reverence (1 Pet. 3:15, NASB).

Gentleness and reverence is particularly essential, for some people's strongest passions are kindled through debates over creation and evolution. By maintaining a content, honest, and caring attitude — in spite of others' arguments and accusations — you will earn respect and credibility.

So pray about your opportunities, that both your temperament and your words will be trustworthy, that your audience will be receptive and open-minded, and that the Holy Spirit will be at work. These notes and quotes, joined with a healthy attitude and prayerful preparation, will help you to motivate people to both understand the truth about creation and to personally trust the Creator.

PART ONE

—

PRESENT
THE
POSITIONS

CHAPTER TWO

CREATION DEFINED

T he first step in preparing a creative defense is to thoroughly understand both the truth and the opposition. In the next two chapters we will review the concepts of both creation and evolution. It is essential that you be thoroughly familiar with them both.

No other plausible explanation exists for how life began, aside from creation or evolution. A third possibility is sometimes mentioned: that life was brought to earth from another planet, such as Mars. In the 1990s, meteorites from Mars were discovered in Antarctica. They were initially thought to contain impressions of tiny creatures, and a wave of speculation abounded. Scientific evidence now disproves this possibility. But even if life came to Earth from another planet, it only moves the question of creation versus evolution further away, and adds the enormous obstacles of transporting such life.

Douglas Futuyma is candid in presenting the options:

> Creation and evolution, between them, exhaust the possible explanations for the origin of living things. Organisms either appeared on the earth fully developed or they did not. If they did not, they must have developed from pre-existing species by some process of modification. If they did appear in a fully developed state, they must indeed have been created by some omnipotent intelligence.[1]

George Sim Johnston, in his book *The Genesis Controversy*, further explains:

In other words, it's natural selection or a Creator. There is no middle ground. This is why prominent Darwinists like G.G. Simpson and Stephen Jay Gould, who are not secretive about their hostility to religion, cling so vehemently to natural selection. To do otherwise would be to admit the probability that there is design in nature — and hence a Designer.[2]

The appearance of the universe (the solar system, planets, and stars) prompts many people to believe there must be a Designer behind it all. Investigations into human physiology and our genetic code persuade certain thinkers to concur with the impossibility that life originated by chance. Examining the conflicting claims and fragile support for evolution convinces a great many people to hold out for a more realistic explanation for their own existence.

The Christian perspective is that the universe and all forms of life were intentionally designed and created by God. Many scientists, religious people of other faith, and philosophers also agree.

Unfortunately today, even many people who identify themselves as Christians are calling into question the Bible's obvious explanation of our origins. Davis Young, in *Christianity and the Age of the Earth*, explains:

> It cannot be denied, in spite of frequent interpretations of Genesis One that departed from the rigidly literal, that the almost universal view of the Christian world until the eighteenth century was that the Earth was only a few thousand years old. Not until the development of modern scientific investigation of the Earth itself would this view be called into question within the church.[3]

THE "ORIGINAL" EXPLANATION: GENESIS CHAPTER ONE

God, by definition, is unlimited in power, knowledge, and insight. There are no boundaries on what He can do or what process He chooses. God could have formed the universe by any method, over any period of time He desired. No "laws of nature" could impede His choices, when in fact He himself is the Creator and controller of these laws.

Amid truly infinite options, how did God actually create life and the universe? Genesis, the first book of the Bible, gives the only eyewitness account — God's account — of our origins. It is essential that each of us defending the truth of creation be very familiar with the seven days of Genesis.

• **Day One** — Genesis 1:1–5

In the beginning God created the heavens and the earth. Now the earth was formless and empty, darkness was over the surface of the deep, and the Spirit of God was hovering over the waters. And God said, "Let there be light," and there was light. God saw that light was good, and he separated the light from the darkness. God called the light "day," and the darkness he called "night." And there was evening, and there was morning — the first day.

These very first sentences from the Bible describe the origin of the four obvious dimensions: time, energy, space, and matter: "In the beginning" (time) "God created" (energy) "the Heavens" (space) "and the Earth" (matter). Genesis initially characterizes our planet as only a formless mass suspended in the empty universe.

• **Day Two** — Genesis 1:6–8

And God said, "Let there be an expanse between the waters to separate water from water." So God made the expanse and separated the water under the expanse from the water above it. And it was so. God called the expanse "sky." And there was evening, and there was morning — the second day.

God gave greater form to the earth in the second day. Many scholars believe that at that time our atmosphere contained very dense water vapor which blanketed the planet, similar to the gases covering Venus today. This water vapor blanket is sometimes referred to as a "canopy," one which likely produced a greenhouse effect, causing tropical-like climate over the entire planet. It is further proposed that this canopy protected earth's inhabitants from cosmic radiation, and may even be credited with promoting the remarkable life expectancy of the first humans.

• **Day Three** — Genesis 1:9–13

And God said, "Let the water under the sky be gathered to one place, and let dry ground appear." And it was so. God called the dry ground "land," and the gathered waters he called "seas." And God saw that it was good. Then God said, "Let the land produce vegetation: seed-bearing plants and trees on the land that bear fruit with seed in it, according to their various kinds." And it was so. The land produced vegetation: plants bearing seed according to their kinds and trees bearing fruit with seed in it according to their kinds. And God saw that it was good. And there was evening, and there was morning — the third day."

God further added form to the earth on the third day by raising up the continents from the ocean floor, causing the appearance of dry land. Also on this day, God created all plant life, mature vegetation ready to reproduce "according to its kind," meaning to multiply repeatedly its very own species.

- **Day Four** — Genesis 1:14–19

And God said, "Let there be lights in the expanse of the sky to separate the day from the night, and let them serve as signs to mark seasons and days and years, and let them be lights in the expanse of the sky to give light on the earth." And it was so. God made two great lights — the greater light to govern the day and the lesser light to govern the night. He also made the stars. God set them in the expanse of the sky to give light from darkness. And God saw that it was good. And there was evening, and there was morning — the fourth day."

The entire universe outside the earth, the sun, moon, solar system, and billions of galaxies containing stars, was produced on the fourth day. It is remarkable to note that the plants created on day three would have been dependent upon the sunlight that appeared the following day. God also apparently recognized that soon humans would be using the sun and stars as a means of measuring time.

- **Day Five** — Genesis 1:20–23

And God said, "Let the water teem with living creatures, and let birds fly above the earth across the expanse of the sky." So God created the great creatures of the sea and every living and moving thing with which the water teems, according to their kinds, and every winged bird according to its kind. And God saw that it was good. God blessed them and said, "Be fruitful and increase in number and fill the water in the seas, and let the birds increase on the earth." And there was evening and there was morning — the fifth day.

On the fifth day, God filled the earth with very specialized creatures, fish appropriately designed for life under water, and birds with all the unique features required for flight through the skies.

- **Day Six** — Genesis 1:26–31

And God said, "Let the land produce living creatures according to their kinds: livestock, creatures that move along the ground, and wild animals, each according to its kind." And it was so. God made the wild animals according to their kinds, the livestock according to their kinds, and all the creatures that move along the ground according to their kinds. And God saw that it was good.

Then God said, "Let us make man in our image, in our likeness, and let them rule over the fish of the sea and the birds of the air, over the livestock, over all the earth, and over all the creatures that move along the ground." So God created man in his image, in the image of God he created him; male and female he created them. . . . God saw all that he had made, and it was very good. And there was evening, and there was morning — the sixth day."

The sixth day marks the introduction of God's most complex creatures. With dry land for habitation and plants for food, the stage was set for creation of varieties of mammals, reptiles, and other land dwellers. Finally, God wrapped up His creative work by producing the first man and woman. Unlike any of the earlier living things, God said that humans were created in His image, indicating that men and women most closely reflect God himself and that we share important characteristics with our Creator.

• **Day Seven** — Genesis 2:1–3

Thus the heavens and the earth were completed in all their vast array. By the seventh day God had finished the work he had been doing; so on the seventh day he rested from all this work. And God blessed the seventh day and made it holy, because on it he rested from all the work of creating that he had done.

Seemingly as a way of marking and celebrating the events of creation, God reserved the seventh day as an interval for reflection and refreshment and as a model for humankind to follow in the future.

In summary, Genesis chapter 1 provides us a consolidated description of our origins — God's step-by-step report on the beginnings of our universe and life itself. God's design and initiation of the universe is often termed "special creation." While Genesis leaves unanswered any number of questions concerning just "how" God created it all (His technique or processes), the description emphasizes that it all happened suddenly, and under God's clear control.

CREATED SPECIES COMPLETED

In biological terms, a particular species is defined as those similar creatures which can reproduce offspring with one another. All house cats, for example, are members of the same species, *Felis catus*. They can

THE SIX DAYS OF CREATION

DAY 1

DAY 2

DAY 3

DAY 4

DAYS 5 AND 6

mate with one another and produce kittens. Genesis chapter 1 refers to God creating groups of creatures according to their "kind," according to their unique characteristics. From the context of Genesis, the term "kind" is very closely equivalent to the biological term "species."

Among invertebrates, protozoa, worms, snails, sponges, jellyfish, lobsters, and bees are all different basic species. Among the vertebrates, the fishes, reptiles, amphibians, and birds are clearly different species. Within reptiles, turtles, crocodiles, and snakes are recognized as different species. Among the mammals we have bats, hedgehogs, rabbits, rats, dogs, cats, lemurs, monkeys, orangutans, chimpanzees, and gorillas, each of which can also be easily assigned to different species.

All creatures lived together.

Genesis makes clear that each "kind" (each species) that has ever existed was created, and therefore lived together, during the six days of creation. What's more, on the seventh day, God "finished the work He had been doing," and "rested from all the work of creating that He had done." This clearly indicates that no new species were forthcoming. God had finished producing all the "kinds" of creatures that were ever to roam the earth.

The fact that God finished completing the species does not exclude the possibility that varieties may occur within those species. Many species seem to have been outfitted from the beginning with enough genetic diversity to allow for several varieties. Today among the species of house cats, *Felis catus*, we find numerous varieties, or breeds, including Burmese cats, Persian cats, rag doll cats, Siamese cats, exotic short-hair cats, and a host of others. But regardless of their breed, they are all still members of the same species, *Felis catus*.

Similarly, all human beings belong to one species, *Homo sapiens*. There exists some variation among us, variation that we frequently refer to as ethnicity. But whether Blacks, Caucasians, Latinos, or Asians, we all possess the same fundamental genetic makeup. We are all still distinctly human, all part of the species *Homo sapiens*, and very unique compared with any other species.

Genesis declares that species are each unique, and that all were created at the beginning of the universe. No new species have appeared since that time. Variations we observe within species do not present a challenge to this position.

In stark contrast, however, evolution holds that transformation takes place from one species into another. Evolution explains that over many millions of years a primitive cell reproduced itself into progressively more complex species, leading to the divergence of life forms we witness today. This will be discussed more in chapter 3.

Early History of the World

Genesis goes on to explain some very important events that help us understand the world as we know it today. A grasp of Genesis chapters 2 through 8 can have a profound impact on how we view geology, human history, and God's relationship with humankind.

• Genesis Chapter 2

In the Middle East region of modern-day Iran, God selected a special location. Popularly termed the "Garden of Eden," it was here that the first created humans, Adam and Eve, were situated. It is clear from Genesis that God desired a personal relationship with the first couple. He spoke with them and strolled with them in the Garden.

But God also established some guidelines. Adam and Eve were free to consume fruit from any tree in the Garden expect for one, the Tree of the Knowledge of Good and Evil. Alternatively, there also existed another special tree, the Tree of Life. From this tree they were invited to eat without limitation.

• Genesis Chapter 3

Later in the Bible we learn of a cataclysmic event that had earlier taken place in heaven. One of God's leading angels, Satan, had challenged God's authority, and as a result was banished from heaven. On earth, Satan disguised himself in the form of a serpent and taunted Adam and Eve, enticing them to disobey God's single command. The couple eventually gave in and ate the fruit from the restricted tree. Immediately the two sensed disgrace and tried to conceal themselves from God. But the deed could not be undone. Trust (the very essence of their relationship with God) was dissolved. Adam and Eve were banished from both the presence of God and from life in the Garden.

• Genesis Chapters 4 and 5

These chapters document the turbulent life of the very first family. Adam and Eve had children, initially two boys named Cain and Abel. Their relationship, however, was marked by extreme jealousy; jealousy to the point that Cain ultimately killed his own brother. In spite of this crisis, the extended family of Adam and Eve continued to multiply over several generations, highlighted by the birth of Noah, a remarkable individual in the history of humankind.

• Genesis Chapters 6 through 8

God became very disappointed with the people He had created, noting that "the wickedness of man was great on the earth, and that every intent of the thoughts of his heart was only evil continually." God was sorry He had ever made humankind, and chose to wipe out our entire species, as well as the other creatures.

But there remained a very bright spot. Noah "was a righteous man, blameless in his time," and "found favor in the eyes of the Lord." So God instructed Noah to construct a gigantic boat, the ark, and to fill it with a male and a female of each species of animal. Genesis indicates that this huge project took Noah 120 years to complete.

Once Noah, his family, and the animals were shut inside the finished ark, it began to rain. The vast canopy of moisture in the atmosphere showered downward, causing the flood waters to rise above earth's highest mountains. In the process, every living animal (with likely exception of the fish) was killed, and the geography of the globe was greatly altered by the powerful torrential waves.

In spite of the chaos outside, those in the ark remained safe. Genesis explains that after 150 days the water began to recede and dry land appeared once again. The ark was pried open and the creatures set free to replenish the planet. Research has uncovered significant and fascinating geological and anthropological evidence that is consistent with Noah's flood. More about this will be presented in later chapters.

SEARCHING FOR SCIENTIFIC EVIDENCE

For many Christians, confidence in the Genesis account is taken at face value. They do not feel that further scientific evidence is necessary to collaborate the events described. This perspective, however, will not fulfill the legitimate questions of most non-Christians, particularly those of a scientific persuasion. In addition, some Christians have very honest doubts about the Genesis account and desire to reconcile their faith with these doubts.

The most reliable scientific support for a hypothesis comes from observing and testing it in the here and now. Ideally, several different investigators would examine the hypothesis at different times. If the hypothesis were indeed true, all the researchers would come to the same conclusion.

When it comes to studying past, non-repeatable events in history, however, the usual scientific support is impossible. In the case of creation, the event is not repeatable and there were no human eyewitnesses. Multiple experts cannot test it in a laboratory.

From a scientific perspective, the only reasonable approach is to look for signs of what happened in the past and draw the best conclusions possible. When dealing with the origin of life and the universe, evidence can be gleaned from three main sources: probability of the events ever happening by chance alone, the age of the earth, and the fossil record of these earlier events. If everything were indeed created according to the Genesis account, we would expect to find:

> • The probability of spontaneous life is extremely low. Since living beings are so unique and enormously complex, we should find that the mathematical probability of them appearing due to chance alone is very, very low.
> • The age of the earth is quite young. The age of the earth and the universe described in the Bible is essentially very short, on the order of 6,000–10,000 years. Since all life was created simultaneously, a longer time frame is unnecessary to explain

its existence by means of evolution. Our scientific findings should confirm that our planet is indeed quite young.

• The fossil record shows only modern creatures. God created all species at the beginning of time, and no new species have appeared since then. Therefore, we would expect to find only fossils that demonstrate modern creatures, accounting for those species that have become extinct over the years. Fossils should reveal only fully formed plants and animals, with no sign of any primitive or transitional life forms, new species that evolution proposes lead up to all modern creatures.

IT'S A BATTLE!

Surveys show that the majority of Americans believe that life and the universe were supernaturally created. The remarkable attributes of our planet and living creatures just cannot be reasonably explained by any other means. George Washington expressed this view when he stated:

> It is impossible to account for the creation of the universe without the agency of a Supreme Being. It is impossible to govern the universe without the aid of a Supreme Being. It is impossible to reason without arriving at a Supreme Being.[4]

Still, people hold a wide difference of opinion concerning the details of creation: the identity of the creator, how long ago creation took place, and the development of life since that time. Often, these are the result of evolution's not-so-subtle influence.

Other people entirely reject creation as a rational alternative and advocate, sometimes radically, an entirely atheistic approach to origins. Charles Darwin, credited with the theory of evolution, clearly expressed his bias when proclaiming:

> The Old Testament, from its manifestly false history of the earth, was no more to be trusted than the sacred books of the Hindoos, or the beliefs of any barbarian. The New Testament is a damnable doctrine. [I can] hardly see how anyone ought to wish Christianity to be true.[5]

As a spokesperson for the Christian view, it is essential to understand, present, and defend the Bible's explanation, not some amalgamation with other ideas. An effective defense demands that we familiarize ourselves with other positions. But when it comes our turn to present the truth, we can make no concession, no compromise over the origin of the universe or of life itself.

CHAPTER THREE

EVOLUTION DEFINED

Any defense of a position must include a thorough understanding of the opposition. "Creationists," those people who hold that life and the universe were intentionally designed and produced by God, must also understand evolution, its beliefs, history, and supposed evidence. The process will help us solidify our own position, and make us much better prepared to present our case to others who are uncertain or who flatly disagree.

Before the widespread introduction of evolution, the great majority of people took for granted that God directly created the earth and all living species, just as the Genesis account explains. History records that most of our great scientists of the 17th and 18th centuries concurred with this viewpoint.

But this was all about to change. In 1859, the book *Origin of Species by Means of Natural Selection* was published by Charles Darwin. The subtitle was both equally important and revealing: *The Preservation of Favored Races in the Struggle for Life*. In this book, and subsequent editions, Darwin proposed that in the ancient past a single cell formed at random from the chemicals that happened to be present. Over the ensuing millions of years this first cell repeatedly mutated and reproduced, adapting to its environment and becoming more complex over time. Today, the visible result of this evolutionary process is many thousands of extremely varied and complex species.

ANCIENT EVOLUTIONISTS

Charles Darwin did not originate the theory of evolution, though he is frequently credited with doing so. Ernest L. Abel explains:

> Although it is customary to credit the inception of this theory to Charles Darwin and his immediate predecessors, a rudimentary form of this notion can be traced back to the beginnings of written history itself. In fact, the belief that life had its origins in a single basic substance is so widespread among the various peoples of the world, primitive or civilized, that it can be considered one of the few universal themes in the history of ideas.[1]

Prior to the influence of Christianity, evolutionary thought was almost universal among ancient religions and philosophies. In Greece and Rome, the Gnostics, Stoics, and Epicureans denied creationism and instead viewed the universe as eternal, without beginning or cause. Their predecessors, ancient religious leaders of Egypt and Babylonia, viewed origins in a similar light. Noted author Michael Denton summarizes this history:

> Even some primitive mythologies express the idea that life in all its diverse manifestations is not the creation of the gods but a purely natural phenomenon being the result of normal flux of the world. The ancient Norse, for example, held that the first living beings, the giant Ymir and the primordial cow Audumla, were formed gradually from the ice melted by the action of a warm wind which blew from a southern land Muspellsheim, the land of fire.[2]

Most noted among ancient evolutionists, the famous Greek philosophers perpetuated their views:

> Aristotle believed in a complete gradation in nature, a progressive development corresponding with the progressive life of the soul. . . . He put his facts together into an Evolution system which had the teaching of Plato and Socrates for its primary philosophical basis.[3]

Some influential writers preceded Darwin himself by a few years. One prominent evolutionist was Alfred Russel Wallace, a self-taught naturalist and leader of a spiritualist movement. Another was Edward Blyth, who in 1835 and 1837 published two papers in which he considered the effects of natural selection.

Origin of the "Origin"

Nevertheless, it is Darwin who is widely credited with the theory of evolution. How did Darwin's ideas originate? His grandfather was a noted physician, who became famous in his own right for literature addressing evolution, among other subjects. Charles initially considered a career in medicine, in spite of his poor scholastic record. He entered Cambridge University in 1828, and ultimately graduated with a degree, not in medicine, but in theology. His memoirs show that, while not entirely satisfied with his career choice, Darwin intended to become a minister somewhere in rural England.

Darwin's immediate career plans were placed on hold when he received a letter from Captain Fitzroy. This noted Christian commander offered Darwin the position of naturalist on an upcoming five-year, round-the-world ocean voyage. Darwin signed up for the journey on the sailing vessel *Beagle*. During the years away, Darwin in particular recorded observations of island natives, varieties of birds, and geographic landmarks.

Though Darwin was profoundly influenced by this voyage, it was not until three decades later that he published his philosophy of origins. He suggested that varieties within species, such as the birds he observed, originated by chance. In the fight to survive in a world of predators and limited food, some varieties were better suited to survive than were others. Those of the superior variety survived and reproduced, while those who were weaker died or were killed off. Darwin proclaimed that this process of spontaneous variation and "survival of the fittest" had been in progress over many millions of years. He declared that this evolutionary process is responsible for the tremendous varieties of life we find today; not God's work of special creation.

Charles Darwin

Deep Impact

Though evolutionary thought had been an underground movement for hundreds of years, by the time Darwin's *Origin of the Species* was published, many people in western Europe seemed especially ripe to receive its message. Darwin was accepted as an authority, though he had no scientific qualifications, and within 50 years most of the scientific community, and indeed much of the world, had complete confidence in his leading. His theory of evolution impacted many scientific fields beyond biology, including cosmology and geology. Stanley Beck correctly observes:

> Twentieth century biology rests on a foundation of evolutionary concepts. . . . The evolutionary basis is also apparent in peripheral independent fields such as chemistry, geology, physics, and astronomy. No central scientific concept is more firmly established in our thinking, our methods, and our interpretations, than that of evolution.[4]

But the impact of evolution did not stop with the sciences. It also effected ethics, religion, psychology, philosophy, politics, and economics. Evolution rapidly displaced creation in schools and colleges throughout the world. It became the world view, the ruling paradigm, of nearly every discipline of study. Darwin's influence was so profound that even Karl Marx, the father of Marxism, offered to dedicate one of his most influential books to none other than Charles Darwin. The impact of evolution on our society remains as strong as ever, a point emphasized by Rene Dubos, one of America's top ecologists:

> Most enlightened persons now accept as a fact that everything in the cosmos from heavenly bodies to human beings has developed and continues to develop through evolutionary processes. The great religions of the West have come to accept a historical view of creation. Evolutionary concepts are applied also to social institutions and to the arts. Indeed, most political parties, as well as schools of theology, sociology, history, or arts, teach these concepts and make them the basis of their doctrines.[5]

Evolution's Rationale

In its most elementary form, evolution states that the first living cell formed spontaneously from a dead, inanimate world. Then this cell reproduced itself and random mutations took place within the new cells, causing some to be more fit for survival than others, and this process of mutation and competition over many millions of years accounts for the variety of creatures that exist today.

According to evolution, all living creatures are connected by a common ancestor. Humans and apes, for example, are believed to have begun from a common animal 5 to 20 million years ago. Likewise, primates (which include humans, apes, monkeys, and lemurs) are believed to have begun from a single animal approximately 75 million years ago. Modern birds are proposed to be descendants of reptiles and dinosaurs. Whales are viewed as descendants of land mammals. The study of these hypothetical relationships is called phylogeny, and they are frequently illustrated by so-called phylogenetic trees.

Descent from a Common Ancestor

The theory of evolution rests upon four primary processes that must exist for it to be plausible. In their most elementary form, these processes include the following.

• **Spontaneous generation.** This term refers to life randomly arising from non-life. Evolution depends on the proposition that in a pond or other moist environment (commonly termed "the pre-biotic soup") an ideal solution of molecules happened to be present at the same instant. Denying all rules of probability, a functioning DNA genetic code, a cell wall, and energy-generating apparatus (the absolute minimum requirements for a viable cell) were all randomly present in the same place, at exactly the same time. This "living" cell then reproduced itself and continued to multiply.

• **Random mutation.** Evolution goes on to explain that spontaneous changes take place within the genetic code of all living things.

Most of these are thought to be due to errors occurring when an organism's genetic code is copied at the time of reproduction. Radiation and chemicals are also believed to induce such changes. The impact of these random mutations is a slightly modified creature, one who is either better or less suited to live in its habitat. Evolutionists recognize that almost every mutation is ultimately detrimental, and that the probability of a positive mutation is remote. Therefore, an extremely high number of mutations are essential to increase the likelihood of a positive outcome.

• **Natural selection.** In the evolution perspective, natural selection is the "engine" that causes advancement in the complexity of species. Random mutations that result in "weaker" creatures will ultimately lead to an early demise for that particular variety of plant or animal. On the other hand, random mutations that increase the health or virility of creatures will make them superior and successful in the struggle for survival.

• **Enormous time.** The above processes by definition demand a vast period of time. Evolutionists confess that the reason is straightforward: these are very rare events. The probability of spontaneous generation is remote. Therefore, time is essential to increase the chances. Random mutations do not occur very often, and almost every single mutation is damaging. Yet many positive mutations are necessary to give rise to a new species of creatures. The solution? Add more time. Natural selection, likewise, requires domination of entire populations of plants and animals over other populations. What is needed to make these processes plausible is immense time.

To account for enough time to make evolution believable, its proponents promote time lines such as the following:

4.5 billion to 570 million years ago — formation of the universe and earth. No life forms present.

Paleozoic ("ancient life") era — 570 million to 225 million years ago. This era includes the Precambrian and Cambrian periods. The first living cell appears, followed by trilobites (a tiny, shelled animal), and later by fish, coral, land plants, insects, amphibians, and reptiles.

Mesozoic ("middle life") era — 225 million to 65 million years ago. This era includes the Triassic, Jurassic, and Cretaceous periods. Dinosaurs and turtles appear, along with ancient mammals, birds, and flowering plants. Dinosaurs then mysteriously disappear.

Cenozoic ("recent life") era — 65 million years ago to present. Modern-day animals appear, along with humans about 2.5 million years ago.

Evolution as a scientific explanation is dependent upon these four processes, all occurring at random and continuously, independent from any coordination or directing purpose. Eliminate or disprove any one of these processes and the rationale for evolution comes unraveled.

"MICRO" DOES NOT EQUAL "MACRO"

Two broad types of evolution are claimed to occur. "Macroevolution," the best known of the two, refers to one species transforming into another entirely new species. This resource book is focused primarily upon concepts surrounding macroevolution.

"Microevolution" is the term given for small changes or variations that take place within a single species. Biologists of all persuasions agree that such adaptations do in fact occur and are commonplace. Unfortunately, a common error is made in scientific reasoning when adaptations or variation (microevolution) are used as evidence that "macroevolution" (evolution from one species into another) must also occur.

Each species of living creature has its own unique gene pool or genetic code. Within this genetic code lies potential for small changes within the particular species. Within the human species, *Homo sapiens*, tiny variations may occur, such as varieties of eye color, height, hair distribution, hair texture, and skin color. But we still all remain distinctly *Homo sapiens*. Within the corn species, *Zea mays*, variations have occurred that today give produce a diversity of corn, including pepper corn, barley corn, Indian corn, sweet corn, and a host of others. Yet these are all still distinctly corn, *Zea mays*.

A vast difference lies between limited variations such as hair color within a species, and transformation into an entirely different species. That the former does occur is in no way proof that the latter is a possibility. Microevolution does not require any significant change in the genetic code, and such changes do not alter the distinction of that particular species. Macroevolution demands permanent and profound alterations in the genetics of the new creature.

Some will refer to the subtle changes within a species as evidence of evolution in progress, that many such tiny changes could eventually lead to a new species. The critical evidence for evolution, however, lies not in proving tiny changes, but in proving that transformation of one species into another does in fact take place.

Searching for Scientific Evidence

It is impossible to turn back time and scientifically observe the proposed evolution of life forms. The next best evidence would come from constructing an experiment to test whether or not evolution seems to be currently happening. However, evolution by definition requires many millions of years, making such an experiment impossible to undertake.

Similar to the case for creation, the only scientific evidence can come from indirect sources, including: probability of the events ever happening by chance alone, the age of the earth, and the fossil record of these earlier events. If evolution were indeed true, we would expect to find the following.

• Probability of spontaneous life is high. Mathematically speaking, spontaneous generation and random

GEOLOGIC

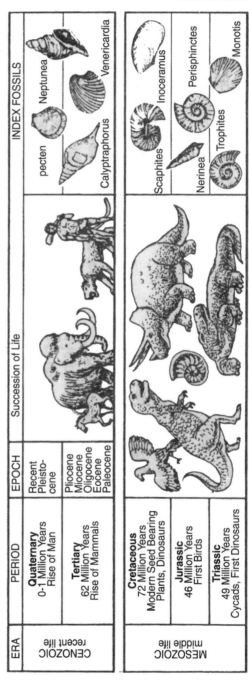

	INDEX FOSSILS	Succession of Life	EPOCH	PERIOD	ERA
	Neptunea, Venericardia, pecten, Calyptraphorus		Recent, Pleistocene	**Quaternary** 0-1 Million Years Rise of Man	CENOZOIC recent life
			Pliocene, Miocene, Oligocene, Eocene, Paleocene	**Tertiary** 62 Million Years Rise of Mammals	
	Inoceramus, Perisphinctes, Monotis, Scaphites, Nerinea, Trophites			**Cretaceous** 72 Million Years Modern Seed Bearing Plants, Dinosaurs	MESOZOIC middle life
				Jurassic 46 Million Years First Birds	
				Triassic 49 Million Years Cycads, First Dinosaurs	

TIME SCALE

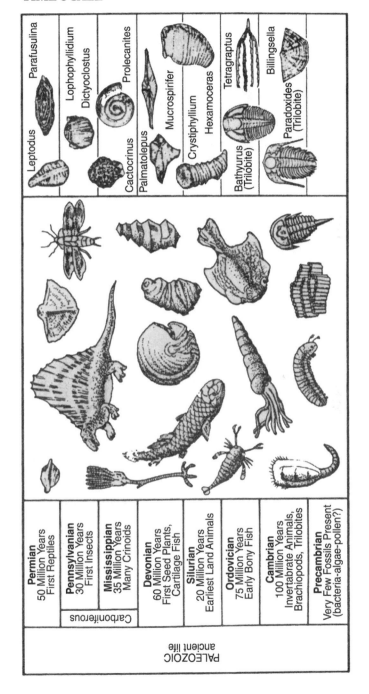

Parafusulina

Leptodus

Lophophyllidium

Dictyoclostus

Prolecanites

Cactocrinus

Palmatolepus

Mucrospirifer

Crystiphyllium

Hexamoceras

Tetragraptus

Bathyurus (Trilobite)

Billingsella

Paradoxides (Trilobite)

Permian 50 Million Years First Reptiles	
Pennsylvanian 30 Million Years First Insects	Carboniferous
Mississippian 35 Million Years Many Crinoids	
Devonian 60 Million Years First Seed Plants, Cartilage Fish	
Silurian 20 Million Years Earliest Land Animals	
Ordovician 75 Million Years Early Bony Fish	
Cambrian 100 Million Years Invertabrate Animals, Brachiopods, Trilobites	
Precambrian Very Few Fossils Present (bacteria-algae-pollen?)	

PALEOZOIC ancient life

mutations are events that can be statistically predicted. Even natural selection can be analyzed using the laws of probability. If indeed these three processes do account for evolution, we should find that the mathematical probability is reasonable. In most scientific research today, acceptable results demand an accuracy of at least 95 percent probability. Similarly, if evolution is true, we would expect the mathematical odds favoring evolution to be quite favorable.

• Age of the earth is very advanced. Spontaneous generation, random mutation, and natural selection all demand enormous time to increase the odds of them ever taking place. Therefore, proof of evolution should reveal that the earth is extremely old, on the order of billions of years. But not only is advanced age essential. We should also discover that throughout the earth's long life, physical conditions, including temperature, oxygen concentration, and sunlight, were appropriate for life to thrive.

•Fossil record demonstrates evolution. If evolution has actually occurred, investigations should reveal fossils that illustrate a steady transformation of one species into another. For example, whales are proposed to have evolved from land mammals. Therefore, we would expect to uncover fossils of transitional creatures whose hind legs gradually became smaller until they disappeared, whose nose gradually moved upward toward to the top of its head, whose tailbone expanded into a giant fin. We would also expect that the shallowest fossils encountered would show the more advanced, modern forms of whales, while the deepest layers of fossils would contain the earliest, more primitive types.

With respect to origins, evolution is the dominant view. But in spite of its popularity, if evolution is really true it must stand up to these three tests. In the coming chapters we will review the concepts, rationale, and evidence that demonstrate evolution's failure on all three tests.

PART TWO

—

PRESENT THE EVIDENCE

CHAPTER FOUR

EXTREME COMPLEXITY OF LIFE

INTRODUCTION

All living things are characterized by incredible complexity. The genetic code of DNA, upon which all creatures depend, is elaborate beyond description. The internal organs and systems upon which plants and animals depend are also enormously intricate. These facts make absolutely zero the possibility that life arose simply by chance.

Living creatures do possess some similarities with one another. Every living thing, for example, is made up of cells, each containing a genetic code. Some creatures have much more in common. Mammals, for instance, all breathe air, are warm-blooded, and nurse their young. But similarities do not necessarily indicate that one species evolved from another. Such similarities can be more readily explained by a common creator who incorporated common features of design.

CONCEPT 4-1: BOTH LIVING CREATURES AND THEIR DNA ARE ENORMOUSLY COMPLEX.

RATIONALE

Even the simplest life form requires enormous intricacy of structures and functions. The more we appreciate the complexity of living things, the more we can also comprehend the likelihood of life beginning by random means of evolution. The eye, the brain, the kidney, the beating heart, and the liver are organs elaborate almost beyond description. Yet at the core of each cell within these organs lies an object far

Parts of a Typical Cell

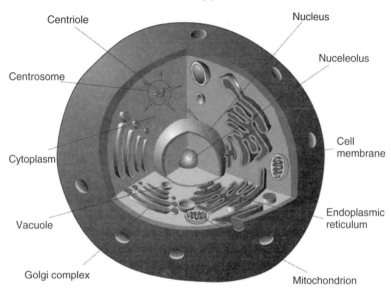

more complex than the organ itself: deoxyribonucleic acid, commonly known as DNA.

DNA contains the genetic code that determines all functions of the cell — what structures it will build, what chemicals or hormones it will produce, how and when the cell will replicate. In fact, all the genetic code necessary to form an entirely new creature is housed within each cell. To appreciate this quantity of information, consider the fact that human DNA stores enough information to fill 1,000 books, each with 500 pages of very small print — a total of about 3 billion letters!

What's more, there exist no "simple" living cells. Even the most miniature one-celled creature is vastly complex and requires elaborate DNA coding to be able to function and reproduce. The study of single-cell organisms is challenging enough to keep researchers busy for a lifetime. Multiply this effort times one trillion and we can just begin to understand the complex challenges of understanding human genetics and cellular physiology. Each advance in biotechnical understanding only broadens scientists' appreciation for the enormous intricacies of life.

EVIDENCE

* That evolutionary enigma, the duck-billed platypus, has more than its egg-laying to distinguish it from other mammals. It now appears that in common with some species of fish and amphibians, it can detect weak electric fields (of a few hundred microvolts or less). Not only that, but it uses its electric sense to locate its prey, picking up the tiny electrical signals passing between nerves and muscles in the tail of a shrimp.[1]

* In man is a three-pound brain which, as far as we know, is the most complex and orderly arrangement of matter in the universe.[2]

All veins, arteries, and capillaries lined end-to-end would extend 80,000 miles. A single drop of blood can be delivered anywhere in the body within 20 seconds.[3]

The brain has 10,000,000,000 circuits and a memory of 1,000,000,000,000,000,000,000 bits.[4]

The human body has 100 trillion cells. All the cells in the human body lined up side-by-side would encircle the earth 200 times.[5]

* There is enough information capacity in a single human cell to store the *Encyclopedia Britannica*, all 30 volumes of it, three or four times over.[6]

* It is in biology that we find the most striking examples of self-organization. I need only cite the astonishing ability of an embryo to develop from a single strand of DNA, via an exquisitely well-orchestrated sequence of formative steps, into an exceedingly complex organism.[7]

* The structure of the human brain is enormously complex. It contains about 10 billion nerve cells (neurons), which are interlinked in a vast network through 1,000 billion junctions (synapses). The whole brain can be divided into subsections, or sub-networks, which communicate with each other in network fashion. All this results in intricate patterns of intertwined webs, networks nesting within larger networks.[8]

* Perhaps in no other area of modern biology is the challenge posed by the extreme complexity and ingenuity of biological adaptations more apparent than in the fascinating new molecular world of the cell. . . . To grasp the reality of life as it has been revealed by molecular biology, we must magnify a cell a thousand million times until it is twenty kilometers in diameter and resembles a giant airship large enough to cover a

great city like London or New York. What we would then see would be an object of unparalleled complexity and adaptive design. On the surface of the cell we would see millions of openings, like the portholes of a vast space ship, opening and closing to allow a continual stream of materials to flow in and out. If we were to enter one of these openings we would find ourselves in a world of supreme technology and bewildering complexity. . . .

Altogether, a typical cell contains about ten million million atoms. Suppose we choose to build an exact replica to a scale one thousand million times that of the cell so that each atom of the model would be the size of a tennis ball. Constructing such a model at the rate of one atom per minute, it would take fifty million years to finish, and the object we would end up with would be the giant factory, described above, some twenty kilometers in diameter, with a volume thousands of times that of the Great Pyramid. . . .

Altogether the total number of connections in the human brain approaches 10^{15} or a thousand million million. Numbers in the order of 10^{15} are of course completely beyond comprehension. Imagine an area about half the size of the USA (one million square miles) covered in a forest of trees containing ten thousand trees per square mile. If each tree contained one hundred thousand leaves the total number of leaves in the forest would be 10^{15}, equivalent to the number of connections in the human brain. . . .

The capacity of DNA to store information vastly exceeds that of any other known system; it is so efficient that all the information needed to specify an organism as complex as man weighs less than a few thousand millionths of a gram. The information necessary to specify the design of all the species of organisms which have ever existed on the planet, a number according to G.G. Simpson of approximately one thousand million, could be held in a teaspoon and there would still be room left for all the information in every book ever written. . . .

Is it really credible that random processes could have constructed a reality, the smallest element of which — a functional protein or gene — is complex beyond our own creative capacities, a reality which is the very antithesis of chance, which excels in every sense anything produced by the intelligence of man? Alongside the level of ingenuity and complexity exhibited by the molecular machinery of life, even our most advanced artifacts appear clumsy. . . .

It would be an illusion to think that what we are aware of at present is any more than a fraction of the full extent of biological design. In practically every field of fundamental biological research, ever-increasing levels of design and complexity are being revealed at an ever-accelerating rate. [9]

* Not only is the amount of information in cellular DNA staggering. It's also incredibly compact.[10]

* Of all creatures on earth, only man has the ability to use language. Not only does man have the ability to remember the past, to cope with complicated problems in the present, and to plan for the future, but he has the ability to express all of these thoughts both verbally and in written form. The human brain, with its twelve billion brain cells and 120 trillion connections, is the most complex arrangement of matter in the universe. Thus endowed, man's ability to express himself verbally and in written form is truly incredible.[11]

* Evolution is strongly constrained by the conservative nature of embryological programs. Nothing in biology is more complex than the production of an adult vertebrate from a single fertilized ovum. Nothing much can be changed very radically without discombobulating the embryo. The order of life, and the persistence of nearly all basic anatomical designs throughout the entire geological history of multi-cellular animals, record the intricacy and resistance to change of complex development programs, not the perfection of adaptive design in local environments.[12]

In a day, the eye moves 100,000 times. (The body would have to walk 50 miles to exercise the leg muscles at an equal amount.) 137 million nerve endings within each eye pick up every visual message the eye sends to the brain. . . .

A single inner ear contains as many circuits as the telephone system of a large city. [13]

Whales and dolphins can locate tiny objects in the water from great distances by making clicking sounds and then listening for the time and direction of the echo. But for this system to work, cetaceans must be able to focus the clicking sound in a particular direction.

This is the purpose of the small lump, or "melon," on the

head of whales and dolphins. This melon is constructed from special fats (lipids) arranged in just the right shape and order. As sound is created by the animal, it travels through the melon, and then exits as a focused beam.[14]

* In the realm of the senses, animals continue to amaze scientists. No longer impressed by a dog's ability to hear high-pitched whistles or a cat's ability to see in dim light, researchers have gone on to document far more unexpected animal perceptions in such animals as the platypus and praying mantis.

Take the bill of the duck-billed platypus. It serves as an antenna to pick up weak electrical signals, scientists report in the January 30 *Nature*. This is the first report of electro-reception in mammals, say Henning Scheich of the technical University of Darmstadt, West Germany, Anna Guppy of the Australian National University in Canberra City and their colleagues.

The praying mantis provides another sensory surprise — a single "ear" that is a groove in the underside of its thorax. Long thought to be deaf, the insect possesses a "sensitive and specialized acoustic sense," David D. Yager and Ronald R. Hoy of Cornell University report in the February 14 *Science*.

What the mantis hears is ultrasonic frequencies, perhaps wings rubbing abdomen during courtship or the sonar signals of insect-eating bats. The sensitivity to ultrasound is shared by some other insects that detect sound with more conventional organs. But all other insects that hear have two "ears," widely separated on the body.[15]

* We do not yet understand even the general features of the origin of the genetic code. . . . The origin of the genetic code is the most baffling aspect of the problem of the origins of life, and a major conceptual or experimental breakthrough may be needed before we can make any substantial progress.[16]

* But let us have no illusions — our research would still leave us quite unable to grasp the extreme complexity of the simplest of organisms.[17]

The information in the brain equals that contained in 20 million separate books.[18]

A single cell contains enough information to fill 10 million books.[19]

* We know a lot about the structure and function of the cells and fibers of the human brain, but we haven't the ghost of an idea about how this extraordinary organ works to produce awareness; the nature of consciousness is a scientific problem, but still an unapproachable one.[20]

The DNA from one human cell contains a billion biochemical steps. If all DNA in a human were placed end-to-end it would reach the sun and back 400 times. . . .

The human eye can handle 1.5 million simultaneous messages. . . .

The human heart beats 40,000,000 times a year. In a lifetime, the heart will pump 600,000 metric tons of blood.[21]

* Insects include some of the most versatile of all flying machines. . . . some insects — through a combination of low mass, sophisticated neurosensory systems and complex musculature — display astonishing aerobatic feats.[22]

CONCEPT 4-2: LIVING CREATURES ARE COMPLEX OUT OF NECESSITY.

RATIONALE

Life is impossible without the existence of intricate systems. In other words, life is complex out of necessity. DNA does not simply contain an enormous quantity of information. Nearly all that information must be present for the cell to live. Consider some comparisons: An intricate laptop computer can be rendered useless if only the battery is removed. A motor boat is dead in the water if the propeller is missing. A car is paralyzed if only a speck of dirt gets into the fuel injection system. Similarly, living cells can expire immediately if only a small component is deactivated or removed.

Each machine has an "irreducible complexity," the minimal number of components necessary for it to function. In the mechanical world, this is easy to appreciate. Take one gear from an automobile transmission and the car will be immobilized. At the cellular level, irreducible complexity is also critically important. Separate the mitochondria and the cell has no energy. Displace the nucleus and most chemical functions of the cell cease immediately. Remove the cell membrane and the cell collapses.

Beyond the realm of individual cells, organ systems also demonstrate irreducible complexity. All of their components must be functioning for the organ to perform its role. Interrupt a few fibers of the heart's conduction system, and the organ ceases to pump. Cause a few abnormal cells to grow within the liver, and it no longer produces digestive fluids. Allow a miniature blood clot to form in a vessel of the brain and immediate paralysis or coma will result.

Irreducible complexity is an unequivocal characteristic of all living beings. Remove even a small functional feature and the organism becomes crippled or expires immediately.

EVIDENCE

Biochemist Michael Behe explains that in the mechanical world, if one essential component (such as a spark plug or wing flap) is missing, the entire machine won't operate.[23]

* It is the sheer universality of perfection, the fact that everywhere we look, to whatever depth we look, we find an elegance and ingenuity of an absolutely transcending quality, which so mitigates against the idea of chance. Is it really credible that random processes could have constructed a reality, the smallest element of which — a functional protein or gene — is complex beyond our own creative capacities, a reality which is the very antithesis of chance, which excels in every sense anything produced by the intelligence of man? Alongside the level of ingenuity and complexity exhibited by the molecular machinery of life, even our most advanced artifacts appear clumsy.[24]

Mycoplasma genitalium is a bacterium with the smallest amount of genetic material of any known organism. Yet this microscopic cell has 580,000 base pairs on its 482 genes. Even with this vast quantity of biogenetic information, *Mycoplasma genitalium* can only survive by parasitizing other more complex organisms, which provide for it nutrients, a cell membrane, and DNA replication — all things *Mycoplasma genitalium* can't do for itself.[25]

* Now we know that the cell itself is far more complex than we had imagined. It includes thousands of functioning enzymes, each one of them a complex machine itself. Furthermore, each enzyme comes into being in response to a gene, a strand of DNA. The information content of the gene (its complexity) must be as great as that of the enzyme that it controls.

A medium protein might include about 300 amino acids. The DNA gene controlling this would have about 1,000 nucleotides in its chain. Since there are four kinds of nucleotides in a DNA chain, one consisting of 1,000 links could exist in 4^{1000} different forms. Using a little algebra (logarithms) we can see that $4^{1000} = 10^{600}$. Ten multiplied by itself 600 times gives the figure 1 followed by 600 zeroes! This number is completely beyond our comprehension.[26]

* What is the bare minimum amount of genetic code necessary for a cell to "live"? Recently, Eugene Koonin and others attempted this calculation and came up with 256 genes. But they expressed doubt that their hypothetical cell could survive in reality. It would have no means to repair DNA damage or digest complex compounds, and would need to live in a near "perfect" environment.[27]

CONCEPT 4-3: SIMILARITIES AMONG DIFFERENT SPECIES AND THEIR DNA DO NOT PROVE EVOLUTION.

RATIONALE

A growing trend in scientific circles is to search for molecular or DNA similarities between creatures in an effort to establish evolutionary links. This field is known as "molecular evolution." Chemical or DNA similarities between creatures are termed "molecular homologies." Given the inability to prove evolution through analysis of fossils and recent advances in genetic research, evolutionists were initially hopeful that molecular homologies would prove evolutionary progress. Initial enthusiasm for this line of evidence, however, is largely waning because of so many contradictions in its results.

DNA contains information essential to form the chemicals and structures of life. Therefore, one would reasonably anticipate that the most similar creatures would have the most similar DNA and other bodily chemicals. This is, in fact, the case. Apes and humans have numerous physical similarities, and have somewhat similar DNA. The DNA of scorpions is more different from that of humans, but still contains some resemblances. The DNA of bacteria is only slightly similar to that of humans or other animals.

Initially, evolutionists used these similarities as an argument in favor of their theory. But this proposal has run into serious trouble, namely, the discovery of DNA and other chemical similarities among creatures that evolutionists insist evolved separately. Such similarities cannot be explained through evolutionary connections, for the creatures involved are not at all related.

For example, we now know that human lysozyme, an enzyme for

digesting food, is more similar to chicken lysozyme than to the lysozyme of apes and other primates. Did humans evolve from chickens instead of apes? Evolutionists would completely disagree. Hemoglobin, the molecule that carries oxygen in blood, is found in all vertebrates, including humans. But hemoglobin also exists in earthworms, crustaceans, starfish, and even in some microorganisms. Did humans evolve from earthworms and starfish? Again, evolutionists would flatly deny the claim.

Analysis of molecular homologies is not a useful proof of evolution. In fact, it raises far more questions than answers. But there does exist a reasonable explanation for chemical similarities between widely divergent creatures: they had a common Creator who chose this method of design.

Leaving chemistry for a moment, evolutionists look at the physical similarities between creatures and abstractly insist that one must have transformed into another. But there is another reasonable explanation: They have a common Designer and Creator.

Consider the Cessna series of private airplanes. The 152 seats two persons, has a high wing, an engine on the nose, and the Cessna logo. The 172 seats four persons, has a high wing, an engine on the nose, and the Cessna logo. The 210 seats six persons, has a high wing, an engine on the nose, and the Cessna logo.

What accounts for these similarities? Did the 152 evolve into the 172, and then the 210? The likelihood seems pretty distant. What's more, search all the airports in the world, and you will find no sign of Cessna "transitional forms" that demonstrate one aircraft evolving into another.

A much more reasonable and provable explanation is that Cessnas are alike because they have a common designer and manufacturer. Using the same line of reasoning, we shouldn't be surprised if the Creator of living creatures used similar biochemistry and physical structures in His designs.

EVIDENCE

* Similarity does not equal relationship. Evolutionists often use similarity between animals and man to "prove" Darwinism. They point to the legs, neck, ears, etc., of apes and remind us how similar they are to those of men. Creationists likewise use similarities to support creation. . . . So God used His blueprint for many of His creatures. Similarities don't mean common ancestry but a common Architect![28]

* Adrian Friday and Martin Bishop of Cambridge have analyzed the available protein sequence data for tetrapods. . . .

To their surprise, i   ⁀n (the mammal) and
chicken (the bird)   ⌐⁀ives, with the
crocodile as next nearest ⌐⌐

　　* Thousands of different sequen⌐⌐
acid, have now been compared in hundreds ⌐
cies but never has any sequence been found to be in a⌐⌐
the lineal descendant or ancestor of any other sequence. . . .
There are hundreds of different families of proteins and each
family exhibits its own unique degree of interspecies variation, some greater than hemoglobin, some far less than the
cytochromes . . . each ticking at its own unique and highly
specific rate.[30]

　　* Proteins with nearly the same structure and function
(homologous proteins) are found in increasing numbers in
phylogenetically different, even very distinct taxa (e.g., hemo-
globins in vertebrates, in some invertebrates, and even in certain plants). . . . The probability . . . of the convergent evolution of two proteins with approximately the same structure
and function is too low to be plausible, even when all possible
circumstances are present which seem to heighten the likelihood of such a convergence. If this is so, then the plausibility
of a random evolution of two or more different but function-
ally related proteins seems hardly greater.[31]

　　* Thus, the similarities between species in anatomy and
protein structure can be interpreted in two entirely different
ways. The evolutionists say that the similarity between features of, for example, humans and apes reflects the fact that
these features were "copied" from a common ancestor; the creationists say that the two species were created independently
but were designed with similar features so that they would
function similarly. Both views seem consistent with the similarity data, but which view is correct?[32]

　　Hemoglobin, the molecule that carries oxygen in blood,
is found in all vertebrates, including humans. But hemoglobin also exists in earthworms, crustaceans, starfish, and even
in some microorganisms.

　　Crocodile hemoglobin is more similar to chicken hemoglobin than it is to the hemoglobin of snakes and other reptiles.

　　Human lysozyme, an enzyme for digesting food, is more

similar to chicken lysozyme than to the lysozyme of apes and other primates.[33]

An identical particular protein is found on the cell wall of both camels and nurse sharks. Yet, speaking in terms of evolution, these animals are completely unrelated.[34]

* Morphology and molecular data are congruent in indicating that *Homo* and African apes are more closely related to each other than to the orang. The position of chimps is equivocal, however; amino acid sequencing links them with humans, morphology links them with gorillas, and DNA sequencing has produced ambiguous results.

An intriguing picture develops in this volume in which molecular and morphological phylogenies sometimes agree and sometimes not. Different philosophies and methods complicate the comparison and may themselves be responsible for much of the conflict. Nevertheless, there is general agreement that both molecular and morphological phylogenetics face similar fundamental problems and that a "touchstone" has not been found.[35]

* The relaxin and insulin families do not stand alone as exceptions to the orderly interpretation of molecular evolution in conventional monophyletic terms. It is instructive to look at additional examples of purportedly anomalous protein evolution and note that the explanations permissible under the molecular clock theories cover a range of ad hoc explanations apparently limited only by imagination. These examples include the egg white lysozymes of goose, chicken, chachalaca, and duck. . . .

This phylogenetic hopscotching of b2 microglobulin and many hormones can be taken together with amino acid sequence data for relaxins, insulins, and some other molecules, to show incompatibility with the monophyletic molecular clock models of evolution. As noted earlier, the positive selectionist neo-Darwinian views of molecular evolution are in principle unfalsifiable, but such evidence as we have presented does not strengthen the positive selectionist interpretation of the data. However, the major conclusion to which we wish to draw attention is that these findings strongly suggest that many of the genes purportedly produced by gene duplication have been present very early in the development of life. In fact, we can ask if they were not present so early that we must question whether any gene has come about by duplication or whether all have been there, from the beginning, as a potential for species development. [36]

* Molecular evolution is about to be accepted as a method superior to paleontology for the discovery of evolutionary relationships. As a molecular evolutionist I should be elated. Instead it seems disconcerting that many exceptions exist to the orderly progression of species as determined by molecular homologies; so many in fact that I think the exception, the quirks, may carry the more important message.

The early existence of some molecules of highly complex function cannot be denied and the question arises whether there are any molecules that have not already been in existence at the time of the origins of life.[37]

* Hypotheses about the origin of *Homo sapiens*, genetic differentiation among human populations, and changes in population size are quantified. None of the hypotheses seems compatible with the observed DNA variation. . . .

Even with DNA sequence data, we have no direct access to the processes of evolution, so objective reconstruction of the vanished past can be achieved only by creative imagination. [38]

CHAPTER FIVE

SPONTANEOUS GENERATION: IMPOSSIBLE ODDS

INTRODUCTION

Have you ever heard of the "theory of spontaneous generation"? Probably not, because it is rarely spoken of in such
definite terms. The reason is simple. The idea of life beginning on its own, with no design, intent, or control is so remote it is
considered impossible by the majority of scientists, as well as by the
public at large.

Yet spontaneous generation is essential. Evolution depends upon
natural selection and other processes we'll discuss in the following chapters. Rarely mentioned by evolutionists, however, is that for evolution to
ever get started, there first must be a very highly complex, intact, living,
self-reproducing creature. And this requires spontaneous generation.

CONCEPT 5-1: NO SCIENTIFIC EVIDENCE EXISTS FOR SPONTANEOUS
GENERATION.

RATIONALE

Evolution first depends upon spontaneous generation, the theory
that the first life arose impromptu from the random chemicals that
happened to be present. All the minimum (and enormously complex) cellular structures necessary for a living cell just happened to be
in the same place at the same time, and the first amoebae-like cell

came into existence. The *Encyclopedia Britannica* explains the event as follows:

> * Whether the earth cooled from a molten mass or con-
> densed out of cold dust, life could not have existed when the
> earth was formed some 5,000,000,000 years ago; it must have
> originated since. As both processes (automatic synthesis and
> ultraviolet light energy) are the characteristics of life, it is not
> unreasonable to suppose that life originated in a watery "soup"
> of prebiological organic compounds and that living organisms
> arose later by surrounding quantities of these compounds by
> membranes that made them into "cells." This is usually con-
> sidered the starting point of organic ("Darwinian") evolution.[1]

Spontaneous generation is, however, only a hypothesis. No evidence exists that spontaneous generation ever actually occurred. Scientists have laboriously attempted to synthesize life in the laboratory,
under the most artificial and controlled conditions. Yet they have failed
every single time.

This should come as absolutely no surprise. For even the simplest
cell to ever get started requires an awesomely complex assembly of
chemical structures. That this could have happened through random
chance is statistically impossible.

Spontaneous generation is, in fact, simply speculation. Evolutionists are forced to assume the most imaginary of scenarios: that intricate
molecules formed by some unknown process, in an imaginary "primeval soup," under stimulation from unknown electrical charges, in a
non-existent, ancient earth atmosphere.

The notion is ridiculous. Louis Pasteur proved experimentally over
a century ago that non-life cannot produce life, that dead objects cannot produce living ones, that each organism requires parents, and that
only parents produce the new life. This is recognized as the law of
biogenesis. Universally upheld since Pasteur is the fact that life always
arises from life of the same kind.

The vast majority of the world's most respected and honored scientists agree with this law and totally reject the theory of spontaneous
generation. Others continue to grapple with their own inconsistencies.
What Louis Pasteur proved over a century ago is still true: non-life
cannot produce life.

EVIDENCE

* Considering the way the pre-biotic soup is referred to in
so many discussions of the origin of life as an already estab-

lished reality, it comes as something of a shock to realize that there is absolutely no positive evidence for its existence.[2]

* An honest man, armed with all the knowledge available to us now, could only state that in some sense, the origin of life appears at the moment to be almost a miracle, so many are the conditions which would have had to have been satisfied to get it going.[3]

* In spite of many attempts, there have been no breakthroughs during the past 30 years to help to explain the origin of chirality in living cells. . . .

Considerable disagreements between scientists have arisen about detailed evolutionary steps. The problem is that the principal evolutionary processes from prebiotic molecules to progenotes have not been proven by experimentation and that the environmental conditions under which these processes occurred are not known. Moreover, we do not actually know where the genetic information of all living cells originates, how the first replicable polynucleotides (nucleic acids) evolved, or how the extremely complex structure-function relationships in modern cells came into existence.[4]

* The problems of reconstructing possible pathways of prebiotic evolution in the absence of any kind of fossil evidence are indeed formidable. Successful attack on these problems will require, on the one hand, the boldness to imagine and create new concepts describing the organization of not-yet-living populations of molecules and, on the other hand, the humility to learn the hard way, by laborious experiment, which molecular pathways are consistent with the stubborn facts of chemistry. We are still at the very beginning of the quest for understanding of the origin of life. We do not yet have even a rough picture of the nature of the obstacles that prebiotic evolution has had to overcome. We do not have a well-defined set of criteria by which to judge whether any given theory of the origin of life is adequate.[5]

* A natural and fundamental question to ask on learning of these incredibly interlocking pieces of software and hardware is: "How did they ever get started in the first place?" It is truly a baffling thing. One has to imagine some sort of bootstrap process occurring, somewhat like that which is used in

the development of new computer languages — but a bootstrap from simple molecules to entire cells is almost beyond one's power to imagine. There are various theories on the origin of life. They all run aground on this most central of all central questions: "How did the genetic code, along with the mechanisms for its translation (ribosomes and RNA molecules), originate?" For the moment, we will have to content ourselves with a sense of wonder and awe, rather than with an answer.[6]

* DNA cannot do its work, including forming more DNA, without the help of catalytic proteins, or enzymes. In short, proteins cannot form without DNA, but neither can DNA form without proteins.

But as researchers continue to examine the RNA-world concept closely, more problems emerge. How did RNA arise initially? RNA and its components are difficult to synthesize in a laboratory under the best of conditions, much less under plausible prebiotic ones.[7]

* No matter how large the environment one considers, life cannot have had a random beginning. Troops of monkeys thundering away at random on typewriters could not produce the works of Shakespeare, for the practical reason that the whole observable universe is not large enough to contain the necessary monkey hordes, the necessary typewriters, and certainly not the waste paper baskets required for the deposition of wrong attempts. The same is true for living material.

The likelihood of the spontaneous formation of life from inanimate matter is one to a number with 40,000 noughts after it. . . . It is big enough to bury Darwin and the whole theory of evolution. There was no primeval soup, neither on this planet nor on any other, and if the beginnings of life were not random, they must therefore have been the product of purposeful intelligence.[8]

* I don't know how long it is going to be before astronomers generally recognize that the combinatorial arrangement of not even one among the many thousands of biopolymers on which life depends could have been arrived at by natural processes here on the earth. Astronomers will have a little difficulty at understanding this because they will be assured by biologists that it is not so, the biologists having been assured in their turn by others that it is not so. The "others" are a group of

persons who believe, quite openly, in mathematical miracles. They advocate the belief that tucked away in nature, outside of normal physics, there is a law which performs miracles (provided the miracles are in the aid of biology). This curious situation sits oddly on a profession that for long has been dedicated to coming up with logical explanations of biblical miracles.

If there were a basic principle of matter which somehow drove organic systems toward life, its existence should easily be demonstrable in the laboratory. One could, for instance, take a swimming bath to represent the primordial soup. Fill it with any chemicals of a non-biological nature you please. Pump any gases over it, or through it, you please, and shine any kind of radiation on it that takes your fancy. Let the experiment proceed for a year and see how many of those 2,000 enzymes [proteins produced by living cells] have appeared in the bath. I will give the answer, and so save the time and trouble and expense of actually doing the experiment. You would find nothing at all, except possibly for a tarry sludge composed of amino acids and other simple organic chemicals. How can I be so confident of this statement? Well, if it were otherwise, the experiment would long since have been done and would be well known and famous throughout the world. The cost of it would be trivial compared to the cost of landing a man on the moon.[9]

* In short there is not a shred of objective evidence to support the hypothesis that life began in an organic soup here on the earth.[10]

* It was already clear that the genetic code is not merely an abstraction but the embodiment of life's mechanisms; the consecutive triplets of nucleotides in DNA (called codons) are inherited but they also guide the construction of proteins.

So it is disappointing that the origin of the genetic code is still as obscure as the origin of life itself.[11]

* Since the time of Louis Pasteur, the origin of optical activity in biological systems has attracted a great deal of attention. Two very different questions must be answered. First, why do all amino acids in proteins or all nucleotides in nucleic acids have the same handedness? Secondly, why are the amino acids all left-handed (L-) and the nucleotides all right-handed (D-)? We do not know the answer to either question, but we can make a number of plausible suggestions.[12]

* It is extremely improbable that proteins and nucleic acids, both of which are structurally complex, arose spontaneously in the same place at the same time. Yet it also seems impossible to have one without the other. And so, at first glance, one might have to conclude that life could never, in fact, have originated by chemical means.[13]

* Take some matter, heat while stirring and wait. That is the modern version of Genesis. The "fundamental" forces of gravity, electromagnetism and the strong and weak nuclear forces are presumed to have done the rest. . . . But how much of this neat tale is firmly established, and how much remains hopeful speculation? In truth, the mechanism of almost every major step, from chemical precursors up to the first recognizable cells, is the subject of either controversy or complete bewilderment. . . .

In their more public pronouncements, researchers interested in the origin of life sometimes behave a bit like the creationist opponents they so despise — glossing over the great mysteries that remain unsolved and pretending they have firm answers that they have not really got. . . . We still know very little about how our genesis came about, and to provide a more satisfactory account than we have at present remains one of science's great challenges.[14]

* Furthermore, no geological evidence indicates an organic soup ever existed on this planet. We may therefore with fairness call this scenario "the myth of the pre-biotic soup."[15]

* It is emphatically the case that life could not arise spontaneously in a primeval soup from its kind.[16]

* The novelty of a scientific theory of creation ex nihilo [Latin for "creation from nothing"] is readily apparent, for science has long taught us that one cannot make something from nothing.[17]

* There are only two possible explanations as to how life arose: Spontaneous generation arising to evolution or a supernatural creative act of God . . . there is no other possibility. Spontaneous generation was scientifically disproved 120 years ago by Louis Pasteur and others, but that just leaves us with only one other possibility . . . that life came as a supernatural act of creation by God, but I can't accept that philosophy because I do not want to believe in God. Therefore I choose to

believe in that which I know is scientifically impossible, spontaneous generation leading to evolution.[18]

* The calculations presented in this paper show that the origin of a rather accurate genetic code, not necessarily the modern one, is a *pons asinorum* which must be crossed to pass over the abyss which separates crystallography, high polymer chemistry and physics from biology. The information content of amino acid sequences cannot increase until a genetic code with an adaptor function has appeared. Nothing which even vaguely resembles a code exists in the physico-chemical world. One must conclude that no valid scientific explanation of the origin of life exists at present.[19]

CONCEPT 5-2: SPONTANEOUS GENERATION IS STATISTICALLY IMPOSSIBLE.

RATIONALE

DNA, containing the genetic code for the first hypothetical living cell, is very complex and does not randomly occur in nature. Its existence can only be reasonably explained by some external, organizing force. Even the "simplest" one-celled organism has more exactly programmed data stored within it than all of the letters in all the books in the largest library in the world! It is impossible that an encyclopedia could have occurred at random, without intelligent design behind it. Similarly, it's just as impossible that life could have begun without intelligent design.

In spite of these truths, evolutionists contend that spontaneous generation was a random, chance event, with no outside, purposeful influence. Let's take a look at "chance." If you role a die, the probability of rolling the number six is one in six. The probability of rolling two straight sixes is six times six, or 36. The probability of rolling three straight sixes is six times six times six, or 216. Rolling nine straight sixes would be one chance in ten million.

In the case of complex molecules like DNA there are literally trillions times trillions times trillions of different ways that the molecule could come together. Yet only one way would lead to a functional DNA molecule.

Imagine walking into a pharmacy, taking all the drugs off the shelves and pouring them into a bucket. Now warm the contents and mix it around. What do you suppose is the chance that a living cell would form in the bucket?

Spontaneous generation, the chance origin of life from dead material, is likewise scientifically indefensible. A chorus of respected

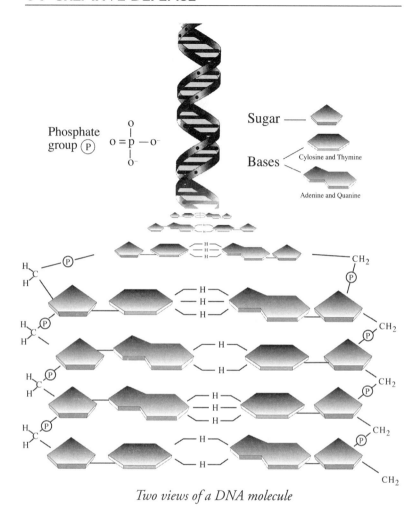

Phosphate group $\textcircled{P}$

$$O = \overset{\overset{\displaystyle O}{|}}{\underset{\underset{\displaystyle O^-}{|}}{P}} - O^-$$

Sugar ——

Bases

Cylosine and Thymine

Adenine and Quanine

Two views of a DNA molecule

scientists lifts its voice in agreement. All attempts to calculate the probability of the chance origin of even the simplest form of life show it to be strictly impossible. There is truth in the concept that nothing produces nothing. Non-life produces only non-life; zero times zero is zero even if you give it a billion trillion years.

EVIDENCE

* The essence of his argument last week was that the information content of the higher forms of life is represented by the number $10^{40,000}$ — representing the specificity with which some 2,000 genes, each of which might be chosen from 10^{20} nucleotide sequences of the appropriate length, might be defined. Evolutionary processes would, Hoyle said, require several Hubble times to yield such a result. The chance that higher life forms might have emerged in this way is comparable with the chance that "a tornado sweeping through a junk-yard might assemble a Boeing 747 from the materials therein."[20]

* The occurrence of any event where the chances are beyond one in ten followed by 50 zeros is an event which we can state with certainty will never happen, no matter how much time is allotted and no matter how many conceivable opportunities could exist for the event to take place.[21]

The most renowned atheist in the latter 20th century, Dr. Carl Sagan, estimated that the mathematical probability of the simplest form of life emerging from non-living matter has the unbelievable odds of one chance in ten to the two billionth power (1 in 10 with two billion zeros after it) — even less probability than predicted by Sir Hoyle or Dr. Morowitz. The enormity of this figure is revealed by the fact that it would take 6,000 books of 300 pages each just to write the number![22]

* The probability of life originating from accident is comparable to the probability of the unabridged dictionary resulting from an explosion in a printing shop.[23]

* If a particular amino acid sequence was selected by chance, how rare an event would this be? . . . Suppose the chain is about two hundred amino acids long; this is, if anything, rather less than the average length of proteins of all types. Since we have just twenty possibilities at each place, the number of possibilities is twenty multiplied by itself some two hundred times. This is approximately equal to . . . a one followed by 260 zeros. . . .

Moreover, we have only considered a polypeptide chain of rather modest length. Had we considered longer ones as well, the figure would have been even more immense. . . . The great majority of sequences can never have been synthesized at all, at any time. . . .

An honest man, armed with all the knowledge available to us now, could only state that in some sense, the origin of life appears at the moment to be almost a miracle, so many are the conditions which would have had to have been satisfied to get it going. [24]

* Even today we have no way of rigorously estimating the probability or degree of isolation of even one functional protein. It is surely a little premature to claim that random processes could have assembled mosquitoes and elephants when we still have to determine the actual probability of the discovery by chance of one single functional protein molecule. [25]

* The complexity of the simplest known type of cell is so great that it is impossible to accept that such an object could have been thrown together by some kind of freakish, vastly improbable event. Such an occurrence would be indistinguishable from a miracle. [26]

* Why then does the scientific theory of evolution hold on to the concept of chance to the degree it does? I suspect it is the fact that there is no alternative whatsoever which could explain the fact of universal evolution, at least in principle, and be formulated within the framework of natural science. If no alternative should be forthcoming, if chance remains overtaxed, then the conclusion seems inevitable that evolution and therefore living beings cannot be grasped by natural science to the same extent as non-living things — not because organisms are so complex, but because the explaining mechanism is fundamentally inadequate. [27]

* The 15,000 or more atoms of the individual sub-assemblies of a single DNA molecule, if left to chance as required by the evolutionary theory, would go together in any of 10^{87} (1 in 10 to the 87th power) different ways. [28]

* One must conclude that, contrary to the established and current wisdom, a scenario describing the genesis of life on earth by chance and natural causes which can be accepted on the basis of fact and not faith has not yet been written. [29]

* The likelihood of the formation of life from inanimate matter is one to a number with 40,000 noughts after it ($10^{40,000}$). . . . It is big enough to bury Darwin and the whole theory of evolution. There was no primeval soup, neither on this planet nor any other, and if the beginnings of life were

not random, they must therefore have been the product of purposeful intelligence. . . .

At all events, anyone, even a nodding acquaintance with the Rubik's cube will concede the near impossibility of a solution being obtained by a blind person moving the cubic faces at random. Now imagine 10^{50} (that's a number 1 with fifty zeros after it) blind people, each with a scrambled Rubik's cube, and try to conceive of the chance of them all simultaneously arriving at the solved form. You then have the chance of arriving by random shuffling at just one of the many biopolymers on which life depends. The notion that not only biopolymers but the operating program of a living cell could be arrived at by chance in a primordial organic soup here on the earth is evidently nonsense of a high order. [30]

* Precious little in the way of biochemical evolution could have happened on the earth. It is easy to show that the two thousand or so enzymes that span the whole of life could not have evolved on the earth. If one counts the number of trial assemblies of amino acids that are needed to give rise to the enzymes, the probability of their discovery by random shufflings turns out to be less than 1 in $10^{40,000}$.[31]

* Supposing the first cell originated by chance is like believing a tornado could sweep through a junkyard filled with airplane parts and form a Boeing 747.[32]

It is extremely improbable that proteins and nucleic acids, both of which are structurally complex, arose spontaneously in the same place at the same time. Yet it also seems impossible to have one without the other. And so, at first glance, one might have to conclude that life could never, in fact, have originated by chemical means.[33]

* To describe the burgeoning life of our planet as improbable may seem odd. But imagine that some cosmic chef takes all the ingredients of the present Earth as atoms, mixes them and lets them stand. The probability that those atoms would combine into the molecules that make up our living Earth is zero. The mixture would always react chemically to form a dead planet like Mars or Venus.

We do not yet understand even the general features of the origin of the genetic code. . . . The origin of the genetic code is the most baffling aspect of the problem of the origins of life, and a major conceptual or experimental breakthrough may be needed before we can make any substantial progress.[34]

* The possibility of life arising spontaneously was virtually zero.[35]

* The probability for the chance of formation of the smallest, simplest form of living organism known is 1 to $10^{340,000,000}$.[36]

* To insist, even with Olympian assurance, that life appeared quite by chance and evolved in this fashion, is an unfounded supposition which I believe to be wrong and not in accordance with the facts.[37]

* The idea of spontaneous generation of life in its present form is therefore highly improbable even on the scale of the billions of years during which prebiotic evolution occurred.[38]

* The "warm little pond" scenario was invented ad hoc to serve as a materialistic reductionist explanation of the origin of life. It is unsupported by any other evidence and it will remain ad hoc until such evidence is found. . . . One must conclude that, contrary to the established and current wisdom, a scenario describing the genesis of life on earth by chance and natural causes which can be accepted on the basis of fact and not faith has not yet been written.[39]

CHAPTER SIX

RANDOM MUTATION/ NATURAL SELECTION: IMPOSSIBLE ODDS

INTRODUCTION

Assuming spontaneous generation did in fact occur, the theory of evolution goes on to state that two continuous processes made the first organisms become progressively more advanced:

• **Random mutation.** Minor changes in a cell's DNA are said to result from outside radiation, chemical contamination, and "accidents" that occur when a cell's genetic code is copied. The result of such random mutations is a new, slightly altered creature.

• **Natural selection.** This "new" creature will either be better or less capable of surviving. A mutation that results in a "weaker" creature would prompt its demise. Similarly, any random mutation which increases the power or virility of the creature will help it, and its offspring, to flourish.

Today scientists recognize that random mutations are actually rare events. They almost always kill the creature, or at least make it incapable of reproducing. What's more, minor improvements would be unlikely to help a creature to survive. For example, a pit in the forehead (claimed to be a first step in the development of eyes) is functionless. It makes the creature no more likely to survive. For an eye to give a creature an advantage, it must be fully functional. Yet classical evolution depends upon such small "developments" to explain the advance of creatures. A growing number of scientists are going public with such fallacies in the theory of evolution.

CONCEPT 6-1: EVOLUTION CONTRADICTS THE SECOND LAW OF THERMODYNAMICS.

RATIONALE

The physical world is governed by certain "laws," that is, rules that always apply. Gravity, for example, is a physical law. If you release an object into the air, it will fall. Every single time. It is a law.

One particular physical law is especially relevant to the notion of evolution. Known as the law of increasing entropy or the second law of thermodynamics, it simply declares that, left to itself, everything is becoming more and more disordered over time. "Entropy" is derived from the two Greek words *en* (meaning "in") and *trope* (meaning "turning"), or literally "in-turning," or "winding down."

It does not take much imagination to appreciate the law of increasing entropy. Just look at an abandoned house. When newly constructed, it was a fine example of planning and organization. But over the years of neglect this organized structure begins to crumble. Paint peels. The roof sags. The foundation cracks. Termites move in. Within a couple of decades, you may not even be able to tell that it used to be a house.

The law of increasing entropy is very relevant to the subject of evolution. Evolution, a "natural process," claims to be causing an enormous complexity of living beings, a process that can never go backwards. But the law of increasing entropy, also a "natural process," causes the universe to become less complex and more random over time.

The law of increasing entropy is widely recognized as an impenetrable barrier to "upward" evolution, from spontaneous generation all the way to natural selection. Although evolutionists have tried various ways of getting around this barrier, the fact remains that no proof of true upward evolution has ever been found. The law of increasing entropy provides a good explanation as to why it never will be found, for entropy and evolution are completely opposite concepts.

EVIDENCE

* Another way of stating the second law, then, is: "the universe is constantly getting more disorderly." Viewed that way, we can see the second law all about us. We have to work hard to

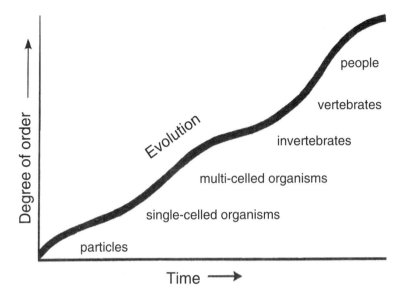

(a) Evolution proposes an increase in order over time.

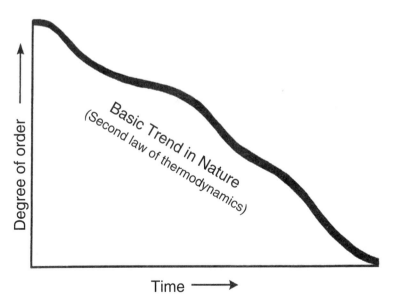

(b) The second law of thermodynamics, which applies in every process, shows that over time all systems, including living systems, decrease in order.

Time is the **enemy** of evolution, not its hero.

straighten a room, but left to itself, it becomes a mess again very quickly and very easily. Even if we never enter it, it becomes dusty and musty. How difficult to maintain houses, and machinery, and our own bodies in perfect working order; how easy to let them deteriorate. In fact, all we have to do is nothing, and everything deteriorates, collapses, breaks down, wears out, all by itself — and that is what the second law is all about. . . .

You can argue, of course, that the phenomenon of life may be an exception [to the second law of thermodynamics]. Life on earth has steadily grown more complex, more versatile, more elaborate, more orderly, over the billions of years of the planet's existence. From no life at all, living molecules were developed, then living cells, then living conglomerates of cells, worms, vertebrates, mammals, finally Man. And in Man is a three-pound brain, which, as far as we know, is the most complex and orderly arrangement of matter in the universe. How could the human brain develop out of the primeval slime? How could that vast increase in order (and therefore that vast decrease of entropy) have taken place?[1]

  * It should be clear that the claim for an inherent evolutionary increase in entropy and organization is based on an arbitrary model which shows signs of having been constructed simply to yield the desired result. . . . There is nothing in evolutionary or developmental biology that justifies their assumptions that a successful mutation (which seems merely to mean a selectively neutral one in their model) is always associated with an increase in some global measure of phenotype. Nor is there anything to support the assumption that new species arise as the result of single gene mutations and are initially genetically uniform. If these assumptions are removed, the whole edifice collapses.[2]

  * Because of the mysterious way the entropy law is usually formulated and because the great physicist A.S. Eddington hailed it as the supreme law of nature, that law has had an unusually strong appeal. The concept of entropy has also been transplanted into virtually all other domains — communications, biology, economics, sociology, psychology, political science, and even art. . . .

Thermodynamics teaches what Boltzmann and, quite recently, Erwin Schrödinger said, namely, that any organism needs to continuously suck low entropy from the environment; otherwise, it would very quickly degrade entropically. But no loophole has yet been discovered in the entropy law to justify the impressive claim that the existence of life-bearing structures is a necessary conclusion of thermodynamic laws.[3]

* Being a generalization of experience, the second law could only be invalidated by an actual engine. In other words, the question, "Can the second law of thermodynamics be circumvented?" is not well worded and could be answered only if the model incorporated every feature of the real world. But the answer can readily be given to the question, "Has the second law of thermodynamics been circumvented?" Not yet.[4]

* There is a factor called "entropy" in physics, indicating that the whole universe of matter is running down, and ultimately will reduce itself to uniform chaos. This follows from the second law of thermodynamics, which seems about as basic and unquestionable to modern scientific minds as any truth can be.

At the same time that this is happening on the physical level of existence, something quite different seems to be happening on the biological level: structure and species are becoming more complex, more sophisticated, more organized, with higher degrees of performance and consciousness. . . .

How can the forces of biological development and the forces of physical degeneration be operating at cross purposes?

It would take, of course, a far greater mind than mine even to attempt to penetrate this riddle. I can only pose the question — because it seems to me the question most worth asking and working upon with all our intellectual and scientific resources. Our other quests seem trivial and time-bound compared with the fate of our species, and of all life in the universe.[5]

* There is another question which has plagued us for more than a century: What significance does the evolution of a living being have in the world described by thermodynamics, a world of ever-increasing disorder?[6]

* Citing Albert Einstein: "Classical thermodynamics . . . is the only physical theory of universal content concerning which I am convinced that, within the framework of its basic concepts, it will never be overthrown."[7]

* [There is a] general natural tendency of all observed

systems to go from order to disorder, reflecting dissipation of energy available for future transformation—the law of increasing entropy.[8]

* The entropy law says that evolution dissipates the overall available energy for life on this planet. Our concept of evolution is the exact opposite. We believe that evolution somehow magically creates greater overall value and order on earth. Now that the environment we live in is becoming so dissipated and disordered that it is apparent to the naked eye, we are for the first time beginning to have second thoughts about our views on evolution, progress, and the creation of things of material value. More about the implications of this in later sections.[9]

CONCEPT 6-2: RANDOM MUTATIONS ARE RARE AND HARMFUL.

RATIONALE

Until the 1950s and 1960s, relatively little was known about mutations or even the genetic code. Fortunately today, we have vast information on these subjects compared with the time when Darwin formulated the theory of evolution. One fact appreciated today is that the structure of genes is extremely stable. Almost without exception, they remain absolutely unchanged and are accurately copied to their offspring at the time of reproduction.

Exceptionally, however, the molecular structure of a gene does alter. This is a phenomenon termed "mutation." Scientists have analyzed nature for signs of mutations, and created many in the laboratory. There exist several known causes of mutations, including ultraviolet light, cosmic radiation, environmental chemicals, and copying errors during reproduction. Mutations most commonly result in but one chemical change amid the thousands of molecular components of a particular gene. In fact, the DNA itself is usually changed so slightly that it can't even be detected in the laboratory.

But even such subtle molecular alterations have drastic consequences. Almost all mutations are harmful, and very often prove lethal to the creature. Of all the mutations studied, scientists conclude that no single one clearly increases the survivability of the living creature.

It appears that the Creator realized the inherent danger of mutations, and designed cellular features to combat them. Research demonstrates that cells have many special safeguards to protect against genetic errors. For example, DNA cannot be copied except by particular enzymes, which chemically "check" one another to detect errors. For example, one enzyme rejects new amino acids if they are too large,

A two-headed turtle.

while the other rejects those that are too small. Using their own minds, scientists conclude that they are unable to imagine a cellular system of checks and safeguards that could be any better at protecting the integrity of DNA.

All the while, evolution depends upon mutations producing "new" creatures. Assume, for the sake of argument, that the first cell did come into existence on its own. To travel up the evolutionary ladder from this simple beginning to a complete human being requires the cell to generate enormous quantities of new genetic information. New DNA code is essential to manufacture skin, eyes, nerves, bones, hearing, muscles, blood cells, and so forth.

But the study of modern genetics shows that mutations lead to a net loss of information, not any overall gain. Mutations, when they do occur, do not increase the total amount of information contained by a cell. Rather, if they don't kill the cell in the process, they clearly decrease the amount of information it contains. So how can mutations possibly account for the enormous amount of new information required by advanced creatures? Furthermore, since most mutant genes produce sterile offspring, how can this mutated cell pass its "new" genetic information to its offspring?

The truth is that "beneficial" mutations are only wishful thinking. Mutations do not produce new information or superior creatures. No scientific evidence exists to the contrary.

EVIDENCE

* The process of mutation ultimately furnishes the materials for adaptation to changing environments. Genetic variations that increase the reproductive fitness of a population to its environment are preserved and multiplied by natural selection. Deleterious mutations are eliminated more or less rapidly depending on the magnitude of their harmful effects. High-energy radiations, such as x-rays, increase the rate of mutations. Mutations induced by radiations are random in the sense that they arise independently of their effects on the fitness of the individuals which carry them. Randomly induced mutations are usually deleterious. In a precisely organized and coupled system like the genome of an organism, a random change will most frequently decrease, rather than increase, the orderliness or useful information of the system.[10]

* It therefore seems clear that, contrary to Darwin's conception, most of the genetic variation in populations arises not from new mutations at each generation but from the re-shuffling of previously accumulated mutations by recombination. Although mutation is the ultimate source of all genetic variation, it is a relatively rare event, providing a mere trickle of new alleles into the much larger reservoir of stored genetic variation. Indeed, recombination alone is sufficient to enable a population to expose its hidden variation for many generations without the need for new genetic input by mutation.[11]

* It has been estimated that those chance errors occur at a rate of about one per several hundred million cells in each generation. This frequency does not seem to be sufficient to explain the evolution of the great diversity of life forms, given the well-known fact that most mutations are harmful and only very few result in useful variations.[12]

* There is nothing in evolutionary or developmental biology that justifies their assumptions that a successful mutation (which seems merely to mean a selectively neutral one in their model) is always associated with an increase in some global measure of phenotype. Nor is there anything to support the assumption that new species arise as the result of single gene mutations and are initially genetically uniform. If these assumptions are removed, the whole edifice collapses.[13]

* All these children are mutant offspring of the same parent, differing from their parents with respect to one gene each. This very high mutation rate is a distinctly unbiological feature of the computer model. In real life, the probability that a gene will mutate is often less than one in a million. The reason for building a high mutation rate into the model is for the benefit of human eyes, and humans haven't the patience to wait a million generations for a mutation.[14]

* Since the vast majority of detectable mutations are deleterious, an artificially increased human mutation rate would be expected to be harmful in proportion to the increase.[15]

* We have to face one particular fact, one so peculiar that in the opinion of some people it makes nonsense of the whole theory of evolution: Although the biological theory calls for incorporation of beneficial variants in the living populations, a vast majority of the mutants observed in any organism are detrimental to welfare. Some are lethal, causing incurable diseases or fatal deaths; others are sub-lethal, killing off or incapacitating most of the carriers but allowing some to escape; still others are sub-vital, damaging health, resistance or vigor in a variety of ways.[16]

* The opportune appearance of mutations permitting animals and plants to meet their needs seems hard to believe. Yet the Darwinian theory is even more demanding: a single plant, a single animal would require thousands and thousands of lucky, appropriate events. Thus, miracles would become the rule: events with an infinitesimal probability could not fail to occur. . . . There is no law against daydreaming, but science must not indulge in it.[17]

* The mass evidence shows that all, or almost all, known mutations are unmistakably pathological and the few remaining ones are highly suspect.[18]

* Scientists are convinced that the cells system of checks and safeguards is the best possible for protecting against DNA errors.[19]

* Of all the mutations that have been analyzed, it is doubtful that a single one can be clearly said to have increased the survivability of the plant or animal.[20]

* Evolutionists assert, however, that a very small number of these mutations may be beneficial; perhaps one in 10,000. This opinion, however, is not based on any evidence of favorable mutations. So why do evolutionists make the claim? The only reasonable explanation is that they know evolution must be ascribed to mutations, and that evolution is impossible unless favorable mutations do occur.[21]

* It is entirely in line with the accidental nature of

mutations that extensive tests have agreed in showing the vast majority of them detrimental to the organism in its job of surviving and reproducing, just as changes accidentally introduced into any artificial mechanism are predominantly harmful to its useful operations. . . . Good ones are so rare that we can consider them all bad.[22]

* Research has uncovered that fact that cells have many special safeguards to protect against genetic errors from ever occurring. DNA information cannot be copied except with many different enzymes, which "check" one another for errors. These include double-sieve enzymes to make sure the right amino acid is linked to the right tRNA. One sieve rejects amino acids too large, while the other rejects those too small.[23]

* In this chapter I'll bring several examples of evolution, [i.e., instances alleged to be examples of evolution] particularly mutations, and show that information is not increased. . . . But in all the reading I've done in the life sciences literature, I've never found a mutation that added information. All point mutations that have been studied on the molecular level turn out to reduce the genetic information and not to increase it. The NDT [neo-Darwinian theory] is supposed to explain how the information of life has been built up by evolution. The essential biological difference between a human and a bacterium is in the information they contain. All other biological differences follow from that. The human genome has much more information than does the bacterial genome. Information cannot be built up by mutations that lose it. A business can't make money by losing it a little at a time.[24]

* Some mutations are "beneficial," that is, the individual in whom they are expressed is better able to adapt to a given set of environmental circumstances. The large majority of mutations, however, are harmful or even lethal to the individual in whom they are expressed. Such mutations can be regarded as introducing a "load," or genetic burden, into the pool. The term "genetic load" was first used by the late H.J. Muller, who recognized that the rate of mutations is increased by numerous agents man has introduced into his environment, notably ionizing radiation and mutagenic chemicals.[25]

CONCEPT 6-3: TIME IS INSUFFICIENT FOR ENOUGH BENEFICIAL MUTATIONS TO OCCUR.

RATIONALE

Acknowledging the scientific evidence, supporters of evolution admit that the number of beneficial mutations must be extremely small. The figure of 1 in 10,000 is often quoted, though this is not based upon any evidence confirmed by research. Nevertheless, evolutionists insist upon this claim. Why is this the case? Simply because evolution, they admit, must be attributed to mutations, and that evolution is impossible unless at least some favorable mutations take place.

Following along this same reasoning, the higher the total number of mutations, the greater the chance that a positive mutation might occur. Evolutionists, with few exceptions, believe that these proposed favorable mutations must result in only slight changes. A mutation that would result in more than a slight change would be too disruptive, and certainly harmful or lethal to the plant or animal. Yet given many thousands of generations, the new "improved" creature would eventually replace the original one. Natural selection would be a success.

Assume for a moment it is true that 1 out of 10,000 mutations leads to a "better" creature (though the actual number may be on the order of one in a million, if it ever happens at all). For this mutation to be passed on, it cannot occur just anywhere within the creature. It must occur in the genes of the specific reproductive cells, and these make up only a small fraction of most creatures' bodies. What's more, this mutation must be somehow overlooked by the cells' safeguards against DNA mutation.

Truly an extraordinary amount of time would be necessary to increase the chances of this process ever being successful. Evolutionists claim that to slightly change one species into a new species requires many thousands of these hypothetical favorable mutations, and at least hundreds of thousands, if not millions, of years. Greater changes, such as transforming a reptile into a bird, would require an extremely large number of beneficial mutations, and demand billions of years. To mutate from a lower form of life to a higher form of life would require an exponentially large number of positive mutations. There is not enough time in the proposed 570 million years since evolution is said to have begun.

In an attempt to close the time gap necessary for evolution to take place, some point out the similarity between DNA of various creatures, emphasizing that the change is not so great after all. The similarity between human and ape DNA, for example, is said to be 96 percent by one limited technique. But even a four percentage difference (if this number is actually true) means that tremendous quantities of new information would be required. Since humans have an amount of information equivalent to 1,000 500-page books, a 4 percent difference amounts to 40 large books. Evolution claims that random mutation plus natural selection generated the information equivalent to these 40 large books, 12 million words arranged in intelligible sentences. Creating this amount of new genetic code is quite impossible, even if we allow the 10 million years for ape/human transformation that evolutionists claim.

To additionally illustrate the time challenge of "creating" new genetic information, consider this. Population genetics calculations show that animals with 20 years between each generation could pass on no more than about 1,700 mutations in these 10 million years. But only perhaps 1 mutation in 10,000 is beneficial. Therefore, not even one positive mutation is likely to be incorporated into the species. So how could mutation and natural selection ever achieve all the millions of beneficial mutations needed to transform reptiles into birds, land mammals into whales, or apes into humans? Even trillions upon trillions of years would not be enough.

Evidence

* Darwin's own bulldog, Huxley, as Eldredge reminds us again, warned him against his insistent gradualism, but Darwin had good reason. His theory was largely aimed at replacing creationism as an explanation of how living complexity could arise out of simplicity. Complexity cannot spring up in a single stroke of chance: that would be like hitting upon the combination number that opens a bank vault. But a whole series of tiny chance steps, if non-randomly selected, can build up almost limitless complexity of adaptation. It is as though the vault's door were to open another chink every time the number on the dials moved a little closer to the winning number. Gradualness is of the essence. In the context of the fight against creationism, gradualism is more or less synonymous with evolution itself. If you throw out gradualness you throw out the very thing that makes evolution more plausible than creation.[26]

* Bacteria, the study of which has formed a great part of the foundation of genetics and molecular biology, are the organisms which, because of their huge numbers, produce the most mutants. . . . Bacteria, despite their great production of intra-specific varieties, exhibit a great fidelity to their species.

The bacillus *Echerichia coli,* whose mutants have been studied very carefully, is the best example. The reader will agree that it is surprising, to say the least, to want to prove evolution and to discover its mechanisms and then to choose as a material for this study a being which practically stabilized a billion years ago.[27]

* No matter how numerous they may be, mutations do not produce any kind of evolution. The opportune appearance of mutations permitting animals and plants to meet their needs seems hard to believe. Yet the Darwinian theory is even more demanding. A single plant or a single animal would require thousands and thousands of lucky, appropriate events. Thus, miracles would become the rule: events with infinitesimal probability could no longer fail to occur. . . . There is no law against daydreaming, but science must not indulge in it.[28]

* How do major evolutionary changes get started? Does anyone still believe that populations sit around for tens of thousands of years, waiting for favorable mutations to occur (and just how does that happen, by the way?), then anxiously guard them until enough accumulate for selection to push the population toward new and useful change? There you have the mathematical arguments of neo-Darwinism that Waddington and others rightly characterized as "vacuous."[29]

* Population genetics calculations show that animals with 20 years between each generation could pass on no more than about 1,700 mutations in these 10 million years.[30]

* Dr. George G. Simpson, an American champion of evolutionary dogma, admitted that if there was an effective breeding population, of say, 100 million individuals, and they could produce a new generation every single day, the likelihood of obtaining good evolutionary results from mutations could be expected only about once in 274 billion years. This, needless to say, is beyond the currently estimated 4.5 billion-year-old earth![31]

* As Professor Pierre Grassé, who for 30 years held the chair in evolution at the Sorbonne, has written: "The probability of dust carried by the wind reproducing Dürer's 'Melancholia' is less infinitesimal than the probability of copy errors in the DNA molecules leading to the formation of the eye."[32]

* Barring extinction, a typical established species — whether a species of land plants, insects, mammals, or marine

invertebrates — will undergo little measurable change in form during 105–107 generations.[33]

CONCEPT 6-4: NATURAL SELECTION DOES NOT LEAD TO NEW SPECIES.

RATIONALE

Competition among species is claimed as the process that leads to new species. But after 160 years of extensive study since Darwin described this formula, science has uncovered no proof that species actually do change.

Natural selection does take place at times, but only on a very limited scale, and just the opposite of what evolutionists are looking for. It causes species not to grow in number, but to become extinct! Many species, dinosaurs for example, have become extinct over the years, a feature of natural selection. They were incapable of surviving in the changing environment of earth.

It is understandable that the fastest, most agile, and strongest creatures will survive longer than the sick, the weakened, and the crippled. But while natural selection may explain the survival of the fittest within a particular group of plants or animals, it does not explain transformation from one species into another. Actually, natural selection is conservative, not creative. It weeds out the mutated varieties and conserves the status quo of a species.

One reason new species do not appear is this: For natural selection to work, the new "creature feature" must be clearly superior to the former one. But mutation-induced changes occur only incrementally at best. If the new feature is incomplete and functionless, the creature

Animals battling for supremacy.

Can this bird fly?

will have no advantage, and may well be less likely to survive. What benefit, for example, is half a wing or an incomplete ear that can't hear?

A seldom-publicized fact is that in later editions of his books, Darwin himself expressed the unlikelihood of mutation and natural selection actually producing new organ systems and new species. The eye, Darwin initially proposed, evolved from a dimple in the forehead all the way to the most complex organ in the human body. With a list of features like those of a modern camera, the eye has an aiming mechanism, focusing, and aperture adjustment — all automatic. And this amazing product just happened by chance?

A slight "positive" mutation must make the creature more likely to survive, and therefore perpetuate more positive mutations. But a mutation leading to eventual development of the eye would have been useless without its complete system. Vision requires everything to be functioning including the lens, retinal cells, optic nerves, and brain vision centers. Every component is essential. If any is lacking, vision (accompanied by increased survival) is impossible. Therefore, the eye could not possibly have evolved through natural selection, a conclusion expressed by Colin Patterson, chief paleontologist at the British Museum of Natural History:

> * The adaptive value of the perfected structure is easily seen,
> but intermediate steps seem to be useless, or even harmful. For

example, what use is a lens in the eye unless it works? A distorting lens might be worse than no lens at all. . . . How can the segments of an animal like the earthworm or centipede arise bit-by-bit? An animal is either segmented or it is not. The usual answer to such a question is that they are due only to the failure of the imagination.[34]

Carefully controlled laboratory experiments have been conducted for years, attempting to demonstrate natural selection. If successful under artificial circumstances, it might at least lend support to the idea of natural selection occurring in nature. Yet no new species have ever been developed. They should have listened to Darwin, who eventually declared:

* Natural selection is incompetent to account for the incipient stages of useful structures.[35]

EVIDENCE

* To propose and argue that mutations even tandem with "natural selection" are the root causes for 6,000,000 viable, enormously complex species is to mock logic, deny the weight of evidence, and reflect the fundamentals of mathematical probability.[36]

* To suppose that the eye with all its inimitable contrivances for adjusting the focus to different distances, for admitting different amounts of light, and for the correction of spherical and chromatic aberration, could have been formed by natural selection, seems, I freely confess, absurd in the highest sense.[37]

* It was not only his general theory that was almost entirely lacking in any direct empirical support, but his special theory was also largely dependent on circumstantial evidence. A striking witness to this is the fact that nowhere was Darwin able to point to one bona fide case of natural selection having actually generated evolutionary change in nature, let alone having been responsible for the creation of a new species.[38]

* But how do you get from nothing such an elaborate something if evolution must proceed through a long sequence of intermediate stages, each favored by natural selection? You can't fly with 2% of a wing or gain much protection from an iota's similarity with a potentially concealing piece of vegetation. How, in other words, can natural selection explain these incipient stages of structures that can only be used (as we now

observe them) in much elaborated forms? . . . One point stands high above the rest: the dilemma of incipient stages. Mivart identified this problem as primary and it remains so today.[39]

* Even though we have no direct evidence for smooth transitions, can we invent a reasonable sequence of intermediate forms, that is, viable, functioning organisms, between ancestors and descendants? Of what possible use are the imperfect incipient stages of useful structures? What good is half a jaw or half a wing?o[40]

* The order of life and the persistence of nearly all basic anatomical designs throughout the entire geological history of multi-cellular animals record the intricacy and resistance to change of complex development programs, not the perfection of adaptive design in local environments.[41]

* How then are we to account for the evolution of such a complicated organ as the eye? . . . If even the slightest thing is

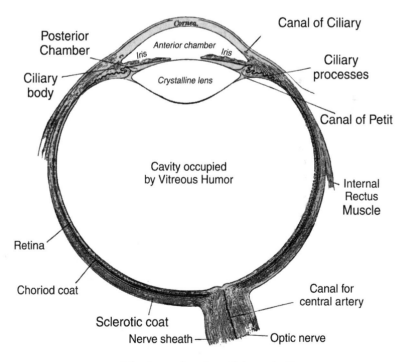

A horizontal section of the eyeball

wrong — if the retina is missing, or the lens opaque, or the dimensions in error — the eye fails to form a recognizable image and is consequently useless. Since it must be either perfect, or perfectly useless, how could it have evolved by small, successive, Darwinian steps?[42]

* Darwin must have begun to realize the impossibility of his own theory. The eye, he initially proposed, evolved from a hole in the head all the way to an organ far more sophisticated than the most modern camera! The human eye has automatic aiming mechanism, automatic focusing, and automatic aperture adjustment. It can function in almost total darkness one moment and in bright sunlight the next. And while we sleep, our eyes perform their own maintenance work! And this all happened by chance? Not![43]

* Once upon a time, it all looked so simple. Nature rewarded the fit with the carrot of survival and punished the unfit with the stick of extinction. The trouble only started when it came to defining fitness. . . . Thus natural selection looks after the survival and reproduction of the fittest, and the fittest are those which have the highest rate of reproduction . . . we are caught in a circular argument which completely begs the question of what makes evolution evolve.[44]

* The adaptive value of the perfected structure is easily seen, but intermediate steps seem to be useless, or even harmful. For example, what use is a lens in the eye unless it works? A distorting lens might be worse than no lens at all. . . . How can the segments of an animal like the earthworm or centipede arise bit-by-bit? An animal is either segmented or it is not. The usual answer to such a question is that they are due only to the failure of the imagination.[45]

* No one has ever produced a species by mechanisms of natural selection. No one has ever gotten near it and most of the current argument in neo-Darwinism is about this question: How can a species originate and is it there that natural selection seems to be fading out and chance mechanisms of one sort or another are being invoked? . . . All one can learn about the history of life is learned from systematics, from groupings one finds in nature. The rest of it is storytelling of one sort or another. We have access to the tips of a tree; the

tree itself is theory, and people who pretend to know about the tree and to describe what went on with it, how the branches came off and the twigs came off are, I think, telling stories.[46]

* No one has ever produced a species by mechanisms of natural selection. No one has ever gotten near it.[47]

* Neither observation nor controlled experiment has shown natural selection manipulating mutations so as to produce a new gene, hormone, enzyme system, or organ.[48]

* Instead of finding the gradual unfolding of life, what geologists of Darwin's time and geologists of the present day actually find is a highly uneven or jerky record; that is, species appear in the sequence very suddenly, show little or no change during their existence in the record, then abruptly go out of the record. And it is not always clear (in fact it's rarely clear) that the descendants were actually better adapted than their predecessors. In other words, biological improvement is hard to find.[49]

Gradualism replaced by the "hopeful monster" theory.

CONCEPT 6-5: SUDDEN DEVELOPMENT OF A NEW SPECIES (PUNCTUATED EQUILIBRIUM) IS SCIENTIFICALLY IMPOSSIBLE.

RATIONALE

The idea of gradual change is an essential part of evolutionary thinking. But scientists acknowledge several seemingly insurmountable obstacles to proving evolution. These include the improbability of beneficial mutations, the illogic and nil evidence of natural selection, and as we will discuss in chapters 9 through 11, the absence of fossil proof.

One proposition to

overcome these obstacles would be for creatures to make sudden leaps in development. Harvard's revered evolutionist Dr. Stephen J. Gould favors the concept that one time, for example, a lizard egg hatched and out popped the first complete bird — so called "punctuated equilibrium," "quantum speciation," or even "hopeful monsters." Dr. Gould proposes that all the required mutations simply occurred in one creature at the same time, and at birth it became a new species. He insists, "Major structural transitions can occur rapidly without a smooth series of intermediate stages."

He is not alone. Faced with the same lack of evidence for gradual evolution, the trend among biologists and paleontologists today is to abandon the idea of mutation-induced slow change and natural selection, and to replace it with instantaneous new species. The journal *American Biology Teacher* explains punctuated equilibrium in the following way:

> * On this view, there is little evidence of modification between species, or of forms intermediate between species, because neither generally occurred. A species forms and evolves almost instantaneously (on the geological time scale) and then remains virtually unchanged until it disappears, yielding its habitat to a new species.[50]

However attractive punctuated equilibrium is for overcoming the obstacle of gradual evolution, the concept is nonsense nevertheless. Punctuated equilibrium is not based on factual evidence, but actually on the absence of evidence.

Just consider a few of the challenges to this scenario. First of all, there is no known genetic mechanism that would allow for such enormous genetic changes. Secondly, punctuated equilibrium has never been observed to take place, nor replicated in the laboratory. Thirdly, the concept raises some remarkably difficult questions. For example, for the hypothetical "new species" to reproduce, a second bird of the opposite sex and the same new species must also have hatched in the next nest in order for the new species to reproduce itself. How likely is this to occur?

The truth is that no speck of evidence has been found to support punctuated equilibrium. Its only rationale is the need for some evolutionary process to explain the existence and diversity of life, some explanation aside from special creation. But to the person willing to consider creationism, however, intentional design is clearly the superior explanation for the presence and complexity of life.

EVIDENCE

* Eldredge and Gould, by contrast, decided to take the record at face value. On this view, there is little evidence of modification between species, or of forms intermediate between species, because neither generally occurred. A species forms and evolves almost instantaneously (on the geological time scale) and then remains virtually unchanged until it disappears, yielding its habitat to a new species.

Gould and Eldredge contend that: "Phyletic gradualism was an a priori assertion from the start — it was never 'seen' in the rocks; it expressed the culture and political bias of 19th century liberalism." By the same token, while many feel that punctuated equilibrium postulates how speciation occurs, its occurrence is not based on empirical evidence but on the apparent lack of evidence — gaps in the fossil record. . . . Bodnar, Jones, and Ellis suggested that one would not see intermediate forms in simple eukaryotes in the fossil record because there are no intermediate forms. A single mutation in a regulatory gene caused the change in one leap of evolutionary development.[51]

* I can understand the inherent difficulty in attempting to discover intermediate forms. My problem concerns the methodology of science: If an evolutionist accepts gaps as a prerequisite for his theory, is he not arguing from a lack of evidence? If a biologist teaches that between two existing fossils there was a non-existing third (and perhaps several others), is he not really like the man of religious faith who says: "I believe, even though there is not evidence"?[52]

* By definition, a new species arises when it splits off from a parent species. But a species is a species only if it doesn't interbreed with other species, including the one from which it arose. The critical question in species formation is how the barrier to reproduction is erected and maintained. As it turns out, the species barrier is a two-layered defense. There are pre-mating mechanisms — behavioral, ecological, and physical differences that make it difficult for two species to mate. If that line of defense fails, second-line, post-mating mechanisms ensure that the progeny of the barrier-crashers are either rendered sterile (like mules) or they die before reaching maturity.[53]

* Did life on earth change steadily and gradually through time? The fossil record emphatically says "no." For millions of years, life goes along uneventfully; then suddenly, a series of natural disasters disrupts the status quo and disturbs and re-structures vast segments of existing ecosystems.[54]

* It should be clear that the claim for an inherent evolutionary increase in entropy and organization is based on an arbitrary model which shows signs of having been constructed simply to yield the desired result. . . . There is nothing in evolutionary or developmental biology that justifies their assumptions that a successful mutation (which seems merely to mean a selectively neutral one in their model) is always associated with an increase in some global measure of phenotype. Nor is there anything to support the assumption that new species arise as the result of single gene mutations and are initially genetically uniform. If these assumptions are removed, the whole edifice collapses.[55]

* Darwin's own bulldog, Huxley, as Eldredge reminds us again, warned him against his insistent gradualism, but Darwin had good reason. His theory was largely aimed at replacing creationism as an explanation of how living complexity could arise out of simplicity. Complexity cannot spring up in a single stroke of chance: that would be like hitting upon the combination number that opens a bank vault. But a whole series of tiny chance steps, if non-randomly selected, can build up almost limitless complexity of adaptation. It is as though the vault's door were to open another chink every time the number on the dials moved a little closer to the winning number. Gradualness is of the essence. In the context of the fight against creationism, gradualism is more or less synonymous with evolution itself. If you throw out gradualness you throw out the very thing that makes evolution more plausible than creation.[56]

* Major structural transitions can occur rapidly without a smooth series of intermediate stages.[57]

* It is the nature of biological evolution that it always proceeds slowly.[58]

* Ruse (along with others among Gould's critics) has no hesitation in assigning Gould's advocacy of punctuated equilibrium theory and the support it has received in large part to politics, both internal and external to science. He identifies an internal struggle among paleontologists and other evolution-

ists, especially geneticists, for cognitive standing in evolutionary theorizing. . . . Gould's advocacy of punctuated equilibrium theory, Ruse claims, is connected with its congruency with the Marxist ideology of dialectical materialism.[59]

* The Eldredge-Gould concept of punctuated equilibrium has gained wide acceptance among paleontologists. It attempts to account for the following paradox: Within continuously sampled lineages, one rarely finds the gradual morphological trends predicted by Darwinian evolution: rather, change occurs with the sudden appearance of new, well-differentiated species. Apart from the obvious sampling problems inherent to the observations that stimulated the model, and apart from its intrinsic circularity (one could argue that speciation can occur only when phyletic change is rapid, not vice versa), the model is more ad hoc explanation than theory, and it rests on shaky ground.[60]

* There are a number of problems with hypothetical schemes capable of producing rapid, large, coherent changes in phenotypes. Equally large immediate changes in the genotype might be needed, and any large change in genotype or phenotype must surely be sufficiently disruptive to be lethal. And where would a large change in a phenotype or genotype come from? Moreover, suppose an oddity were to be produced, how would a population be established and maintained?[61]

* The reorganization required for the origin of the highest categories may seem so great that only "hopeful monsters" will do. Here, however, we must consider the size and complexity of the organisms. Such changes would probably have been impossible except in an organism of very small size and simple anatomy. I have recorded more than 100,000 newborn guinea pigs and have seen many hundreds of monsters of diverse sorts but none were remotely "hopeful," all having died shortly after birth if not earlier.[62]

* We conclude that the probability that species selection is a general solution to the origin of higher taxa is not great, and that neither of the contending theories of evolutionary change at the species level, phyletic gradualism or punctuated equilibrium, seem applicable to the origin of new body plans.[63]

CHAPTER SEVEN

YOUNG AGE OF THE EARTH

INTRODUCTION

The true age of the earth is essential information. For evolution to have occurred (to go from primitive one-cell creatures to modern humans) is said to require (among many other things) an inhabitable planet "billions of years old" to give enough time for life to emerge and develop. Actually, the statistics for the number of necessary mutations demands a time period on the order of trillions of years!

Age of the earth is estimated using several measuring techniques, which will be examined below. It is essential to first understand the concept of uniformitarianism — the idea that geologic processes have always occurred at the same rate. For example, uniformitarianism claims that the layers of rock we see today, the drift between continents, and the formation of river valleys are extremely slow processes that have been proceeding at a constant rate since time began.

Geologists are recognizing today, however, that uniformitarianism does not always apply. We've been taught, for example, that sedimentary rock indicates an old planet. Today, however, we know that sedimentary rock can actually form very quickly. A great worldwide flood can certainly explain many features found in geology. What's more, other processes that were once thought to take millions of years to occur are now recognized to happen very quickly at times. These include the formation of coal beds, stalactites, salt deposits, coral reefs, and river valleys. This conclusion has profound implications on measuring the age of the earth. Rather than looking at a canyon and being convinced of how many millions of years it took to form, geologists are now realizing that given the right catastrophic conditions, it may have formed in a matter of months or years.

Radiometric dating, long considered a gold standard, is actually a flawed and unreliable technique. For accuracy, it requires information about the ancient world that we have no way of knowing today. This helps to explain why the results of such tests are so often in conflict with one another.

Geochronology is the study of assigning age based upon geologic findings. Many geochronologic methods are available. To draw accurate conclusions, we must gather as much data as possible from several reliable sources, and draw the best conclusions we honestly can. Contrary to what is commonly taught, the greatest weight of scientific evidence does not point toward a four-to-five-billion-years-old earth. Scientific evidence actually supports a very young planet, on the order of only six to ten thousand years old, far too young for evolution to have had any chance to occur.

CONCEPT 7-1: SEDIMENTARY ROCK AND CANYONS CAN FORM QUICKLY, AND DO NOT PROVE THE EARTH IS ANCIENT.

RATIONALE

Sedimentary rock is formed by water depositing layers of solid material on the earth's surface. During this process, heavier elements drop to the bottom, while lighter ones remain at the top. The final layers are then cemented together by pressure from overlying earth and by the minerals dissolved within the water. Mature sedimentary rock looks like layers of blankets laid flat on top of one another.

Such rock can be formed in two ways. The first is by a small amount of water depositing a layer of dirt and sand over a long period of time. The second is by a vast amount of water making such deposits over a short time period.

When we see sedimentation occurring today, the process is usually slow, small amounts of water depositing layers of dirt and sand in tiny quantities. This observation led some scientists to presume that it has always been this way. If this constant rate has always been the case, then the layers of rock would indeed have taken enormous time to form.

Recent observations and experiments, however, demonstrate that sedimentation and sedimentary rock can also form very rapidly. Much in this regard was learned from the Mount St. Helens eruption on

Sedimentary rock

May 18, 1980. Located in Washington, this volcano deposited 25 feet of finely layered sediment around its base in just six hours.

Furthermore, experiments by several different scientists show that differently sized particles within sediment can quickly sort themselves into layers like those found in sedimentary rock today. To these layers, add time and pressure from the earth above and the result is sedimentary rock. It is quite plausible that thick sedimentary rock was quickly formed through a catastrophic event — such as the huge, globe-covering flood described in Genesis. Such a flood would have picked up vast quantities of sediment, deposited them, and led to the formation of today's sedimentary rock.

The speed with which sedimentary rock forms is also disclosed by the many fossils it contains. To understand the process, consider the following scenario: When a plant or animal dies and falls onto the ground, it quickly decays or is consumed. After a few weeks, often little remains of the creature. Within a few months, even the bones of a larger animal disintegrate.

To prevent such disintegration, the plant or animal must be buried very quickly by mud, volcanic dust, or another protecting substance. If conditions are right — if minerals in the mud, dust, soil, or rock are absorbed by the buried body — the body becomes hard and fossilized over time.

If fossil-containing sedimentary rock was formed by laying down dirt and sand over millions of years, then the remains of the living things would easily have rotted long before they were covered and fossilized. The only way to explain the presence of fossils within rock is for these plants and animals to have been buried very quickly. These facts suggests that the vast quantities of fossil-containing sedimentary rock must have been formed rapidly over days or weeks, not millions of years.

The very form of some fossils tells us how very quickly they formed. Fossils have been discovered, for example, of a marine reptile giving birth, and also of fish eating other fish.

Still clinging to uniformitarianism and slow processes, some geologists have declared that, given its depth, the Grand Canyon and other geological strata must have taken more than one billion years to form. However, we know today that some comparatively small "natural disasters" can have the same affect much more quickly.

The Mount St. Helens' volcano exploded with the force of 20,000 Hiroshima-sized atom bombs. One aftermath of the eruption was a 140-feet-deep canyon that was formed in just one day. At this rate, the entire Grand Canyon could have been formed in only 40 days; not 40 million years! Observations since the eruption have revealed new rock layered strata, similar to the walls of the Grand Canyon, forming at the rate of 100 feet per year. In one case, such a wall descended 25 feet in depth over just one day.

Altitude is another challenge to the formation of the Grand Canyon by the proposed "slowly flowing river" theory. The top of the Grand Canyon is over 6,000 feet above sea level. But the river that supposedly "carved" these walls "billions of years ago" enters the canyon at only 2,800 feet above sea level. To "carve" those walls, the river would have had to flow uphill over 3,200 feet vertically. Clearly, the river did not form the Grand Canyon, for rivers do not flow uphill!

The argument that the formation of sedimentary rock proves an ancient earth is not reliable. Neither is the conclusion that canyons take millions of years to form. Both phenomena could easily have been formed very quickly by a great flood.

EVIDENCE

* In the late Carboniferous Coal Measures of Lancashire, a fossil tree has been found, 38 feet high and still standing in its living position. Sedimentation must therefore have been fast enough to bury the tree and solidify before the tree had time to rot. Similarly, at Gilboa in New York state, within the

deposits of the Devonian Catskill delta, a flashflood (itself an example of a modern catastrophic event) uncovered a whole forest of in situ Devonian trees up to 40 feet high.[1]

* Probably the most convincing proof of the local rapidity of terrestrial sedimentation is provided by the presence in the coal measures of trees still in position of life. . . .

We cannot escape the conclusion that sedimentation was at times very rapid indeed and that at other times there were long breaks in sedimentation, though it looks both uniform and continuous. . . .

One of the most remarkable geological sights I have ever seen was at Mikulov in Czechoslovakia where an excavation in Danubian loess shows the remains of literally dozens of mammoths.[2]

* Experiments and observations also tell us that sedimentation and sedimentary rock can form very rapidly. Take the Mount St. Helens eruption as an example. Located in Washington state, this volcano deposited 25 feet of finely layered sediment around its base in just six hours.[3]

* The bones were obviously human and "in situ," that is, in place and not washed or fallen into the stratum where they rested from higher, younger strata. The portions of the two skeletons that were exposed were still articulated, indicating that the bodies were still intact when buried or covered. . . .

In addition, the dark organic stains found around the bones indicated that the bones had been complete bodies when deposited in the ancient sandstone. . . .

Mine metallurgist Keith Barrett of the Big Indian Copper Mine that owned the discovery site recalled that the rock and sandy soil that had been removed by dozer from above the bones had been solid with no visible caves or crevices. He also remembered that at least 15 feet of material had been removed, including 5 or 6 feet of solid rock. This provided strong, but not conclusive, evidence that the remains were as old as the stratum in which they were found.

And that stratum was at least 100 million years old. Due to considerable local faulting and shifting, the site could either be in the lower Dakota or the still older upper Morrison formation. . . .

Somehow, the university scientists never got around to

age-dating the mystery bones. Dr. Marwitt seemed to lose interest in the matter, then transferred to an eastern university. No one else took over the investigation. . . .

We may never know exactly how human bones came to be in place in rock formations more than 100 million years old. It is highly probable that the bones are, indeed, this old. Yet, who knows? . . .

Part of the mystery, of course, is why the University of Utah scientists chose not to age-date the mystery bones and clear up at least the question of their actual age.[4]

* Lin Ottinger, Moab back-country tour guide and amateur geologist and archaeologist, made a find early last week that could possibly upset all current theories concerning the age of mankind on this planet. While searching for mineral specimens south of Moab, Ottinger found traces of human remains in a geological stratum that is approximately 100 million years old. . . . He carefully uncovered enough of what later proved to be the parts of two human skeletons.

Dr. Marwitt [J.P., prof. of anthropology, Utah University] pronounced the discovery "highly interesting and unusual" for several reasons. As the bones were uncovered, it soon became obvious that they were "in place" and had not washed in or fallen down from higher strata. . . . The rock and soil that had been above the remains had been continuous before the dozer work, with no caves or major faults or crevices visible. Thus, before the mine exploration work, the human remains had been completely covered by about fifteen (15) feet of material, including five or six feet of solid rock. . . . Due to some local shifting and faulting, it was uncertain, without further investigation, whether the find is in the lower Dakota, or still older upper Morrison formation.

Of course, despite evidence that these human remains are "in place" in a formation 100 million years old, the probability is very low that they are actually that old. The bones appeared to be relatively modern in configuration, that is, of *Homo sapiens* rather than one of his ancient, semi-animal predecessors.[5]

* The continuous deposit of a heterogranular sediment in still water was studied. 1. It was noted that the deposited material organized itself immediately after deposition into periodic graded laminae giving the appearance of successive beds.

2. One of the more striking features of these laminae formed in the sediment itself was their regular periodicity. 3. The thickness of the laminae is measured in millimeters. It is independent of the speed of sedimentation and varies according to the extreme difference in the size of the mixed particles. 4. When deposition took place in a water flow, the lamination phenomenon was also observed. The geometry of lamination was modified by the water flow, but the latter was not the cause of the modification. 5. The periodic graded laminae were similar to the laminae or varves observed in nature, which are interpreted as a superposition of seasonal or annual beds. Their origin, however, was quite different arising from periodic structuring after deposit. 6. The question now is to study a number of laminated or varved formations in relation to this mechanism for physical structuring obtained from experimentation.[6]

* In 1959 Broadhurst and Magraw described a fossilized tree, in position of growth, from the Coal Measures at Blackrod near Wigan in Lancashire. This tree was preserved as a cast, and the evidence available suggested that the cast was at least 38 feet in height. The original tree must have been surrounded and buried by sediment which was compacted before the bulk of the tree decomposed, so that the cavity vacated by the trunk could be occupied by new sediment which formed the cast. This implies a rapid rate of sedimentation around the original tree.[7]

* We define stratigraphic disorder as the departure from perfect chronological order of fossils in a stratigraphic sequence. Any sequence in which an older fossil occurs above a younger one is stratigraphically disordered. Scales of stratigraphic disorder may be from millimeters to many meters. Stratigraphic disorder is produced by the physical or biogenic mixing of fossiliferous sediments, and the reworking of older, previously deposited hard parts into younger sediments. Since these processes occur to an extent in virtually all sedimentary systems, stratigraphic disorder at some scale is probably a common feature of the fossil record.[8]

* Since the eruption, new rock layered strata (like walls of the Grand Canyon) have also continued to form at the rate of 100 feet per year (in one case 25 feet in one day).[9]

* Substantive uniformitarianism as a descriptive theory

has not withstood the test of new data and can no longer be maintained in any strict manner.[10]

* It is hereby submitted that most scientists are guilty of an overly zealous interpretation of the doctrine of uniformitarianism. Many instructors dismiss the possibilities of global catastrophes altogether, whereas others ridicule and scoff at the early ideas. These same instructors will implore their students to think scientifically and to develop the principles of multiple-working hypotheses. The fact is, the doctrine of uniformitarianism is no more "proved" than some of the early ideas of worldwide cataclysms have been disproved.[11]

* On sites reaching from Virginia and Pennsylvania, through Kentucky, Illinois, Missouri, and westward toward the Rocky Mountains, prints similar to those shown above, and from 5 to 10 inches long, have from time to time been found on the surface of exposed rocks, and more and more keep turning up as the years go by. What made these prints? As yet the answer is unknown to science. They look like human footprints and it often has been said, though not by scientists, that they really are human footprints made in the soft mud before it became rock.

If man made these prints in this manner, then man's antiquity is no matter of a mere million years or so, as scientists think, but a quarter of a billion years, for they are found in rocks of the Carboniferous Period and those rocks were laid down about 250,000,000 years ago.

If man, or even his ape ancestor, or even that ape ancestor's early mammalian ancestor, existed as far back as in the Carboniferous Period in any shape, then the whole science of geology is so completely wrong that all the geologists will resign their jobs and take up truck driving. Hence, for the present at least, science rejects the attractive explanation that man made these mysterious prints in the mud of the Carboniferous Period with his feet.[12]

* Furthermore, experiments by several different scientists show that differently sized particles within sediment can quickly sort themselves into layers like those found in sedimentary rock today.[13]

* No terrestrial rocks closely approaching an age of 4.6

billion years have yet been discovered. The evidence for the age of the earth is circumstantial, being based upon . . . indirect reasoning.[14]

* A stream moving from side to side, or alternately fast and slow over one area for several hours or days would inevitably sort its material and deposit them in horizontal layers one above another, and we do not see what else could possibly do so.[15]

* The rocks do date the fossils, but the fossils date the rocks more accurately. Stratigraphy cannot avoid this kind of reasoning, if it insists on using only temporal concepts, because circularity is inherent in the derivation of time scales.[16]

* To become fossilized, a plant or animal must usually have hard parts, such as bone, shell or wood. It must be buried quickly to prevent decay and must be undisturbed throughout the long process.[17]

* How can we be so sure that these great masses of rock, weighing untold millions of tons, have really been moved across the surface of the earth for distances that may range up to 25 miles?

The answer to this question is provided by nature herself. Where ages of erosion have stripped away enough of the overlying rocks, geologists can look through the resulting erosion-openings, or "windows," and see the younger rocks below, with their younger fossils — a contradiction of one of the established rules of the science of geology.[18]

CONCEPT 7-2: ANALYSIS OF FOSSILS IN SEDIMENTARY ROCK IS AN UNRELIABLE METHOD OF DATING.

RATIONALE

From time to time scientists analyze fossils in sedimentary rock and "determine" just how old they are, usually on the order of many millions of years. But in truth, assigning an age to fossils in sedimentary rock is very tricky business.

The problems erupt when attempting to date either the age of fossils or the rock that contains them, for neither the age of the fossil nor the age of the rock is certain. This leads inevitably to a situation of circular reasoning.

For example, when determining the age of certain rocks, geologists look for clues in the fossils those rocks contain. If the paleontologists say

A fish fossilized while swallowing another fish.

that creature lived a certain number of years ago, the geologists often give the rock that particular age. In doing so, paleontologists frequently refer to radiometric dating of the fossils. But as we'll see below, radiometric methods are highly unreliable. One simply can't prove the age of a rock by the fossils it contains, for the primary method that assigns age to the fossils is flawed.

Next, when paleontologists are determining the age of certain fossils, they consider the strata of the rock in which the fossils were found. If the geologists say that the rock is a certain age based upon its depth, the paleontologists often assign the fossil that particular age. But this line of reasoning is upset when we realize that deep sedimentary rock can be formed very quickly.

The truth remains that determining the true age of sedimentary rocks and fossils is inexact at best. Neither the fossils nor the rocks nor the combination of the two tell us how old they actually are.

EVIDENCE

* Paleontologists cannot operate this way. There is no way simply to look at a fossil and say how old it is unless you know the age of the rocks it comes from. . . .

And this poses something of a problem: if we date the rocks by their fossils, how can we then turn around and talk about patterns of evolutionary change through time in the fossil record? [19]

* The rocks do date the fossils, but the fossils date the rocks more accurately. Stratigraphy cannot avoid this kind of reasoning, if it insists on using only temporal concepts, because circularity is inherent in the derivation of time scales. [20]

* It cannot be denied that from a strictly philosophical standpoint geologists are here arguing in a circle. The succession of

organisms has been determined by a study of their remains embedded in the rocks, and the relative ages of the rocks are determined by the remains of organisms that they contain.[21]

Note: Especially appreciate the conflict between the following two quotes by the same author:

* Scientists determine when fossils were formed by finding out the age of the rocks in which they lie.[22]

* Paleontology (the study of fossils) is important in the study of geology. The age of rocks may be determined by the fossils found in them.[23]

* One example illustrates a 7-foot long ichthyosaur (a fish-shaped marine reptile, now extinct) that became fossilized while giving birth. We've also found fossils of a fish in the act of swallowing another fish.

Most striking is a fossilized tree trunk oriented vertically. It extends through several layers of sedimentary rock. Indeed, these layers must have all been laid down all at the same time. Otherwise, if the upper layers had taken millions of years (or even more than one year) to form, the top of the tree would have decomposed long before it was encased in rock.[24]

CONCEPT 7-3: COAL AND PETROLEUM CAN FORM RAPIDLY, AND DO NOT PROVE THE EARTH IS ANCIENT.

RATIONALE

It is widely taught that formation of coal and petroleum is a natural process that requires millions of years to complete. This "fact" is often cited as evidence that the earth must, in fact, be very advanced in age. However, considerable evidence points against such rapid formation. For example, in many places fossilized trees have been discovered which penetrate upward through several different layers of coal. The only way this is possible is for the surrounding coal to have formed so quickly that even insects did not have opportunity to consume the wood. Summing up the conclusions of many researchers is the following statement of E.S. Moore, a geologist specializing in coal:

From all available evidence it would appear that coal may form in a very short time, geologically speaking, if conditions are favorable.[25]

Similar conclusions have been made concerning the origin of oil and natural gas. When organic matter is placed under high pressure

A fossilized tree extending through rapidly formed layers of coal.

and temperature, it relatively quickly decomposes into petroleum. Rather than serving as an argument for an ancient earth, such evidence is entirely consistent with a young planet.

EVIDENCE

* A group at Argonne National Laboratory near Chicago, Illinois, recently uncovered some clues as to the origin of coal. The studies indicate that currently accepted theories of the development of coal probably are wrong. "We made simple coals by duplicating conditions that are known to occur in nature," explained Randall Winans, who headed the research team. "But we started with material that was less decomposed than the material nature is thought to have used. . . ."

The group heated undecomposed lignin, the substance that holds plant cells together, in the presence of montmorillite, or illite clay. The process led to simple coals, whose rank depended on the length of exposure to the 300° F temperature. . . .

Although the experiments did not fully reproduce conditions in nature, they do suggest how natural coal could have formed. "It appears that the clay acts as a catalyst to form coal from lignin," explained Winans. Backing that speculation is the fact that montmorillite and illite clays are often found in natural coal.[26]

* For six years, two Australian researchers patiently watched over a set of 1-gram samples of organic materials sealed inside stainless steel "bombs." The samples were derived from brown coal and a type of oil shale called torbanite. Each week, the temperature of the samples was increased by 1º C, gradually heating the material from 100º to 400º C. . . .

The researchers found that after four years a product "indistinguishable from a paraffinic crude oil" was generated from the torbanite-derived samples, while brown coal produced a "wet natural gas."[27]

A group at Argonne National Laboratory near Chicago, Illinois, recently uncovered some clues as to the origin of coal. The studies indicate that currently accepted theories of the development of coal probably are wrong. . . . The group heated undecomposed lignin, the substance that holds plant cells together, in the presence of montmorillite, or illite clay. The process led to simple coals, whose rank depended on the length of exposure to the 300º F temperature.[28]

* To understand this process better, the Exxon group collected samples of oil shale from different parts of the world. The samples included a series from oil shale under the North Sea, where rocks in different locations exhibit different degrees of transformation. Siskin then placed the samples into a pressurized reaction vessel and heated them individually to temperatures ranging from 570º C to 750º C. These hotter-than-natural conditions sped up the transformation from a geologic time frame of millions of years to one measured in days and hours.[29]

* A much greater enigma is presented by the items that have been found in coal. This substance has been deposited on the surface of this earth at various times but most notably in what is called the Carboniferous (and specifically the Upper Carboniferous, so-called, or Pennsylvanian of America) which is calculated to be from 270 to 230 millions of years old; and from the Miocene of the Tertiary Era estimated to be from 26 to 12 million years of age. From it several items have appeared that confound just about everything we believe. For instance, it has been reported that in 1891 a Mrs. Culp of Morrisonville, Illinois, dropped a shovelful of coal in transferring it to her cooking range, and a large lump broke in two,

disclosing a lovely little gold chain of intricate workmanship neatly coiled and embedded.[30]

* In the coal collection of the Mining Academy in Freiberg there is a puzzling human skull composed of brown coal and manganiferous and phosphatic limonite, but its source is not known. This skull was described by Karsten and Dechen in 1842.[31]

CONCEPT 7-4: RADIOMETRIC DATING IS UNRELIABLE.

RATIONALE

Radiometric dating is one of the best known ways of assigning age to an object. Actually, radiometric dating is the term given to several similar techniques. One technique, radiocarbon dating, is especially designed to date fossils of formerly living things.

All the radiometric dating techniques are based on the fact that some radioactive elements undergo decay to produce new elements. In the case of uranium-lead dating, uranium 238 (the "parent element") will eventually decompose to produce lead 206 (the "daughter element").

Ideally, scientists could measure the quantities of radioactive elements in rocks today, know at just what rate they formed, and then determine how old the rock is — or how long ago it cooled from its molten state.

The carbon 14 dating method was developed during the late 1940s and early 1950s by Dr. Willard F. Libby, who won a Nobel Peace Prize for his excellent work. He cautioned, however, that carbon 14 dating is only accurate to about 4,000 years. After that amount of time, the accuracy becomes untrustworthy. Nevertheless, today radiometric dating methods are heavily relied upon. Are their results reliable? In a word, no. The reason is because radiometric dating is based on some fragile, even unanswerable, assumptions.

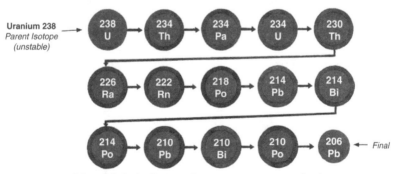

Natural decay from radioactive uranium to lead.

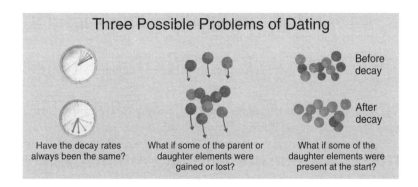

Three Possible Problems of Dating

Have the decay rates always been the same?

What if some of the parent or daughter elements were gained or lost?

What if some of the daughter elements were present at the start?

Before decay

After decay

For radiometric dating to be accurate, several critical factors must be known or be true:

1. The quantity of radioactive elements present when the rock was first formed must be known.
2. The rate of radioactive decay must be constant over time.
3. The rocks must have been insulated from outside factors.

However, this information is either unreliable or unavailable:

1) It is impossible to know the quantity of radioactive elements in a rock when it was first formed, whether thousands, millions, or billions of years ago. We can only speculate. In most calculations, it is assumed that no radioactive element ("daughter element") was present when the rock formed. But there is no way to prove this. We also know from recently "created" rock from lava flow that this assumption is invalid. Sometimes the daughter element is already present.

2) Current evidence suggests that radioactive decay is indeed constant, and is not affected by heat or pressure. However, decay rates have been examined for only about 100 years. Nuclear physicist Dr. Russell Humphreys has presented evidence known as radiohalo analysis which suggests that decay rates used to be faster. We have no assurance of what the radioactive decay rates were thousands, and certainly not billions of years ago.

3) Rocks are rarely insulated from outside factors. Argon, one of the most often measured radioactive elements, is a gas and can easily diffuse out of rock. Potassium and uranium (two other commonly measured elements) are easily dissolved in water. Water seeping in rock could easily dissolve away these

elements, leading to inaccurate measurement. In reality, both parent and daughter elements migrate into the rocks from tectonic, metamorphic, and hydrologic forces. Geochronologists recognize this as a serious drawback to radiometric dating methods.

The public is largely unaware of the unknown assumptions surrounding radiometric dating. By simply changing some of these assumptions, radiometric dates can be brought down to essentially zero. People are also unaware of the fact that many radiometric dating results are wholly inconsistent and are never published.

The bottom line is that no radiometrically determined date is reliable. Radiometric dating, long considered a secure means of determining age, must be viewed realistically. Though the technique has been perfected for many years, the measurements are based upon unverifiable information, and cannot be trusted.

EVIDENCE

A particular rock from Mount St. Helens volcano was obviously formed in 1986 when it cooled. But examination with the potassium-argon (K-Ar) radiometric method, determined it to be as much as 350,000 years old, give or take 50,000 years. This study of Mount St. Helens dacite causes the more fundamental question to be asked — how accurate are K-Ar "ages" from the many other applications?[32]

* Natural processes (including radioactive decay rates) in general do not act at fixed rates. The assumption that an average rate taken over a long period of time can be extrapolated is generally unsatisfactory.[33]

* Radiocarbon analysis of specimens obtained from mummified seals in southern Victoria Land has yielded ages ranging from 615 to 4,600 years. A seal freshly killed at McMurdo had an apparent age of 1,300 years.[34]

* For radiometric dating to be anywhere near accuracy, the rocks being measured must be insulated from outside factors. Argon, one of the most often measured radioactive elements, is a gas and can easily diffuse out of rock. Potassium and uranium (two other commonly measured elements) are easily dissolved in water. Water seeping among rock could easily dissolve away these elements, leading to inaccurate measurement. In reality, both parent and daughter elements mi-

grate into the rocks from tectonic, metamorphic and hydrologic forces. Geochronologists recognize this to be a serious and common drawback to their dating method dogma.[35]

Dr. Willard F. Libby invented the carbon 14 dating method, and developed it during the late 1940s and early 1950s. He won a Nobel Prize for his excellent work. He said in his own book, however, that carbon 14 dating is only accurate to about 4,000 years. After that amount of time, the system becomes unreliable.[36]

* The age of our globe is presently thought to be some 4.5 billion years, based on radiodecay rates of uranium and thorium. Such "confirmation" may be short-lived, as nature is not to be discovered quite so easily. There has been in recent years the horrible realization that radiodecay rates are not as constant as previously thought, nor are they immune to environmental influences. And this could mean that the atomic clocks are reset during some global disaster, and events which brought the Mesozoic to a close may not be 65 million years ago but, rather, within the age and memory of man.[37]

* The troubles of the radiocarbon dating method are undeniably deep and serious. Despite 35 years of technological refinement and better understanding, the underlying assumptions have been strongly challenged, and warnings are out that radiocarbon may soon find itself in a crisis situation. Continuing use of the method depends on a "fix-it-as-we-go" approach, allowing for contamination here, fractionation there, and calibration whenever possible. It should be no surprise, then, that fully half of the dates are rejected. The wonder is, surely, that the remaining half come to be accepted. . . .

No matter how "useful" it is, though, the radiocarbon method is still not capable of yielding accurate and reliable results. There are gross discrepancies, the chronology is uneven and relative, and the accepted dates are actually selected dates. This whole blessed thing is nothing but 13th century alchemy, and it all depends upon which funny paper you read.[38]

* In general, dates in the "correct ball park" are assumed to be correct and are published, but those in disagreement with other data are seldom published nor are discrepancies fully explained.[39]

* Radiocarbon dating is not only subject to errors; like all scientific procedures, it depends on definite assumptions, and these must be understood if the method is to be used properly.

Firstly, it is assumed that the radioactive decay of radiocarbon will take place in a regular way, quite unaffected by physical or chemical conditions such as temperature or contact with the air, and also that the decay rate is known. This is a fundamental principle of modern physics.

Secondly, it is assumed that the samples to be dated have not been contaminated since their death, so that the proportion of carbon-14 to carbon-12 has not been changed, other than by the steady process of radioactive decay. This depends on the careful collection of samples by the archaeologist in the field.

The third assumption is that the small proportion of radiocarbon in all living things at a given time is, in fact, a constant, and that it does not vary from place to place, or among different species. This too is found in practice to be broadly justified.

And finally it is assumed that the concentration of radiocarbon in the earth's atmosphere has remained constant through time. If this is so, by measuring the proportion of radiocarbon present in living things today we can obtain a valid value for the proportion that the sample contained when it was alive.[40]

* By radiocarbon dating, living snails "died" 27,000 years ago![41]

* If a C14 date supports our theories, we put it in the main text. If it does not entirely contradict them, we put it in a footnote. And if it is completely "out of date," we just drop it.[42]

* Studies on submarine basaltic rocks from Hawaii, known to have formed less than 200 years ago, when dated by the potassium-argon method, revealed "ages" from 160 million to almost 3 billion years.[43]

Newly formed rocks from the Mount Ngauruhoe volcano in New Zealand were also examined. The radiometric age of the rocks ranged between 270,000 and 3,500,000 years. However, these rocks were formed during eruptions between 1949 and 1975.[44]

Analysis of wood from Australia by the radiocarbon (C-14) method revealed it to be 45,000 years old. But analysis by the potassium-argon method put the wood at about 45,000,000 years old.[45]

In another find, fossilized wood from Upper Pennian rock layers was found to have radioactive carbon 14 present. The radiometric date assigned to these rock layers was 250,000,000. Yet other research reveals that all detectable carbon 14 should have disintegrated if the wood were older than 50,000 years.[46]

* Several methods have been devised for estimating the age of the earth and its layers of rocks. These methods rely heavily on the assumption of uniformitarianism, i.e., natural processes have proceeded at relatively constant rates throughout the earth's history. . . .

It is obvious that radiometric techniques may not be the absolute dating methods that they are claimed to be. Age estimates on a given geological stratum by different radiometric methods are often quite different (sometimes by hundreds of millions of years). There is no absolutely reliable long-term radiological "clock." The uncertainties inherent in radiometric dating are disturbing to geologists and evolutionists. [47]

* Abstract. Radiocarbon analyses by accelerator mass spectrometric (AMS) techniques on organic fractions of human bone from various North American localities previously assigned ages ranging from about 70,000 to 15,000 years B.P. now suggest that none of these skeletons is older than 11,000 C-14 years B.P.[48]

* Abstract. K, Ar, and mineral analyses of montmorillonite mud samples 4,233 feet to 16,450 feet deep from a well in the Mississippi Delta area show that, with depth, the apparent K-Ar ages of the bulk samples decrease 100 million years.[49]

CONCEPT 7-5: MULTIPLE EVIDENCES SUGGEST THE EARTH IS YOUNG.

Note: In this section the format has changed. Rather than quoting multiple sources, a summary is made of the single overall best publication available on the subject.

RATIONALE: WORLD POPULATION GROWTH SUGGESTS
A YOUNG PLANET

The earth's age would be more certain if we understood just how long humans have existed. Knowing the earth's population at different times in history would help us to estimate a population growth rate. This would then allow extrapolation back to the date for the genesis of humankind. But the estimation of our world's population at different dates in history is difficult, for censuses (such as those of the Roman Empire) were few and limited in scope. Researchers widely disagree on world population estimates prior to the 1750s.

One reasonable solution is to estimate a growth rate, then based upon today's population, extrapolate back to a beginning point. Today, world population growth is estimated by many population experts to be an average of about two percent per year. Taking into account the wars, plagues, and famine of former years, a human population growth rate of one-half percent per year is more reasonable.

Evolutionists estimate that humans have existed for about one million years. If the population only increased one-half percent per year in one million years there would have been 10^{2100} people somehow stacked on the earth. Even if an almost zero population growth rate was assumed, in a million years an impossible total of three trillion people would have lived on the earth!

Assuming the same one-half percent growth rate, however, it would take about 4,000 years to produce today's population from a single couple. This is approximately the amount of time that has passed since Noah's worldwide flood eliminated all but a handful of people.[50]

RATIONALE: ABSENT METEORS SUGGEST A YOUNG PLANET

Each day, hundreds of tons of meteors fall through earth's atmosphere. Most of these meteors burn up before reaching the earth's surface, though as many as 60 tons worth of meteors each day strike land or sea.

If the geological layers that compose the earth's crust were laid down over many millions of years, then they should contain a vast number of meteors. But no such meteors have been found in the geological layers. This evidence would suggest that the earth is young, that there has not been enough time for meteors to strike earth.[51]

RATIONALE: THE CONCENTRATION OF OCEAN SALT SUGGESTS A YOUNG PLANET

The concentration of salt in the oceans is steadily growing. Yet the oceans are not nearly salty enough to have existed for billions of years. Even with generous allowances, the salt concentration suggests they could be no more than 62 million years old at the most.[52]

RATIONALE: PRESERVED RED BLOOD CELLS SUGGEST THAT "ANCIENT" CREATURES LIVED RECENTLY

Preserved red blood cells and hemoglobin have been discovered in unfossilized dinosaur bones. Evolutionists dated the dinosaur as living 65 million years ago. However, research shows that such cells could not survive more than a few thousand years. The dinosaur must have lived recently.[53]

RATIONALE: ATMOSPHERIC HELIUM CONCENTRATION SUGGESTS A YOUNG PLANET

Radioactive decay releases helium into the atmosphere, but not much is escaping. Helium concentration in our atmosphere is gradually increasing. Yet the current amount is only about 1/2000th of what we'd expect if the atmosphere were billions of years old. The helium concentration suggests a much younger atmosphere.[54]

The Age of the Atmosphere

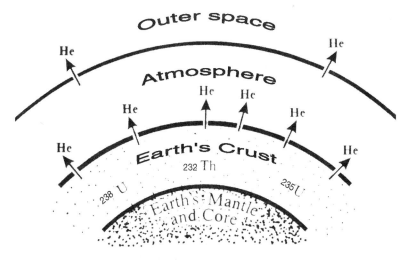

All of the helium now in the atmosphere would accumulate in a maximum of two million years.

Rationale: Top soil depth suggests a young planet

There is an average seven or eight inches of topsoil that sustains all of life on the earth, while the earth beneath the topsoil is as dead as rock itself. Scientists tell us that the combination of plants, bacterial decay, and erosion will produce six inches of topsoil in 5,000 to 20,000 years. If the earth had been here for 5 billion years, we should have much more topsoil than the seven or eight inches; more on the order of 56 miles thick![55]

Rationale: Speedily decaying comets suggest the earth is young

A remarkable event is taking place in outer space. Our solar system's comets are rapidly disintegrating and then disappearing; both so-called short-period comets and long-period comets. This is true of even the most famous comet of all, Halley's Comet. This fact has profound implications for estimating the age of the earth. It is generally accepted that the comets of our solar system are approximately the same age as the solar system itself, including the earth. Yet calculation of the age of these comets reveals that they are young indeed, as explained by John Maddox in the magazine *Nature*:

> * Indeed the rate at which comets such as Halley lose material near perihelion is so great that they cannot have been in their present orbits for very long, either. . . . Their [planetary physicists'] conclusion is that the time Halley's Comet has spent in the inner solar system is a mere 23,000 years, perhaps enough for fewer than 300 revolutions of the orbit.[56]

By analyzing a comet's largest potential size, and the current speed of its disintegration, astronomers can calculate approximately how long it has existed. The compelling conclusion is that the comets, and therefore the earth, are very young.

This data prompts those in the evolution camp to search for some other explanation, for 23,000 years for the age of the earth is completely inconsistent with the time evolution requires. The "Oort Cloud" is proposed as a solution to explain how comets could be constantly present, even though they are rapidly disintegrating. This hypothesis says that many comets are lying just outside of our solar system, occasionally pulled by the sun's gravity, thus keeping the number of comets constant.

The Oort Cloud, however, has never been observed. It remains only a hypothesis formulated to counter the evidence to the contrary. Yet the data is clear. Both comets and our earth are young.

CONCEPT 7-6: THE EARTH'S MAGNETIC FIELD INTENSITY SUGGESTS A YOUNG PLANET.

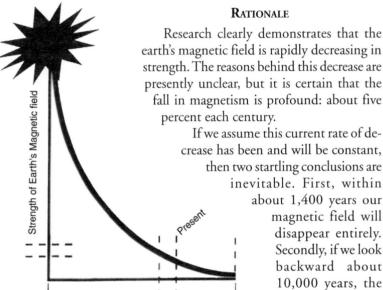

RATIONALE

Research clearly demonstrates that the earth's magnetic field is rapidly decreasing in strength. The reasons behind this decrease are presently unclear, but it is certain that the fall in magnetism is profound: about five percent each century.

If we assume this current rate of decrease has been and will be constant, then two startling conclusions are inevitable. First, within about 1,400 years our magnetic field will disappear entirely. Secondly, if we look backward about 10,000 years, the earth's magnetic field would have been as strong as that of a magnetic star and incapable of supporting life. These conclusions would clearly limit the potential age of the earth today to less than 10,000 years.

EVIDENCE

* Preliminary results from the just-downed Magsat — for Magnetic Field Satellite — confirm a previously detected decrease in the intensity of the earth's magnetic field, NASA scientists said last week. . . .

Measurements of the main field . . . show that the overall intensity of the field is declining at a rate of 26 nanoteslas per year. . . .

If the rate of decline were to continue steadily . . . the field strength would reach zero in 1,200 years. In that event, according to current theory, the magnetic field would be likely to rebuild with a polarity opposite to that of the present, so that compass needles that now point north would point south. . . . Moreover, little is known about what may cause the field, which is created by churning in the earth's molten core, to decline in strength. [57]

* If we went back about ten thousand years, the earth's magnetic field would have been as strong as the field in a magnetic star. A magnetic star is like our sun; it has a nuclear power source. Surely our earth never had a nuclear source like the sun. Surely our earth never had a magnetic field stronger than that of a star. That would limit the age of the earth to ten thousand years.[58]

* The dipole component of the earth's field was considerably stronger 2,000 years ago than it is today. (Dipole decay is evident in Roman ceramic artifacts, which contain iron particles that are magnetized to a greater extent than are those in modern products.) In the next two millennia, if the present rate of decay is sustained, the dipole component of the field should reach zero.[59]

* So we have measured directly the strength of the earth's magnetic field for less than 150 years. . . . Nevertheless, these direct measurements are helpful, and they show that even over this short period the geomagnetic field has been growing weaker by an average of five percent per century. At this rate, the geomagnetic field would disappear in about 3,000 years.[60]

The earth's magnetic field has been decaying so fast that it looks like it is less than 10,000 years old. Rapid reversals during the flood year and fluctuations shortly after would have caused the field energy to drop even faster. . . . Calculations on the magnetic field by other investigators also reveal that it couldn't be more than about 10,000 years old. [61]

CONCEPT 7-7: HISTORICAL EVIDENCE SUGGESTS THE EARTH IS YOUNG.

RATIONALE

What can be learned about the history of our planet by studying actual man-made records? Indeed, such records would provide reliable information since the writers were eyewitnesses of historical events, thus removing much of the uncertainty surrounding more indirect evidence.

Scholars have made extensive study of the rise and fall of world civilizations. In the process, the various researchers have succeeded in formulating a history of human societies which is remarkably consistent.

Just how far back does recorded human history go? Colin Renfrew, the premier living archaeological and linguistic scholar in England, sums up the conclusions of enormous research by declaring that 3100 B.C. is approximately the date of the founding of the world's oldest empire, located in Egypt. There are even some Egyptologists who argue that Egypt's first dynasty did not start until around 2000 B.C. No less a scientist than Isaac Newton came to similar conclusions. Claims regarding any earlier events must be viewed with speculation, since there are no human records to verify them.

If humans have been present on earth for one million years, as evolutionists insist, it remains unexplainable why they left no trace of civilization older than about 3,000 B.C. On this topic, evolutionists have been unable to make justifiable response. The truth is that there is no historical evidence to support the long-age, old-earth claims made by evolutionists. Rather, the world's archaeological, linguistic, and demographic historical evidence is quite consistent with the Bible's accounts of history.

EVIDENCE

* As a matter of fact, however, it may be stated categorically that no archaeological discovery has ever controverted a biblical reference. Scores of archaeological findings have been made which confirm in clear outline or in exact detail historical statements in the Bible. And, by the same token, proper evaluation of biblical descriptions has often led to amazing discoveries. They form tesserae in the vast mosaic of the Bible's almost incredibly correct historical memory.[62]

* Ussher represented the best scholarship in his time. He was part of a substantial research tradition, a large community of intellectuals working toward a common goal under an acceptable methodology.

Moreover, within assumptions of the methodology, this research tradition had considerable success. Even the extreme values were not very discordant, ranging from a minimum for the creation of the earth of 3761 B.C. in the Jewish calendar (still in use) to a maximum of just over 5500 B.C. for the Septuagint. Most calculators had reached a figure very close to Ussher's 4004. The Venerable Bede had estimated 3952 B.C. several centuries before, while J.J. Scaliger, the greatest scholar of the generation just before Ussher, had placed creation at 3950 B.C. Thus, Ussher's 4004 was neither idiosyncratic nor at all unusual; it was, in fact, a fairly conventional estimate developed within a large and active community of scholars.

James Barr explains the problems and complexities in an excellent article, "Why the World was Created in 4004 B.C.: Archbishop Ussher and Biblical Chronology."[63]

* Nor was this belief restricted to the credulous or the excessively devout. No less a thinker than Sir Isaac Newton accepted it implicitly, and in his detailed study of the whole question of dating, *The Chronology of Ancient Kingdoms Amended*, took the ancient Egyptians severely to task, since they had set the origins of the monarchy before 5000 B.C. . . . and "out of vanity have made this monarchy some thousands of years older than the world." This criticism was meant literally; for an educated man in the seventeenth or even eighteenth century, any suggestion that the human past extended back further than 6,000 years was a vain and foolish speculation. . . .

Until the discovery of radiocarbon dating, therefore, there was really only one reliable way of dating events in European prehistory after the end of the last glaciation around 8000 B.C. — only one way, that is, to date the neolithic, bronze age and iron age periods. This was by the early records of the great civilizations, which extended in some cases as far back as 3000 B.C. The records of the Greeks did not go back before the first millennium B.C., but in Mesopotamia the Assyrians and their predecessors, the Sumerians, left records of kings and dynasties extending back well before 2000 B.C. The Egyptian king lists go back to the First Dynasty of Egypt, a little before 3000 B.C. Before that, there were no written records anywhere. . . .

The date in question corresponds to 1872 B.C., so that the reign of Sesostris III is now set with some confidence from 1878 B.C. to 1843 B.C.

This is, in fact, the earliest fixed calendrical date in human history. And while some uncertainties of detail makes possible an error of a decade or so, it is a date which Egyptologists accept with considerable confidence. Using the information from the annals, the end of the Eighth Dynasty, with which the so-called "Old Kingdom" of Egypt terminated, may be set at 2160 B.C. As we have seen, the Turin Royal Canon reports a total duration for the Old Kingdom of 955 years. Some scholars think this may be inaccurate by a couple of centuries or so, but if the figure is accepted, the beginning of the Old Kingdom of Egypt — the founding of Egypt's first historic dynasty — can be set close to 3100 B.C. . . .

The Mesopotamian chronology is less reliable than the Egyptian and it does not go back so far.

This date of 3100 B.C. thus sets the limit of recorded history. No earlier dates can be obtained by calendrical means, and indeed the dates cannot be regarded as reliable before 2000 B.C. There is thus a theoretical limit beyond which the traditional chronology for Europe, based, as it was, ultimately on Egypt, simply could not go. Any dates before 3000 B.C. could be little more than guesswork, however persuasive the arguments and the evidence after that period. . . .

The oldest living tree yet discovered has been alive for 4,900 years — the earth's oldest living thing.[64]

CONCEPT 7-8: DINOSAURS LIVED VERY RECENTLY.

RATIONALE

Most paleontologists claim that dinosaurs began evolving around 235 million years ago. They reached their height in population about 70 million years ago, and then died out at least 60 million years before humans ever evolved.

But if the earth is indeed a young planet, then the question of what became of the dinosaurs becomes even more relevant. Add to this the fact that the Genesis account declares that humans and dinosaurs were created at the same time. What scientific evidence exists to document when the dinosaurs actually lived, and what caused their extinction?

Several research studies on dinosaur remains demonstrate findings, such as fresh blood, that point to their recent existence. History is also filled with reports of dinosaurs living into recent times, being called "dragons" by ancient, even medieval, peoples. Discoveries of paintings with humans and dinosaurs side by side is further evidence of their contemporary survival.

Many scholars believe the "dragons" mentioned in the Bible (at least 25 times) were the dinosaurs of paleontology. The Bible also describes an eyewitness description of an ancient behemoth (widely believed to be a dinosaur) that was recorded about 3,500 years ago:

> Look at the behemoth, which I made along with you and which feeds on grass like an ox. What strength he has in his

loins, what power in the muscles of his belly! His tail sways like a cedar; the sinews of his thighs are close-knit. His bones are tubes of bronze, his limbs like rods of iron" (Job 40:15–18).

Note the accurate description of the animal, with special attention to the description of the animal's tail. Although some skeptics have tried to classify this animal as a modern-day elephant or rhinoceros, the claim is unreasonable, as no such animal has a tail "that sways back and forth like a giant cedar tree."

What led to dinosaur extinction? Numerous hypotheses have been made: epidemic disease, starvation, poison plants, even constipation. Another popular idea is that they were killed when the earth was struck by a giant asteroid many millions of years ago. While they make for a great movie plot, no substantial scientific evidence exists to support any of these proposals.

A widely held explanation consistent with Genesis is the following: Prior to Noah's flood, it's likely that the earth's worldwide climate was subtropical, for the earth was covered by a "water canopy," dense clouds that caused a greenhouse effect. This water canopy collapsed at the time of Noah's flood, causing the earth to become significantly cooler than before. The dinosaurs on the ark left to a completely new and milder climate. Unable to adjust to the temperature and changes in vegetation, many of their species died and became extinct.

EVIDENCE

* A fantastic mystery has developed over a set of cave paintings found in the Gorozomzi Hills, 25 miles from Salisbury. For the paintings include a brontosaurus — the 67-foot, 30-ton creature scientists believed became extinct millions of years before man appeared on earth.

Yet the bushmen who did the paintings ruled Rhodesia from only 1500 B.C. until a couple of hundred years ago. And the experts agree that the bushmen always painted from life. This belief is borne out by other Gorozomzi Hills cave paintings — accurate representations of the elephant, hippo, buck, and giraffe.

The mysterious pictures were found by Bevan Parkes, who owns the land the caves are on.

Adding to the puzzle of the rock paintings found by Parkes is a drawing of a dancing bear. As far as scientists know, bears have never lived in Africa.[65]

* In the swampy jungles of western Africa, reports persist of an elephant-sized creature with smooth, brownish-gray skin, a long, flexible neck, a very long tail as powerful as a crocodile's, and three-clawed feet the size of frying pans. Over the past three centuries, native Pygmies and Western explorers have told how the animals feed on the nutlike fruit of a riverbank plant and keep to the deep pools and subsurface caves of waters in this largely unexplored region.

After a recent expedition there, two American researchers conclude that these stories refer to a real animal, not a myth. Fantastic as it seems, Roy Mackal and James Powell believe that this creature, called "Mokele-Mbembe" by the natives, may actually be a dinosaur, perhaps one resembling brontosaurus, which is thought to have died out 70 million years ago. . . .

There are precedents. No one believed that the prehistoric coelacanth could still be living until one was fished up off the African coast in 1939. The paleotragus, a giraffe-like creature that lived 20 million years ago, was thought to be extinct until one turned up in the Congolese rain forests at the turn of the century. [66]

Discoveries have been made of cave-dwelling humans with drawings and carvings of dinosaurs on the walls of caves in Arizona's Hava Supai Canyon, and in thirty other places worldwide.

Fossilized footprints of man and footprints of dinosaurs have been found in the same geological strata in New Mexico, Arizona, Mexico, Kentucky, Missouri, Russia, Illinois, Texas, and other locations.[67]

* In France, the bohemian tradition goes back a long way. Palaeolithic cave artists of the Lot Valley in southwestern France not only experimented with surrealism, they may also have found inspiration in hallucinogenic drugs. So say Michel Lorblanchet and Ann Sieveking, in an analysis of engravings in the innermost room (IV) of the cave of Pergouset.

Room IV is hard to reach; the passage is narrow, mud-choked and steep. Once there, the explorer faces a sloping ceiling on which a fantastic bestiary is engraved. Part of it is transcribed here, showing a long-necked creature with a horse-like head, and next to it a "monstrous head" that is harder to categorize. Elsewhere there are both less and more peculiar creatures, including one that vaguely resembles a fox's head on two narrow legs.[68]

On March 16, 1982, in Glen Rose, Texas, Dr. Baugh, accompanied by other scientists, removed a layer of limestone twelve inches thick to reveal human and dinosaur prints within inches of each other! By the next day, they had uncovered four more human footprints and twenty-three more dinosaur prints all next to one another![69]

* Many hundreds of pages have been written about how the dinosaurs became extinct without our being any the wiser.[70]

The dragons of legend are strangely like actual creatures that have lived in the past. They are much like the great reptiles which inhabited the earth long before man is supposed to have appeared on earth.[71]

* Look at the behemoth, which I made along with you and which feeds on grass like an ox. What strength he has in his loins, what power in the muscles of his belly! His tail sways like a cedar; the sinews of his thighs are close-knit. His bones are tubes of bronze, his limbs like rods of iron (Job 40:15–18).

* Persistent reports of strange creatures in remote, swampy jungles of western Africa have led two scientists to believe that dinosaurs still may walk the earth. Both historical reports from Westerners and firsthand accounts from natives indicate dinosaur-like creatures may exist today in a virtually unexplored jungle in the People's Republic of the Congo, the researchers said yesterday. Dr. Roy Mackal, a research associate at the University of Chicago, said he believes the animals may be elephant-sized dinosaurs. . . .

In an article in *Science-80* magazine, published by the American Association for the Advancement of Science, the researchers say natives call the creature "Mokele-Mbembe."

"The researchers say they believe it actually may be a dinosaur that looks like a smaller version of the brontosaurus, a giant plant-eater that died out 70 million years ago. Natives shown pictures of many kinds of animals picked illustrations of the brontosaurus as most closely resembling the creatures they say they saw," Mackal said.[72]

* The Gobi Desert of Central Asia is one of the earth's desolate places. . . .

Yet the Gobi is a paradise for paleontologists. Its eroding terrain exposes nearly complete skeletons of creatures hitherto known only through painstaking reconstructions from a few scattered bones. Our expeditions, jointly sponsored by the Mongolian Academy of Sciences and the American Museum of Natural History, have excavated dinosaurs, lizards and small mammals in an unprecedented state of preservation. Freshly exposed skeletons sometimes look more like the recent remains of a carcass than like an 80-million-year-old fossil. . . .

Among them are 25 skeletons of theropod dinosaurs. This group of agile carnivores runs the gamut from the enormous *Tyrannosaurus* and *Allosaurus* through fast-running *Dromaeosaurs* such as *Velociraptor* (the villainous predator of *Jurassic Park*, a title some 60 million years out-of-date) to smaller birdlike creatures such as the oviraptorids. We also gathered an unprecedented rich collection of small vertebrates: more than 200 skulls of mammals — many with their associated skeletons — and an even greater number of lizard skulls and skeletons. . . .

The Cretaceous Gobi is unquestionably one of the world's great dinosaur hunting grounds. The fossils range from complete skeletons of *Tarbosaurus*, a fierce carnivore closely related to the North American *Tyrannosaurus*, to giant sauropods, duck-billed dinosaurs, armored ankylosaurs, frilled ceratopsian dinosaurs such as *Protoceratops* and a magnificent assemblage of smaller carnivores. Birdlike oviraptorids and dromaeosaurs such as *Velociraptor* are better represented in the stratified rocks of the Gobi than anywhere else in the world.[73]

* This spring, an expedition from the Institute of Geology of the Turkmen SSR Academy of Science found over 1,500 tracks left by dinosaurs in the mountains of the southeast of the Republic. Impressions resembling in shape a human footprint were discovered next to the tracks of the prehistoric animals.[74]

Preserved red blood cells and hemoglobin have been discovered in unfossilized dinosaur bones. Evolutionists dated the dinosaur as living 65 million years ago. However, research shows that such cells could not survive more than a few thousand years. The dinosaur must have lived recently.[75]

When Alexander the Great (c. 330 B.C.) and his soldiers marched into India, they found that the Indians worshiped huge hissing reptiles that they kept in caves.

A 10th century Irishman wrote of his encounter with what appears to be a Stegosaurus.

In the 1500s, a European scientific book, *Historia Animalium*, listed several animals that we would call dinosaurs, as still alive. A well-known naturalist of the time, Ulysses Aldrovandus, recorded an encounter between a peasant named Baptista and a dragon whose description fits that of the small dinosaur Tanystropheus. The encounter was on May 13, 1572, near Bologna in Italy, and the peasant killed the dragon.

England has its story of St. George who slew a dragon that lived in a cave.[76]

The belief in dragons seems to have arisen without the slightest knowledge on the part of the ancients of the gigantic and astonishingly dragon-like extinct reptiles of past ages.[77]

CONCEPT 7-9: SCIENTIFIC EVIDENCE IS CONSISTENT WITH NOAH'S FLOOD.

RATIONALE

Many geologic findings cannot be reasonably explained by slow, gradual processes. But a massive flood readily fits with the facts. The multitude of fossilized creatures and sedimentary rock layers all over the world are both consistent with a worldwide, violent, and then slowly settling flood.

The Book of Genesis, chapters 6 through 9, gives an accurate account of God's decision to bring on a worldwide flood. He gave Noah instructions to build an ark according to specifications: 450' long, 80' wide, and 45' high, with 1.5 million cubic feet of storage area (about ten freight trains each pulling 52 boxcars) and deck equal to about 20 basketball courts. Calculations today demonstrate that two of every species of air-breathing animal in the world today could be easily housed in half of that volume.

Genesis 6:3 explains that Noah and his sons constructed the ark over about one hundred years. Then, God caused the animals to come to Noah, where they were placed in the ark, along with Noah and his family. Immediately came the flood, brought on by rain and surfacing underwater currents: "The springs of the great deep burst forth, and the floodgates of the heavens were opened." The water continued rising for 40 days. Then for the next 150 days, it covered the tallest mountains by 15 cubits. (One cubit is about 15 inches.) Finally, the waters began to recede.

This event occurred in approximately 3,000–3,500 B.C. The universal worldwide flood is not only described in the Bible, but is also found in many ancient literatures. Noah's flood was a worldwide catastrophe, unparalleled in the earth's history. Instantly, trillions of tons of mud, all vegetation and all animal life were tumultuously overturned. Finally, after six months of flooding and terrestrial cataclysm, according to Psalm 104:6–8, the basic geography of the world today was formed: the mountains were raised and the valleys were lowered as the oceans, mountains, canyons, plains, and prairies took on their post-flood contours.

Residual effects of Noah's flood can be found all over the world today. Crustaceans have been discovered on 12,000-foot mountaintops. Hippopotamuses, native only to Africa, have been uncovered in England. The Norfolk forest-beds in England contain fossils of northern cold-climate animals, tropical warm-climate animals, and temperate zone plants all mixed together. Hundreds of dinosaurs have been found buried together with other creatures that did not share the same habitat.

The evidence of a worldwide flood is enormous. Moose-deer, native only of America, were found buried in Ireland. Elephants, natives of only Asia and Africa, were found buried in the midst of England. Crocodile fossils, native to the Nile region, were discovered in the heart of Germany. Shellfish were found together with entire skeletons of whales in the most inland regions of England. A whale's skeleton was even found on top of Sanhorn Mountain, which is 3,000 feet high! A vast flood is the only event that could have carried a whale to such a great height. How could such diverse creatures get buried thousands of miles from their normal environments, at unexplainable elevations, except by a devastating universal flood? What's more, geologists discovered a field of pillow lava as high as 15,000 feet on Mt. Ararat. Pillow lava is formed only under water!

The best explanation in all of science for the fossils buried on all seven continents is a flood of cataclysmic proportions. It also helps explain formation of sedimentary rock, coal, oil, canyons, and global climate changes, such as the remnants of warm humid marshes now being dug up from under deserts, and evidence of formerly tropical climates in Antarctica.

EVIDENCE

* The hurricane, the flood or the tsunami may do more in an hour or a day than the ordinary processes of nature have achieved in a thousand years. Given all the millennia we have

to play with in the stratigraphical record, we can expect our periodic catastrophes to do all the work we want of them.[78]

* However, nothing can seriously detract from the fact that during some part of the Jurassic a fairly rich flora of temperate facies flourished within or near both the Arctic and Antarctic Circles, in East Greenland and Grahamland.[79]

* The chances for preservation may be enhanced by severe storms, epidemics, or changes in the temperature, availability, or chemistry of water, all of which can leave large numbers of buried and unburied dead at one time. . . .

Because mass mortality or instantaneous death and burial create the optimal initial conditions for fossilization, it is possible that a significant portion of our fossil record is due to such exceptional events. [80]

* One catastrophic inundation may well have been responsible for worldwide stories of the flood, another for the later events leading up the exodus.[81]

* Now all is changed. We are rewriting geohistory. Where once we saw a smooth conveyor belt, we now see a stepped escalator. Upon that escalator the treads are long periods of relative quiescence when little happens. The risers are episodes of relatively sudden change when the landscape and its inhabitants are translated into some fresh state. Even the most staid of modern geologists are invoking sedimentary surges, explosive phases of organic evolution, volcanic blackouts, continental collisions and terrifying meteoroid impacts. We live in an age of neocatastrophism.[82]

* Further, we know that the deluge of Noah is not mere myth or fancy of primitive man or solely a doctrine of the Hebrew scriptures. The record of the catastrophe is preserved in some of the oldest historical documents of several distinct races of men, and is indirectly corroborated by the whole tenor of the early history of most of the civilized races.[83]

* If the continental lands were leveled down to a uniform sea floor, the mean depth of a completely covering ocean would be roughly 9,000 feet, and its surface would stand at a height about 600 feet above our present sea level. . . . There would be no mountain chains to precipitate rain or snow, and it is prob-

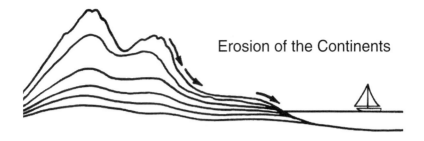

Erosion of the Continents

At present rates, the continents would all be eroded
in no more than 14 million years.

able that a uniform climate would prevail over the face of this
earth ocean.[84]

* After a study which lasted nearly 3 years, it was determined that the average upward growth of these specimens
amounted to 10.7 mm a year. . . . An upward growth of one
foot would take about 28.5 years. . . .

If there is any merit in this estimate, one of the most significant results is the realization of the rapidity at which coral
reef material can accumulate.[85]

* According to computer models of climate, North Dakota and other continental interiors also had relatively harsh
winters in the geologic past, even during periods like the early
Eocene, about 50 million years ago, when global temperatures
were the highest in the past 65 million years. But while the
computers insist on harsh winters, Eocene fossils from continental interiors tell a different story: winters mild enough for
crocodiles to roam through Wyoming and tree ferns to shade
Montana. . . .

The fossil fauna records compiled by Wing and Green-
wood include abundant signs of mild Eocene winters in continental interiors: cold-sensitive land turtles too large to bur-
row for protection during the winter, diverse communities of
tree-living mammals dependent on year-round supplies of fruit
and insects, and crocodile relatives, all found as far into the
continental interior as Wyoming.[86]

Certainly enough water exists to produce a flood of such
proportions. Recent calculations on the quantity of water on

earth show that if the surface of the planet were smooth, the earth would be entirely covered with water to a depth of 1.7 miles (2.7 km).[87]

* In many parts of the geological record fossils are scattered sparsely through the rocks, but in other parts they are densely concentrated on one or more bedding planes. The numbers of fossils may be so great as to suggest abnormal conditions, possibly a catastrophe of some sort. Such an example was described by D.S. Jordan from the Miocene of California. Enormous numbers of the herring Xyne grex were found crowded on a bedding plane in the "Monterey shale." Jordan estimated that more than a billion fish, averaging 6 to 8 inches in length, died on 4 square miles of bay bottom.[88]

Search the earth [and] you will find the moose-deer (native of America) buried in Ireland; elephants (natives of Asia and Africa) buried in the midst of England; crocodiles (natives of the Nile) in the heart of Germany; shell-fish (never known in the American seas) together with the entire skeletons of whales in the most inland regions of England. . . .

A whale's skeleton was even found on top of the Sanhorn Mountain, which is 3,000 feet high! Nothing could have conveyed the whale to that height except a great flood. Sea fossils are found on all the mountains of the world. What's more, geologists have found a field of pillow lava as high as 15,000 feet on Mount Ararat. Pillow lava is formed only under water. How did such diverse creatures get buried thousands of miles from their normal environments, at unexplainable elevation, except by a devastating universal flood? [89]

* The discovery of thousands of well-preserved leaves in Antarctica has sparked a debate among geologists over whether the polar region, rather than being blanketed by a massive sheet of ice for millions of years enjoyed a near-temperate climate as recently as three million years ago.[90]

* Scientists have reported discovering the first set of dinosaur fossils ever to be found in the interior of Antarctica.

The fossils are said to be the remains of a plant-eating dinosaur, 25 to 30 feet long, that lived about 200 million years ago in what geologists call the early Jurassic age.

The bones were spotted at a small section of exposed rock

alongside the mountain, which lies about 400 miles from the South Pole.[91]

* The account of the Genesis flood hardly stands alone. Researchers have described over 100 flood traditions from Europe, Asia, Australia, the East Indies, the Americas, East Africa, and many other places. Almost all accounts agree on these points: universal, worldwide flood, all mankind perished, an ark, and a seed of mankind survived to perpetuate the human race. . . .

Genesis chapters six through nine gives an accurate account of God's decision to bring on a worldwide flood. He gave Noah instructions to build an ark according to specifications: 450' long, 80' wide, and 45' high, with 1.5 million cubic feet of storage area (about ten freight trains each pulling 52 boxcars) and deck equal to about 20 basketball courts. Two of every air-breathing animal in the world today could be housed adequately in half of that space. . . .

Vast animal graveyards and fossiliferous rubble shifts have been found worldwide. Evidence of a great, sudden, and recent water cataclysm, followed by a deep freeze, across the entire great north, accompanied by titanic hydraulic forces and crustal upheavals, burying a host of mammoths, mastodons, elephants, and other great beasts in a region which is now almost totally devoid of vegetation has been documented.

Vast numbers of fossil trees and plants, standing erect, oblique and even inverted while piercing through successive beds of water-laid stone have been discovered. There is abundant evidence of profuse vegetation and a temperate, even subtropical climate prevailing in Antarctica and the north polar regions at some time in the past.

Worldwide fossilization has occurred in vast quantities, including fossils in sedimentary strata, often at great depths and under great pressure. Vast and numerous rifts, fissures, and lava beds have been discovered, scarring the world ocean floor, all clearly recent and speak of some gigantic submarine upheaval of the earth's crust (as in breaking up of the "fountains of the deep"). Marine fossils have been found buried and exposed at almost every altitude. And on and on and on such evidences could be listed.[92]

CHAPTER EIGHT

YOUNG AGE OF THE UNIVERSE

INTRODUCTION

The earth is but one tiny component of the entire universe. If indeed the earth were a young planet, as we discussed in the prior chapter, then we would also expect to find that the entire universe is young as well. Multiple lines of research suggest that the universe is young; not one in the "billions of years old" range, but rather a universe with an age of only thousands of years, as expressed by Dr. Harold Slusher, an astrophysicist and geophysicist:

> * There are a number of indicators that seem to indicate an age of no more than 10,000 years, at the very most, for the solar system and the earth.[1]

Students are often led to believe that a process of evolution is occurring in the stars and galaxies of outer space. We must realize, however, that these ideas are based upon imagination and mathematical models, not upon any direct observations. The fact remains that human observations of stars and constellations have appeared unchanged, with the exception of disintegrating stars, since history began being recorded.

Scientific research is most reliable when dealing with events that can be observed and repeated. However, studying the origin of the universe pushes the limits of science, for the events can neither be duplicated nor directly observed. The reliability of scientific conclusions becomes limited and metaphysical questions loom greater than ever.

CONCEPT 8-1: THE BIG BANG IS SCIENTIFICALLY IMPOSSIBLE.

RATIONALE

Textbooks regularly describe the universe as beginning as a "big bang," a tiny speck of matter (sometimes called a "cosmic egg") packed with incredible energy, which exploded with unimaginable force, and expanded outward to form the stars, planets, and other complex structures of the universe. One typical science textbook describes the event in this way:

> * A fireball exploded 15 to 20 billion years ago. Then matter and energy spread outward in all directions, cooling as it expanded. After about 500,000 years, hydrogen gas formed. The gas collected into clouds which formed galaxies during the next half billion years. Now all that remains are galaxies and radiation. Within the galaxies, stars form and die and new ones form. . . . Probably the most widely accepted theory for the origin of the solar system is the dust cloud theory. According to this idea, a dust cloud began to rotate. . . . When the mass had swept up most of the material in an eddy, a planet was formed.[2]

This is a truly remarkable hypothesis: an uncontrolled explosion resulted in a vast, organized universe consisting of over 100 billion galaxies; our diverse solar system, life-supporting planet Earth, and advanced forms of life of all varieties were all the outcome of a massive detonation in space.

Many evolutionary astronomers and cosmologists have been raising serious doubts about the big-bang theory, finding it both scientifically impossible and intuitively unbelievable. One of the strongest arguments comes from observations and experiments that demonstrate explosions always produce disorder and chaos. Nowhere in history has a single explosion been observed that produced higher order and greater complexity. The entire big-bang theory contradicts the law of entropy, also known as the second law of thermodynamics, which states:

> Complex ordered arrangements and systems naturally become simpler and more disorderly (increased entropy or randomness) with time.

A contradiction to the law of entropy has NEVER been found. Structures that are highly ordered (like our solar system and living beings) require a high degree of energy to be maintained. Yet, the law of entropy states that usable energy in the universe is becoming less and less as

The Milky Way Galaxy

structures become more and more random. Therefore, the structures of the universe should be degenerating, not becoming more orderly. In a sense, the entire universe is like a car slowly running out of gasoline.

Explosions always destroy complexity. They produce chaos. If indeed such an explosion actually did occur at the beginning of time, then matter should have continued expanding outward and dissipated completely, for in outer space there is nothing to stop a moving object once set in motion. Rather than forming well-designed complexities like galaxies and solar systems, a great explosion would have resulted in only microscopic dust, salted through the ever-expanding cosmos.

One of the greatest challenges to the big bang is located just next door to Earth. If the planets of our solar system were simply the result of particulate matter clumping together after the big bang, then we would expect the planets to all be quite similar. However, the make-up of the nine planets in our solar system is extremely varied: gas planets, rock planets, those that rotate sideways, and the one-of-a-kind Earth. These remarkably varied features simply cannot be explained as a result of random clumping.

The big-bang theory simply defies the laws of science, for our universe demonstrates incredible structure and order. Not surprisingly, many scientists do not find sufficient evidence to support the big bang theory. They judge its logic absurd, probability impossible, and evidence unobservable.

The big-bang theory is actually a big bust. What, then, is the most reasonable explanation for the complex structures of our universe? The only alternative explanation is this: The universe must have been designed and created with these features.

EVIDENCE

* The big-bang model offers a universe created in a smooth featureless condition, out of which a highly structured universe is nevertheless supposed to have evolved. Numerous attempts have been made to explain how this miracle is supposed to have happened. They have two features in common, one a retreat into the highest flights of physics and the other an unsatisfactory absence of the immense detail that would be required to support them in a proper manner, from which we suspect the attempts to be little more than ingenious handwaving. Perhaps this is why they are called "scenarios."

Cosmology is unique in science in that it is a very large intellectual edifice based on a very few facts.[3]

* Big-bang cosmology is probably as widely believed as has been any theory of the universe in the history of Western civilization. It rests, however, on many untested, and in some cases untestable, assumptions. Indeed, big-bang cosmology has become a bandwagon of thought that reflects faith as much as objective truth.

This situation is particularly worrisome because there are good reasons to think the big-bang model is seriously flawed. Why then has the big bang become so deeply entrenched in modern thought? Everything evolves as a function of time except for the laws of physics. Hence, there are two immutables: the act of creation and the laws of physics which spring forth fully fashioned from that act. The big bang ultimately reflects some cosmologists' search for creation and for a beginning. That search properly lies in the realm of metaphysics, not science.[4]

* What are the odds that such an explosion could produce the highly organized structures we see in the universe? Carl Sagan [himself an evolutionist and astronomer] gives it the immense odds of 1 to $10^{2,000,000,000}$ (that is 1 followed by 2 billion zeroes). Absolutely impossible![5]

Einstein also agreed, suggesting that the "high degree of order" was somewhat of a "miracle."[6]

* Now, in the 1990s we can still say that we are only on

the verge of understanding how galaxies are born, how they work, and what roles they play in the universe at large. . . . The process by which galaxies clump together poses a significant mystery for astronomers.[7]

* Many cosmologists now feel that the shortcomings of the standard (big bang) theory outweigh its usefulness.[8]

* Everywhere we look in the universe, from the far-flung galaxies to the deepest recesses of the atom, we encounter order.[9]

* Was there ever really a big bang? Even as greater and greater numbers of people have come to believe that the universe began with one great eruption, others have seen a persistent weakness in the theory — a weakness that is becoming ever harder to overlook.

But in a single big bang there are no targets at all, because the whole universe takes part in the explosion. There is nothing for the expanding universe to hit against, and after sufficient expansion, the whole affair should go dead. However, we actually have a universe of continuing activity instead of one that is uniform and inert.

As a result of all this, the main efforts of investigators have been in papering over holes in the big-bang theory, to build up an idea that has become ever more complex and cumbersome. . . .

I have little hesitation in saying that a sickly pall now hangs over the big-bang theory. When a pattern of facts becomes set against a theory, experience shows that the theory rarely recovers.[10]

* An explosion merely throws matter apart, while the big bang has mysteriously produced the opposite effect, with matter clumping together in the form of galaxies.[11]

* Theorists hoped that these traces [of the big bang] would be detected by the sensitive instruments of COBE [Cosmic Background Explorer], a satellite launched last November by NASA. To their surprise, however, the preliminary data from COBE, announced in January, show none of these hypothetical relics of past explosions. There now seems no way to reconcile the predictions of any version of the big bang with the reality of the universe that we observe, no way to get from the perfectly smooth big bang to the imperfect lumpy universe we

136 · CREATIVE DEFENSE

see today. As one COBE scientist, George Smoot of the University of California at Berkeley, put it, "Using the forces we now know, you can't make the universe we now know."[12]

"If we really trust the data (concerning the big bang)," exclaims Stanford astrophysicist Andrei Linde, "then we are in disaster, and we must do something absolutely crazy. But this hasn't stopped the theorists from doing crazy things anyway; they've proposed one mind-stretching idea after another to explain what's going on."[13]

* It is hard to see how galaxies could have formed in a universe which is flying apart so fast.[14]

* The trouble starts right here. There is no unambiguous way of estimating the distance of a galaxy.[15]

* There are even more serious difficulties concerning the cosmic microwave background. The problem is that it is much too smooth. Observations have shown that matter in the universe is in the form of galaxies grouped into clusters and superclusters with long filamentary stretches and giant voids in between. When these structures formed in the early universe, they should have left an imprint on the microwave background, in the same way holiday-makers leave behind footprints on the beach. So far, COBE, the satellite currently investigating the microwave background, has found no evidence for any unevenness in the radiation. These latest observations pose a serious problem for cosmologists dedicated to the big bang. Indeed, a considerable amount of theoretical ingenuity is being devoted toward scenarios that would leave imprints below the observable threshold. Avoiding confrontation with observations is scarcely the hallmark of a good theory.[16]

* Both the "big bang" model and the theoretical side of elementary particle physics rely on numerous highly speculative assumptions. Extrapolating back and forth between the present state of the observable universe and an ultimate cosmological singularity involves an incredible amount of faith in the completeness of our physical knowledge.[17]

* First, the big bang is treated as an unexplainable event without a cause. Secondly, the big bang could not explain convincingly how matter got organized into lumps (galaxies and

clusters of galaxies). And thirdly, it did not predict that for the universe to be held together in the way it is, more than 90 percent of the universe would have to be in the form of some strange, unknown dark form of matter.[18]

* By the end of the 1960s, the big bang had become almost universally accepted, and it has now penetrated the popular consciousness so deeply that at times one forgets it is still just a theory.

In spite of their many successes, proponents of the big bang have lately been forced to acknowledge a growing number of inconvenient observations, and older but still nagging difficulties with the model have refused to go away. In the past twenty years, for instance, astronomers have noticed numerous cosmological objects whose enormous red shifts may be intrinsic properties of the objects themselves; if the red shift is no longer a reliable demonstration of an expanding universe, the big-bang model is left without the phenomenon it was invented to explain. Perhaps more important, some of the most prominent aftereffects of the explosion have been difficult to reconcile with the observation. For example, the motions and shapes of galaxies and clusters of galaxies cannot be explained by the action of gravity alone, as the big-bang model seems to require. To save the basic gravitational mechanism of the big bang itself, astronomers have postulated a variety of exotic but invisible subatomic particles that could fill the interstellar and intergalactic voids with dark but massive amounts of matter.[19]

* The time asymmetry of the universe is expressed by the second law of thermodynamics, that entropy increases with time as order is transformed into disorder. The mystery is not that an ordered state should become disordered but that the early universe was in a highly ordered state.[20]

* Few cosmologists today would dispute the view that our expanding universe began with a bang — a big, hot bang — about 18 billion years ago. Paradoxically, no cosmologist could now tell you how the big bang — the explosion of a superhot, superdense atom — ultimately gave rise to galaxies, stars, and other cosmic lumps.

As one sky scientist, IBM's Philip E. Seiden, put it, "The standard big-bang model does not give rise to lumpiness. That model assumes the universe started out as a globally smooth, homogeneous expanding gas. If you apply the laws of physics to this model, you get a universe that is uniform, a cosmic vastness of evenly distributed atoms with no organization of any kind."

How then did the lumps get there? No one can say.[21]

* West German and American astronomers recently discovered a super super-cluster nearly two and a half billion light years long; to grow to such a scale under the force of gravity alone would have taken more than 100 billion years, five times longer than our big-bang model allows. Furthermore, if the universe turns out to be clumpy on this scale, where is the large-scale uniformity presumed by the big bang?[22]

* When the Cosmic Background Explorer (COBE) satellite produced its first detailed measurements of the cosmic microwave background (the so-called echo of creation), cosmologists cheered. It was a proud moment in the age-old effort to understand our origins, taken as confirmation of the prevailing model of the big bang. Four years later, however, the pages of the *Astrophysical Journal* look much as they did before, full of contentious debate over the age of the universe, the nature of "dark matter" and the ways that mysterious physical laws may have shaped the world around us.

Such obliging flexibility engenders a disturbing sense that cosmological theory resembles an endlessly nested set of Matryoshka dolls. Each refinement of the big bang delves deeper into abstruse theory, which grows progressively harder to prove or disprove.[23]

* The notion that galaxies form, to be followed by an active astronomical history, is an illusion. Nothing forms; the thing [the big-bang theory] is dead as a doornail.[24]

CONCEPT 8-2: EXPLAINING THE PRESENCE OF THE UNIVERSE IS SCIENTIFICALLY IMPOSSIBLE.

RATIONALE

Science can only be exact when dealing with events that are observable and repeatable. The reliability of scientific conclusions diminishes very rapidly when these criteria are not met. When this is the case, mere proposals and hypotheses are often the best that can be offered, with little or no way of proving whether or not they are actually true.

Any hypothesis concerning the origin of the universe ultimately confronts profound and unanswerable questions. In the case of the big bang, what was the origin of the "cosmic egg" itself? Where did this first dense particle come from? From where was the enormous energy supplied? What drastically slowed the speed of the expanding matter? Why did the expanding matter clump together to form stars and planets? The big-bang theory has no answer to these essential queries.

Creation of the universe is neither directly observable, nor is it repeatable. Therefore, it is a subject that science can never answer with any assurance, only conjecture. In the final analysis, creation of the building blocks of the universe (matter, energy, time, physical laws) is a question beyond the normal realm of science. Of necessity, it pushes us to consider the metaphysical.

EVIDENCE

* As an erstwhile cosmologist, I speak with feeling of the fact that theories of the origin of the universe have been disproved by present-day empirical evidence, as have various theories of the origin of the solar system.[25]

* What is a big deal — the biggest deal of all — is how you get something out of nothing. Don't let the cosmologists try to kid you on this one. They have not got a clue either, despite the fact that they are doing a pretty good job of convincing themselves and others that this is really not a problem. "In the beginning," they will say, "there was nothing — no time, space, matter, or energy. Then there was a quantum fluctuation from which. . . ." Whoa! Stop right there. You see what I mean? First there is nothing, then there is something. And the cosmologists try to bridge the two with a quantum flutter, a tremor of uncertainty that sparks it all off. Then they are away and before you know it, they have pulled a hundred billion galaxies out of their quantum hats.

You cannot fudge this by appealing to quantum mechanics. Either there is nothing to begin with, in which case there is no quantum vacuum, no pre-geometric dust, no time in which anything can happen, no physical laws that can effect a change from nothingness into somethingness; or there is something, in which case that needs explaining.[26]

* The greatest puzzle is where all the order in the universe came from originally.[27]

* Since the big-bang theory implies that the entire observed universe can evolve from a tiny speck, it's tempting to ask whether a universe can in principle be created in a laboratory. Given what we know of the laws of physics, would it be possible for an extraordinarily advanced civilization to create new universes at will?[28]

* So, to produce a universe by the standard big-bang description, one must start with the energy of 10 billion universes![29]

* So, in the inflationary theory the universe evolves from essentially nothing at all, which is why I frequently refer to it as the ultimate free lunch.[30]

* From a historical point of view probably the most revolutionary aspect of the inflationary model is the notion that all the matter and energy in the observable universe may have emerged from almost nothing. . . . The inflationary model of the universe provides a possible mechanism by which the observed universe could have evolved from an infinitesimal region. It is then tempting to go one step further and speculate that the entire universe evolved from literally nothing.[31]

* A number of scientists are unhappy with the big-bang theory. . . . For one thing, it leaves unanswered the questions that always arise when a precise date is given for the creation of the universe: Where did the matter come from in the first place?[32]

* The first, and main, problem is the very existence of the big bang. One may wonder, What came before? If space-time did not exist then, how could everything appear from nothing? What arose first: the universe or the laws determining its evolution? Explaining this initial singularity — where and when it all began — still remains the most intractable problem of modern cosmology.[33]

* There is no mechanism known as yet that would allow the universe to begin in an arbitrary state and then evolve to its present highly ordered state.[34]

* And now to the biggest question of all, where did the universe come from? Or, in modern terminology, what started the big bang? Could quantum fluctuations of empty space have something to do with this as well? Edward Tryon of the City University of New York thought so in 1973 when he proposed that our universe may have originated as a fluctuation of the vacuum on a large scale, as "simply one of those

things which happen from time to time." The idea was later refined and updated within the context of inflationary cosmology by Alexander Vilenkin of Tufts University, who proposed that the universe is created by quantum tunneling from literally nothing into the something we call the universe. Although highly speculative, these models indicate that physicists find themselves turning again to the void and fluctuations therein for their answers.[35]

* Thus we reach a general conclusion: there is no philosophy of big-bang cosmology that makes it reasonable to reject the fundamental thesis of big-bang cosmology: that the universe began to exist without a cause.[36]

CONCEPT 8-3: MULTIPLE EVIDENCES SUGGEST THE UNIVERSE IS YOUNG

Note: In this section the format is changed. Rather than quoting multiple sources, a summary is made of the single overall best publication available on the subject.

RATIONALE: THE ABSENCE OF SUPERNOVA SUGGEST A
YOUNG UNIVERSE

Toward the end of a star's life, a tremendous explosion often occurs, given the name "supernova." This explosion creates a brief light far brighter than any other object in a galaxy. Calculations show that the remains of supernovas should continue shining for hundreds of thousands of years. Yet observations of our own Milky Way galaxy do not show any old supernovas. This fact suggests the galaxy has not existed long enough for old supernovas to have formed.[37]

RATIONALE: ABSENT METEORS SUGGEST A YOUNG UNIVERSE

Each day, hundreds of tons of meteors fall through earth's atmosphere. Most of these meteors burn up before reaching the earth's surface, though as many as sixty tons worth of meteors each day strike land or sea.

If the geological layers that compose the earth's crust were laid down over many millions of years, then they should contain a vast number of meteors. But no such meteors have been found in the geological layers. Since the earth is thought to have formed near the beginning of the universe, this evidence would suggest that the earth is young, that there has not been enough time for meteors to strike earth.[38]

RATIONALE: SPEEDILY DECAYING COMETS SUGGEST THE
UNIVERSE IS YOUNG

Observations demonstrate that our solar system's comets are rapidly disintegrating and then disappearing, both so-called short-period comets and long-period comets. This is true of even the most famous comet of all, Halley's comet.

This fact has profound implications for estimating the age of the universe. It is generally accepted that the comets of our solar system are approximately the same age as the solar system itself, and that the solar system has existed since near the beginning of the universe. Yet calculation of the age of these comets reveals that they are young indeed, as explained by John Maddox in the magazine *Nature*:

> * Indeed the rate at which comets such as Halley's lose material near perihelion is so great that they cannot have been in their present orbits for very long, either. . . . Their [planetary physicists'] conclusion is that the time Halley's comet has spent in the inner solar system is a mere 23,000 years, perhaps enough for fewer than 300 revolutions of the orbit.

By analyzing comets' largest potential size, and the current speed of their disintegration, astronomers can calculate approximately how long they have existed. The compelling conclusion is that the comets, and therefore the solar system and universe itself, are very young.

This data prompts those in the evolution camp to search for some other explanation, for 23,000 years for the age of the earth is completely inconsistent with the time evolution requires.

The "Oort cloud" has been proposed as a way to explain how comets could be constantly resupplied to our solar system. This hypothesis says that many comets are lying just outside, and are occasionally pulled by the sun's gravity, and thus keep the number of comets constant. The Oort cloud, however, has never been observed. It remains only a hypothesis formulated to counter the evidence to the contrary. Yet the data is clear. The comets, and the universe by association, have not existed for more than a few thousands of years.[39]

RATIONALE: THE EARTH-MOON DISTANCE SUGGESTS A
YOUNG UNIVERSE

The precise distance of the moon from earth is critical for regulating ocean tides. If it varied by even a few thousand miles the ocean tides would either submerge coastal land, or there would be no tides at all.

Calculations demonstrate that the moon is slowly withdrawing from earth. Each year, the distance increases by about one and a half inches, though the rate was likely greater in the past. Projections show that even if the moon had been in contact with the earth, it would have taken only 1.37 billion years to reach its present distance. This gives a *maximum* possible age of the moon — not the actual age. But 1.37 billion years is in conflict with much older radiometric ages assigned to moon rocks.

In reality, the earth's surface as we know it could not have existed more than a few thousand years ago, for the effect of the moon's nearer location would have daily drowned most all land masses. This suggests that the earth-moon system has not existed for long.[40]

RATIONALE: THE RAPIDLY SHRINKING SUN SUGGESTS A
YOUNG UNIVERSE

Another intriguing approach to dating the universe is to analyze the change in the size of our sun. As the sun burns its fuel, it becomes smaller, revealing clues about its true age. Dr. John A. Eddy, an astrophysicist at the Harvard-Smithsonian High Altitude Observatory in Boulder, Colorado, suggested a solar diameter shrinkage of approximately 10 miles per year. Dozens of the observatory's independent studies from all over the world have confirmed similar rates of shrinkage. At this rate, our sun will disappear in just one hundred thousand years.

Calculations based upon this data indicate that just 20 million years ago the sun would have been so large it would hve been in contact with the earth in its present orbit. What's more, during over 99.8% of the earth's supposed multi-billion-year history, the earth would have been exponentially too hot to support any hope for life. This information lead Dr. Eddy to declare:

> * I suspect . . . that the sun is 4.5 billion years old. However, given some new and unexpected results to

The solar system

the contrary and some time for frantic adjustment, I suspect that we could live with Bishop Ussher's figure for the age of the earth and sun [approximately six thousand years]. I don't think we have much in the way of observational evidence in astronomy to conflict with that.[41]

Long assumed to be billions of years old, newer data show the sun to be consuming itself far faster than was earlier believed. The startling implication of this fact leads many scientists to conclude that the sun is actually very young.[42]

CHAPTER NINE

GEOLOGIC COLUMN: NO EVOLUTION

INTRODUCTION

E volution will remain only a hypothesis until direct evidence is found that it actually occurred. "Proof" of evolution requires the discovery of fossils that document the process.

Evolutionists claim, among other things, that fish evolved into amphibians. So, they reason, there was a gradual transition of fin to foot, gill to lung, and spine to pelvis. Since the transition from fish to amphibian would have required many millions of years (during which time many billions of transitional creatures must have lived), their fossils must be abundantly preserved in the sedimentary rocks of the earth's crust.

Geological evidence, however, fails to demonstrate any sign of such transition. Fossils of many extinct creatures have been found, but they show no sign of transition. What's more, so many fossils and rocks have been studied that many scientists now conclude with certainty that no transitional life forms will ever be found.

KEY TERMS

Fossil record — living things that were petrified and are now used as evidence of previous events.

Geologic column — the layers of rock and other objects found when exploring downward through the earth's crust.

Conventional wisdom says that the older an object is, the deeper it will be found.

Geologic clock — construction of a time line of previous events based upon geologic findings.

Uniformitarianism — the concept that geologic processes are constant, including the proposal that the layers of fossils and rock on the earth's surface have been laid down at a constant rate since time began.

CONCEPT 9-1: FOSSIL EVIDENCE IS ESSENTIAL.

RATIONALE

As we critique evidence of evolution and creation we can utilize the fields of cosmology, physics, statistics, molecular biology, and genetics to predict the probability of these previous events. Ultimately, however, what actually happened to living creatures in the past can only be verified by examining their fossils. Short of studying the fossils, we are only left with speculation about what life was like in the distant past.

Since evolution proposes that living things very slowly transformed from one type into another, we would expect to find fossils that illustrate this transition, fossils of "intermediate" or "transitional" types of creatures sometimes referred to as "missing links." If reptiles, for example, transformed into birds over millions of years, we'd expect to discover many millions of fossils of reptiles whose scales were becoming more feather-like, whose front legs were beginning to fan out like wings, whose mouths were becoming pointed and beak-like, and whose bones were becoming thinner and lighter to optimize flight.

But, if all living things were all created in their mature, modern forms, then the fossils should reveal only fully formed creatures. No evidence of missing links would be discovered.

EVIDENCE

* Creation and evolution, between them, exhaust the possible explanations for the origin of living things. Organisms either appeared on the earth fully developed or they did not. If they did not, they must have developed from pre-existing species by some process of modification. If they did appear in a fully developed state, they must indeed have been created by some omnipotent intelligence.[1]

* The fossil record affords an opportunity to choose between evolutionary and creationist models for the origin of the earth and its life forms.[2]

* Naturalists must remember that the process of evolution is revealed only through fossil forms. A knowledge of paleontology is, therefore, a prerequisite; only paleontology can provide them with the evidence of evolution and reveal its course or mechanisms. Neither the examination of present beings, nor imagination, nor theories can serve as a substitute for paleontological documents. If they ignore them, biologists, the philosophers of nature, indulge in numerous commentaries and can only come up with hypotheses.[3]

* It is sometimes suspected that comparative morphology and molecular biology of living organisms can provide a reliable record of life's history without attention to fossils. Not so! Living organisms tell little or nothing of the environmental setting or oscillations in diversity of past life — nothing about those myriads that died out without issue.[4]

* In any case, no real evolutionist, whether gradualist or punctuationist, uses the fossil record as evidence in favor of the theory of evolution as opposed to special creation.[5]

CONCEPT 9-2: FOSSIL EVIDENCE DOES NOT SUPPORT EVOLUTION.

RATIONALE

Evolution predicts that study of fossils and the geologic column will demonstrate the following:

1. The oldest rocks would contain fossils of the most primitive forms of life.
2. Younger rocks would contain fossils of more complex forms of life.
3. Fossils would demonstrate a gradual change in life forms from simple to complex.
4. Vast numbers of such transitional forms would be discovered.

If evolution is true, then between the amoebae and the jellyfish, between the jellyfish and the vertebrate fish, between the frog and the bird, between the cow and the whale, between the chimpanzee and modern man, there must exist many billions of intermediate steps. This means there must also have existed trillions on trillions of transitional organisms, some of which must certainly have been fossilized in sedimentary rock.

The crust of our planet certainly contains many fossils, the remnants of living creatures whose bodies were encased and preserved.

Evolution says that this "fossil record" occurred through the gradual lying down of fossils of one generation on top of those of the older generation. Thus, the geologic column would also be a geologic clock, telling us about previous events. If this concept is correct, then the layer of oldest fossils, called the Cambrian layer, should be buried deepest. Based upon this unproven concept, the following time periods are commonly illustrated and taught:

4.5 billion to 570 million years ago — formation of the universe and earth. No life forms present.

Paleozoic ("ancient life") era — 570 million to 225 million years ago. This era includes the Precambrian and Cambrian periods. The first living cell appears, followed by trilobites (a tiny, shelled animal), and later by fish, coral, land plants, insects, amphibians, and reptiles.

Mesozoic ("middle life") era — 225 million to 65 million years ago. This era includes the Triassic, Jurassic, and Cretaceous periods. Dinosaurs and turtles appear, along with ancient mammals, birds, and flowering plants. Dinosaurs then mysteriously disappear.

Cenozoic ("recent life") era — 65 million years ago to present. Modern-day animals appear, along with humans about 2.5 million years ago.

What the geologic column actually reveals, however, is no evidence of either transitional forms or less-complex-to-more-complex creatures. Although the earth's crust is a vast museum of trillions of fossils, no such "missing links" have been encountered. The "fossil record" gives no support for the theory of evolution.

Although the "family tree" showing evolution from single-celled creatures up to humans continues to be presented in most schools as accepted scientific fact, many honest and empirical scientists flatly deny its validity. What's more, the lack of fossil evidence for evolution is not a new conclusion. As early as the 1930s and 1940s leaders in paleontology realized this fact.

EVIDENCE

* Paleontologists are traditionally famous (or infamous) for reconstructing whole animals from the debris of death. Mostly they cheat.[6]

* If any event in life's history resembles man's creation

myths, it is this sudden diversification of marine life when multicellular organisms took over as the dominant actors in ecology and evolution. Baffling (and embarrassing) to Darwin, this event still dazzles us and stands as a major biological revolution on a par with the invention of self-replication and the origin of the eukaryotic cell. The animal phyla emerged out of the Precambrian mists with most of the attributes of their modern descendants.[7]

* We have no intermediate fossils between rhipidistian fish and early amphibians.[8]

* No matter how far back we go in the fossil record of previous animal life upon earth, we find no trace of any animal forms which are intermediate between the various major groups or phyla. . . . Since we have not the slightest evidence, either among the living or the fossil animals, of any intergrading types following the major groups, it is a fair supposition that there never have been any such intergrading types.[9]

* Despite these similarities, there is no evidence of any Paleozoic amphibians combining the characteristics that would be expected in a single common ancestor. The oldest known frogs, salamanders, and caecilians are very similar to their living descendants.[10]

* Why then is not every geological formation and every stratum full of such intermediate links? Geology assuredly does not reveal any such finely graduated organic chain; and this, perhaps, is the most obvious and serious objection which can be urged against the theory.[11]

* All of the basic architectures of animals were apparently established by the close of the Cambrian explosion; subsequent evolutionary changes, even those that allowed animals to move out of the sea onto land, involved only modifications of those basic body plans. About 37 distinct body architectures are recognized among present-day animals and from the basis of the taxonomic classification level of phyla.[12]

* It is, indeed, a very curious state of affairs, I think, that paleontologists have been insisting that their record is consistent with slow, steady, gradual evolution where I think that privately, they've known for over a hundred years that such is not the case. . . . It's the only reason why they can correlate

rocks with their fossils, for instance. . . . They've ignored the question completely.[13]

* Paleontologists ever since Darwin have been searching (largely in vain) for the sequences of insensibly graded series of fossils that would stand as examples of the sort of wholesale transformation of species that Darwin envisioned as the natural product of the evolutionary process. Few saw any reason to demur — though it is a startling fact that, of the half-dozen reviews of *On the Origin of Species* written by palaeontologists that I have seen, all take Darwin to task for failing to recognize that most species remain recognizably themselves, virtually unchanged throughout their occurrence in geological sediments of various ages.[14]

* The extreme rarity of transitional forms in the fossil record persists as the trade secret of paleontology. The evolutionary trees that adorn our textbooks have data only at the tips and nodes of their branches; the rest is inference, however reasonable, not the evidence of fossils. Yet to preserve our favored account of evolution by natural selection we view our data as so bad that we never see the very process we profess to study.[15]

* The absence of fossil evidence for intermediary stages between major transitions in organic design, indeed our inability, even in our imagination, to construct functional intermediates in many cases, has been a persistent and nagging problem for gradualistic accounts of evolution.[16]

* All paleontologists know that the fossil record contains precious little in the way of intermediate forms; transitions between major groups are characteristically abrupt.[17]

* Studies that began in the early 1950s and continue at an accelerating pace today have revealed an extensive Precambrian fossil record, but the problem of the Cambrian explosion has not receded, since our more extensive labor has still failed to identify any creature that might serve as a plausible immediate ancestor for the Cambrian faunas.[18]

* Microscopic fossils extracted from rock in upstate New York . . . which include the oldest known centipede, several arachnids, a mite and perhaps the earliest known insect . . . have been analyzed by a team of paleontologists who now conclude that

the diverse sample provides the best evidence anywhere for fully adapted land animals during the so-called Devonian era.[19]

* But some are "remarkably similar" to modern forms, Shear says: the mite can actually be assigned to a living class of animals, indicating an amazing degree of evolutionary stability; the centipede looks very much like a modern centipede, he says, and one of the arachnids resembles the existing daddy longlegs. Another of the collaborators . . . has identified another of the fossils as a machlid, or silverfish; if it is indeed a silverfish . . . it would be the oldest known insect ever found.[20]

* Darwin all but ignored the fossil record, complaining about the imperfections of the geologic record. He and his followers wrote the history of life on the basis of what they thought the history should be. The Darwinistic dictum of variation/adaption/natural selection/speciation has been supposed to be the rule in the history of life. This method of writing history is very much like attempting to develop a history of the antique by studying sociology, psychology, and political science of the present world.[21]

* Of course there are many gaps in the synapsid fossil record, with intermediate forms between the various known groups almost invariably unknown. However, the known groups have enough features in common that it is possible to reconstruct a hypothetical intermediate stage.[22]

* Gaps at a lower taxonomic level, species and genera, are practically universal in the fossil record of the mammal-like reptiles. In no single adequately documented case is it possible to trace a transition, species by species, from one genus to another.[23]

* Despite the bright promise that paleontology provides a means of "seeing" evolution, it has presented some nasty difficulties for evolutionists, the most notorious of which is the presence of "gaps" in the fossil record. Evolution requires intermediate forms between species and paleontology does not provide them.[24]

* The fossil record doesn't even provide any evidence in support of Darwinian theory except in the weak sense that the fossil record is compatible with it, just as it is compatible with other evolutionary theories, and revolutionary theories and special creationist theories and even ahistorical theories.[25]

* The actual percentage of areas showing this progressive order from the simple to the complex is surprisingly small. Indeed formations with very complex forms of life are often found resting directly on the basic granites. Furthermore, I have in my own files a list of over 500 cases that attest to a reverse order, that is, simple forms of life resting on top of more advanced types.[26]

* I fully agree with your comments on the lack of direct illustration of evolutionary transitions in my book [*Evolution*]. If I knew of any, fossil or living, I would have certainly have included them. . . . Yet Gould and the American Museum people are hard to contradict when they say there are no transitional fossils. . . . I will lay it on the line — there is not one single transitional form in the fossil record for which one could make a watertight argument.[27]

* The fossil record of evolutionary change within single evolutionary lineages is very poor. If evolution is true, species originate through changes of ancestral species: one might expect to be able to see this in the fossil record. In fact it can rarely be seen. In 1859 Darwin could not cite a single example.[28]

* In any case, no real evolutionist, whether gradualist or punctuationist, uses the fossil record as evidence in favor of the theory of evolution as opposed to special creation. . . . So just what is the evidence that species have evolved? There have traditionally been three kinds of evidence, and it is these, not the "fossil evidence," that the critics should be thinking about. The three arguments are from the observed evolution of species, from biogeography, and from the hierarchical structure of taxonomy.[29]

* This regular absence of transitional forms is not confined to mammals, but is an almost universal phenomenon, as has long been noted by paleontologists. It is true of almost all orders of all classes of animals, both vertebrate and invertebrate. Absolutely, it is also true of the classes, and of the major animal phyla, and it is apparently also true of analogous categories of plants.[30]

* The fossil record shows very clearly that there is no central line leading steadily, in a goal-directed way, from a protozoan to man. . . .

Neither in its over-all pattern nor in its intricate detail can that record be interpreted in any simply finalistic way. If evolution is God's plan of creation — a proposition that a scientist as such should neither affirm nor deny — then God is not a finalist.[31]

* The known fossil record fails to document a single example of phyletic evolution accomplishing a major morphologic transition, and hence offers no evidence that the gradualistic model can be valid.[32]

If evolution is true, the fossil record should demonstrate:
1. The oldest rocks that bear evidence of life would contain the most primitive forms of life capable of fossilization.
2. Younger rocks would contain evidence of more complex forms of life.
3. There would be a gradual change in life forms from simple to complex.
4. There would be huge numbers of transitional forms.[33]

Contrary to what most scientists write, the fossil record does not support the Darwinian theory of evolution.[34]

CONCEPT 9-3: FOSSIL EVIDENCE IS CONSISTENT WITH CREATION.

RATIONALE

Clearly, a vast difference exists between the geologic column predicted by evolution and the actual geologic findings. There are no transitional forms — no transitions from invertebrates to vertebrates, none from fishes to amphibians, none from amphibians to reptiles, none from reptiles to birds or mammals, and certainly none from apes to men.

The creation model predicts that a study of fossils and the geologic column will demonstrate the following characteristics:

1. A sudden and explosive appearance of very diverse and highly complex forms of life.
2. No evidence of gradual change in life forms from simple to complex.
3. No evidence of transitional forms, since there never were any transitional forms.

What is actually demonstrated by the fossils? The lower four-fifths of the earth's crust shows no sign of life. Then, suddenly, life abruptly appears, seemingly out of nowhere. More than 5,000 species have been discovered in the Cambrian layers, with no evidence of transitional forms; no evidence of evolution. What's more, these fossils demonstrate modern, fully-formed creatures, just what we'd expect to find if they were created this way. The Cambrian layer contains complete jellyfish, trilobites (with eyes as complex as vertebrate eyes), urchins, sponges, and a host of other perfectly formed invertebrates. The fossil record is entirely consistent with the finding predicted by the creation model.

EVIDENCE

* It must be significant that nearly all the evolutionary stories I learned as a student . . . have now been debunked. . . . The point emerges that, if we examine the fossil record in detail, whether at the level of orders or of species, we find, over and over again, not gradual evolution, but the sudden explosion of one group at the expense of another.[35]

Trilobites are referred to as the very earliest life forms, the most "primitive" known creatures. Yet on June 1, 1968, William Meister found the fossils of several trilobites in Utah in what appeared to be the fossilized, sandaled footprint of a man![36]

* The abrupt manner in which whole groups of species suddenly appear in certain formations, has been urged by several paleontologists . . . as a fatal objection to the belief in the transmutation of species. If numerous species, belonging to the same genera of families, have really started into life at once, the fact would be fatal to the theory of evolution through natural selection.[37]

* The Cambrian strata of rocks, vintage about 600 million years [evolutionists are now dating the beginning of the Cambrian at about 530 million years], are the oldest in which we find most of the major invertebrate groups. And we find many of them already in an advanced state of evolution, the very first time they appear. It is as though they were just planted there, without any evolutionary history. Needless to say, this appearance of sudden planting has delighted creationists.[38]

* It remains true, as every paleontologist knows, that most new species, genera, and families . . . appear in the record suddenly and are not led up to by known, gradual, completely continuous transitional sequences.[39]

* The history of most fossil species includes two features

particularly inconsistent with gradualism.

1. Stasis. Most species exhibit no directional change during their tenure on earth. They appear in the fossil record looking much the same as when they disappear; morphological change is usually limited and directionless.

2. Sudden appearance. In any local area, a species does not arise gradually by the steady transformation of its ancestors; it appears all at once and "fully formed."[40]

* The oldest truth of paleontology proclaimed that the vast majority of species appear fully formed in the fossil record and do not change substantially during the long period of their later existence (average durations for marine invertebrate species may be as high as 5 to 10 million years). In other words, geologically abrupt appearance followed by subsequent stability.[41]

* As is now well known, most fossil species appear instantaneously in the record, persist for some millions of years virtually unchanged, only to disappear abruptly — the "punctuated equilibrium" pattern of Eldredge and Gould.[42]

* Most of evolution's dramatic leaps occurred rather abruptly and soon after multicellular organisms first evolved, nearly 600 million years ago during a period called the Cambrian. The body plans that evolved in the Cambrian by and large served as the blueprints for those seen today. Few new major body plans have appeared since that time. Just as all automobiles are fundamentally modeled after the first four-wheel vehicles, all the evolutionary changes since the Cambrian period have been mere variations on those basic themes.[43]

* Before the Cambrian period, almost all life was microscopic, except for some enigmatic soft-bodied organisms. At the start of the Cambrian, about 544 million years ago, animals burst forth in a rash of evolutionary activity never since equaled. Ocean creatures acquired the ability to grow hard shells, and a broad range of new body plans emerged within the geologically short span of 10 million years. Paleontologists have proposed many theories to explain this revolution but have agreed on none.[44]

* *Time* magazine describes the Cambrian period fossils (the very oldest fossils) like this: "In a bust of creativity like nothing before or since, nature appears to have sketched out

the blueprints for virtually the whole of the animal kingdom.
. . . Since 1987, discoveries of major fossil beds in Greenland,
in China, in Siberia, and now in Namibia have shown that the
period of biological innovation occurred at virtually the same
instant in geologic time all around the world. What could
possibly have powered such a radical advance?"[45]

* Instead of finding the gradual unfolding of life, what geologists of Darwin's time, and geologists of the present day actually find is a highly uneven or jerky record; that is, species
appear in the sequence very suddenly, show little or no change
during their existence in the record, then abruptly go out of the
record and it is not always clear, in fact it's rarely clear, that the
descendants were actually better adapted than their predecessors. In other words, biological improvement is hard to find.[46]

* New species almost always appeared suddenly in the fossil
record with no intermediate links to ancestors in older rocks
of the same region.[47]

* In any case, no real evolutionist, whether gradualist or
punctuationist, uses the fossil record as evidence in favor of
the theory of evolution as opposed to special creation. . . .
So just what is the evidence that species have evolved?
There have traditionally been three kinds of evidence, and it is
these, not the "fossil evidence," that the critics should be thinking about. The three arguments are from the observed evolution of species, from biogeography, and from the hierarchical
structure of taxonomy.[48]

* The facts are that many species and genera, indeed the
majority, do appear suddenly in the record, differing sharply
and in many ways from any earlier group, and that this appearance of discontinuity becomes more common the higher
the level, until it is virtually universal as regards orders and all
higher steps in the taxonomic hierarchy.[49]

* Eldredge and Gould, by contrast, decided to take the
record at face value. On this view, there is little evidence of
modification within species, or of forms intermediate between
species because neither generally occurred. A species forms and
evolves almost instantaneously (on the geological timescale)
and then remains virtually unchanged until it disappears, yielding its habitat to a new species.[50]

If creation is true, the fossil record should demonstrate:

1) The fossil record would show a sudden and explosive appearance of very diverse and highly complex forms of life.

2) There would not be a gradual change in life forms from simple to complex.

3) There would be a regular and systematic absence of transitional forms, since there never were any transitional forms.[51]

* Abstract. All three subdivisions of the bony fishes first appear in the fossil record at approximately the same time. They are already widely divergent morphologically, and they are heavily armored. How did they originate? What allowed them to diverge so widely? How did they all come to have heavy armor? And why is there no trace of earlier, intermediate forms?[52]

* If ever we were to expect to find ancestors to or intermediates between higher taxa, it would be in the rocks of late Precambrian to Ordovician times, when the bulk of the world's higher animal taxa evolved. Yet transitional alliances are unknown or unconfirmed for any of the phyla or classes appearing then.[53]

* We conclude that the probability that species selection is a general solution to the origin of higher taxa is not great, and that neither of the contending theories of evolutionary change at the species level, phyletic gradualism or punctuated equilibrium, seem applicable to the origin of new body plans.[54]

Dr. Clifford Burdick, another geologist, found more evidence that men and trilobites did live together when he discovered the footprints of a barefoot child, one of which contained a compressed trilobite![55]

CONCEPT 9-4: SUFFICIENT EVIDENCE EXISTS TO DRAW CONCLUSIONS ABOUT THE FOSSIL RECORD.

RATIONALE

Analysis of fossil evidence is extremely demanding, both from an intellectual standpoint and from the enormous amount of physical labor involved. Fortunately, many respectable scientists have invested decades studying the fossils, trying to learn what they can teach us. For example, scientists have studied literally billions of fossils of ancient invertebrates and fish. In their search, no transitional forms have been identified. Similar conclusions have been made concerning the fossils of many other species.

Still, it remains true that not all fossils on the planet have been studied. Is it possible that science has simply not searched long enough or deep enough? By any account, over the last 150 years we have examined a good selection of the fossils that exist. Best estimation has it that our museums contain at least 250,000 different fossilized species, and that these represent the results of literally billions of fossils examined.

The contents of unstudied fossils can always be speculated. Yet scientists believe we have indeed examined enough fossils to draw accurate conclusions about those yet to be found. Sampling of the fossil record is now so thorough that it is unreasonable to blame the lack of transitional forms on insufficient research. Scientists generally agree that, if they ever did exist, 150 years of intense searching would have revealed a very large number of obvious transitional forms.

EVIDENCE

* It must be significant that nearly all the evolutionary stories I learned as a student . . . have now been "debunked."[56]

* We all know that many apparent evolutionary bursts are nothing more than brainstorms on the part of particular paleontologists. One splitter in a library can do far more than millions of years of genetic mutation.[57]

* The number of intermediate and transitional links between all living and extinct species must have been inconceivably great.[58]

* Since Darwin's time, the search for missing links in the fossil record has continued on an ever-increasing scale. So vast has been the expansion of paleontological activity over the past one hundred years that probably 99.9% of all paleontological work has been carried out since 1860. Only a small fraction of the hundred thousand or so fossil species known today was known to Darwin. But virtually all the new fossil species discovered since Darwin's time have either been closely related to known forms or, like the Poganophoras, strange unique types of unknown affinity.[59]

* There is no need to apologize any longer for the poverty of the fossil record. In some ways it has become almost unmanageably rich, and discovery is out-pacing integration.[60]

* Studies that began in the early 1950s and continue at an accelerating pace today have revealed an extensive Precambrian

fossil record, but the problem of the Cambrian explosion has not receded, since our more extensive labor has still failed to identify any creature that might serve as a plausible immediate ancestor for the Cambrian fauna. . . . Where, then, are all the Precambrian ancestors — or, if they didn't exist in recognizable form, how did complexity get off to such a fast start?[61]

    * There are too many places where the fossil record is complete enough that we ought to see transitions occurring. Even in these cases we see very few good examples of higher taxa evolving by gradual change. There may be a few examples here and there, but by and large we just don't see the steps.[62]

CHAPTER TEN

FOSSIL EVIDENCE: NO EVOLUTION

INTRODUCTION

If evolution has really taken place, there should be multitudes of transitional forms preserved in the rocks. If reptiles turned into birds, as is claimed, then we should expect to find fossils with gradual extending of the front feet into the form of bird-like wings, along with many other reptile/bird intermediate forms. The fossil record ought to be packed with such creatures and they should fill our museums.

In spite of their best efforts, evolutionists have been able to offer only a handful of "evolution-proving" candidates from among the billions of known fossils. These are mainly the lungfishes, the mammal-like reptiles, the archaeopteryx, the horses, and, more recently, the so-called walking whales. As the following examples show, however, these fossils, on closer inspection, show no true signs of evolution.

CONCEPT 10-1: PLANT FOSSILS DO NOT DEMONSTRATE EVOLUTION.

RATIONALE

Flowering plants, also known as angiosperms, abundantly cover the earth. Their fossils are readily discovered. The remarkable facts surrounding flowering plants are that they seem to have appeared suddenly, and in great variety. No traces of ancestors, intermediate forms, or missing links have been found among the fossils. To date, explaining their development in terms of evolution has been only a hypothesis. No trace has been found of more primitive plants developing into these more complex ones. Darwin described their beginning as "an abominable mystery."

EVIDENCE

* Thirty million years ago some green leaves from elm trees in Oregon were rapidly buried under volcanic ash. Some of those leaves are still a vivid green today. . . . So far, they find the chemical profile of the prehistoric leaves surprisingly similar to that of modern leaves.

The Oregon leaves are not the oldest leaves that have been studied: green leaves, at least 60 million years old, were reported previously in Germany.[1]

* It has long been hoped that extinct plants will ultimately reveal some of the stages through which existing groups have passed during the course of their development, but it must freely be admitted that this aspiration has been fulfilled to a very slight extent even though paleobotanical research has been in progress for more than one hundred years.[2]

* Indeed, the mystery of the origin and early evolution of the angiosperms is as pervasive and as fascinating today as it was when Darwin emphasized the problem in 1879. . . . We have no definitive answers, because we are forced to base our conclusions largely on circumstantial evidence, and they must usually, of necessity, be highly speculative and interpretative.[3]

* Much evidence can be adduced in favor of the theory of evolution, from biology, biogeography, and paleontology, but I still think that to the unprejudiced, the fossil record of plants is in favor of special creation. . . . Yet mutations and natural selection are the bricks with which the taxonomist has built his temple of evolution, and where else have we to worship?[4]

* We still lack any precise information concerning the presumed aquatic ancestors from which land plants evolved, and the search for evidence of these precursors and of probable transitional stages continues.[5]

* The evolutionary origin of the now dominant land-plant group, the angiosperms, has puzzled scientists since the middle of the nineteenth century. . . . With few exceptions of detail, however, the failure to find a satisfactory explanation [for the evolutionary origins of angiosperms] has persisted and many biologists have concluded that the problem is not capable of solution by fossil evidence.[6]

* A third fundamental aspect of the record is somewhat different. Many new groups of plants and animals suddenly appear, apparently without any close ancestor. Most major groups of organisms — phyla, subphyla, and even classes — have appeared in this way. . . . The fossil record, which has produced the problem, is not much help in its solution.[7]

* My last doubt concerns so-called parallel evolution. In the angiosperms, the same features of flower structure have apparently appeared independently several times in unrelated evolutionary lines. Indeed, the problem is so severe that no satisfactory classification scheme for flowering plants has yet been devised. Even something as complex as the eye has appeared several times, for example, in the squid, the vertebrates, and the arthropods. It's bad enough accounting for the origin of such things once, but the thought of producing them several times according to the modern synthetic theory makes my head swim.[8]

* Life, the temporary reversal of a universal trend toward maximum disorder, was brought about by the production of information mechanisms. In order for such mechanisms to first arise it was necessary to have matter capable of forming itself into a self-reproducing structure that could extract energy from the environment for its first self-assembly. Directions for the reproduction of plants, for the extraction of energy and chemicals from the environment, for the growth sequence and the mechanism for translating instructions into growth all had to be simultaneously present at that moment. This combination of events has seemed an incredibly unlikely happenstance and often divine intervention is prescribed as the only way it could have come about.[9]

CONCEPT 10-2: BIRD FOSSILS DO NOT DEMONSTRATE EVOLUTION.

RATIONALE

Many evolutionists believe that birds evolved from reptiles, perhaps even a type of small dinosaur. *Archaeopteryx* is thought by some to be an example of a transitional form: half-bird and half-reptile. The book *Teaching About Evolution and the Nature of Science* presents this alleged dinosaur-bird intermediate as evidence for evolution:

* A bird that lived 150 million years ago and had many reptilian characteristics, was discovered in 1861 and helped support the hypothesis of evolution proposed by Charles Darwin in *The Origin of Species* two years earlier.[10]

Other scientists, however, take odds with this claim. Their analysis does not support the possibility that *Archaeopteryx* — or other proposed bird ancestors including *Sinosauropteryx prima*, *Longisquama insignis*, and *Mononykus* — evolved into birds. Their rationale is twofold:

• Physical distinctions separating birds and reptiles are striking. Reptiles and dinosaurs have anatomy that is, for example, completely incapable of flight.

• Analysis of fossils has yet to reveal any creatures with distinct features intermediate between those of reptiles and birds.

Birds are animals well prepared for flight with very unique features. For example, the body of a flying bird is aerodynamically streamlined to decrease wind resistance. Its center of gravity is located in the middle of its wings for balance in flight. A bird has a unique, superefficient breathing system in which air in the lung flows in only one direction. It has powerful muscles and distinct long tendons necessary for flight, keen vision, and most distinctly, feathers.

By stark contrast, the body of a reptile lacks streamlined body features necessary for smooth movement through the air. The body weight is more evenly distributed along its head, torso, and tail. Reptiles have a "bellows" type of lung in which air moves in and out along the same

Archaeopteryx *is actually an extinct bird.*

passageway. Most powerful muscles are located on the hind legs and pelvis for crawling. Reptiles have uniformly poor vision. Close inspection reveals the enormous structural differences between scales and feathers. These distinctions make any proposed evolutionary connection between reptiles and birds virtually impossible.

EVIDENCE

Another proposed reptile-bird "missing link" was based on the fossil discovery of a creature called *Sinosauropteryx prima*. Initial investigators thought this animal had both feathers and reptile-like features. Their opinion was disproved only about one year later by several leading paleontologists who found that the alleged "feathers" were simply fibers of collagen, the thing from which tendons are made.[11]

* Fossil remains of a bird which lived between 142 and 137 million years ago were recently found in the Liaoning province of northeastern China. The discovery, made by a fossil-hunting farmer and announced by a Chinese/American team of scientists, including Alan Feduccia (University of North Carolina, Chapel Hill) and Larry D. Martin (University of Kansas), provide the oldest evidence of a beaked bird on earth yet found.[12]

* The Chinese bird, claim its discoverers, probably lived at the Jurassic-Cretaceous boundary — prior to the arrival of *Deinonychus* and *Mononykus* — and could not possibly be descended from them.

But there are plenty of other reasons to refute the dinosaur-bird connection, says Feduccia. "How do you derive birds from a heavy, earthbound, bipedal reptile that has a deep body, a heavy balancing tail, and foreshortened forelimbs?" he asks. "Biophysically, it's impossible."[13]

* At the morphological level, feathers are traditionally considered homologous with reptilian scales. However, in development, morphogenesis, gene structure, protein shape and sequence, and filament formation and structure, feathers are different. Clearly, feathers provide a unique and outstanding example of an evolutionary novelty.[14]

* Other evidence suggests that *Archaeopteryx* had an advanced aerodynamic morphology. (i) It had the feathers of modern birds, unchanged in structural detail over 150 million years of evolution, including microstructure, like regular

spacing of barbs throughout the feather's length and clear impressions of barbules.[15]

* I conclude that *Archaeopteryx* was arboreal and volant, considerably advanced aerodynamically, and probably capable of flapping, powered flight to at least some degree. *Archaeopteryx* probably cannot tell us much about the early origins of feathers and flight in true protobirds because *Archaeopteryx* was, in the modern sense, a bird.[16]

* But confirming whether the impressions are feathers, scales, or something else may prove to be difficult.[17]

* It's biophysically impossible to evolve flight from such large bipeds (hind legs) with foreshortened forelimbs and heavy, balancing tails.[18]

* The Chinese fossil is too recent — 121 million years old — for the dinosaur to have given rise to the 150-million-year-old Jurassic bird, *Archaeopteryx*.[19]

* But these ideas on the evolution of feathers are, well, for the birds, according to University of North Carolina ornithologist Alan Feduccia, the best-known critic of the theory that dinosaurs gave rise to birds. He sees no proof that the dinosaur had feathers and doubts that any will be forthcoming. Feathered wings were "the most complex appendage produced by vertebrates," he says; it's implausible that an animal would have developed feathers if it did not fly.[20]

Also like other birds, both *Archaeopteryx*'s maxilla (upper jaw) and mandible (lower jaw) moved, while in most reptiles, only the mandible moves. *Archaeopteryx*'s brain had a large cerebellum and visual cortex — the same as that found in today's flying birds.[21]

* Mongolian and U.S. researchers have found a 75-million-year-old bird-like creature with a hand so strange it has left paleontologists grasping for an explanation.[22]

* While other paleontologists hail the new discovery, they remain unconvinced that *Mononychus* fits in the same phylogenetic category as *Archaeopteryx* and all later birds. Paul Sereno of the University of Chicago notes that *Mononychus* had arms built much like those of digging animals. Because moles and other diggers have keeled sternums and wrists remi-

niscent of birds, the classification of *Mononychus* becomes difficult," he says.[23]

* If people can have their 15 minutes of fame, so can dinosaurs. Most recently, the international spotlight has focused on a chicken-size fossil from northeast China, its body apparently fringed with downy impressions. For paleontologists who believe that birds evolved from dinosaurs, this specimen seemed the ultimate feather in their cap.

An international team of researchers that examined the Chinese fossil now concludes that the fibrous structures are not feathers.[24]

* Paleontologists have tried to turn *Archaeopteryx* into an earth-bound, feathered dinosaur. But it's not. It is a bird, a perching bird. And no amount of "paleobabble" is going to change that.[25]

* A bird that lived 150 million years ago and had many reptilian characteristics was discovered in 1861 and helped support the hypothesis of evolution proposed by Charles Darwin in *The Origin of Species* two years earlier.[26]

* It is fascinating to follow the arguments surrounding the evolution and function of feathers. The traditional view is that feathers are unique to birds, and Feduccia robustly defends this view against the feathered dinosaurs hypothesis. He follows the argument through in relation to the problem of the origin of winged flight: why did wings first evolve? As Feduccia says, feathers "have an almost magical structural complexity," which "allows a mechanical aerodynamic refinement never achieved by other means," making them one of the most remarkable structures in biology.[27]

* Remarkably, the wing feathers of the famous 150-million-year-old late-Jurassic bird *Archaeopteryx* are already well advanced and comparable to those of modern birds with an aerodynamic asymmetry and structural fabric that can evolve only as an adaptation for flight.[28]

A third alleged dinosaur-bird "transition form" was *Mononykus*. It was initially described as a "flightless bird," though feathers were never identified within the fossil, and it could not be proven to have been a bird at all.[29]

* *Mononykus* was clearly not a bird. . . . It clearly was a fleet-footed fossorial theropod [a meat-eating dinosaur that dug in the earth with its feet].[30]

* There is no fossil evidence of the stages through which the remarkable change from reptile to bird was achieved.[31]

CONCEPT 10-3: HORSE FOSSILS DO NOT DEMONSTRATE EVOLUTION.

RATIONALE

One of the most widely propagated evolution "stories" is that the first horse was a dog-sized animal with four toes on the front feet, known as *Hyracotherium* (*Eohippus*). It is proposed that this animal evolved to the three-toed *Miohippus*, and finally to the one-toed *Equus* horse of today.

However, there exist many scientists who believe that *Hyracotherium* was actually not a horse at all, and that there is no evolutionary relationship between *Hyracotherium*, *Miohippus*, and *Equus* (modern horse). The physical similarities between them are far too distinct.

An additional challenge to the proposal of horse evolution is that the timing is inconsistent. The theory of evolution is based on the concept that one species is prone to evolve into another because it is better adapted for survival. This leads to extinction of the first species. In the case of horses, the three-toed form must not have been as hearty as the one-toed. Evolution demands millions of years for transition to occur between species — plenty of time for the first species to die out.

However, today we know that three-toed and one-toed horses lived together in North America. The fact that varieties of horses co-existed is completely inconsistent with evolution's explanation. Add to this the fact that missing links between *Hyracotherium*, *Miohippus*, and *Equus* have never been identified. Rather than lending support for evolution, the history of the horse is more consistent with special creation — modern, fully formed beings that were created simultaneously.

EVIDENCE

* Much of this story [the popular scheme of horse evolution] is incorrect.[32]

* The evolution of the foot mechanism proceeded by rapid and abrupt changes rather than gradual ones. The transition from the form of foot shown by miniature *Eohippus* to larger, consistently three-toed *Miohippus* was so abrupt that it even

left no record in the fossil deposits. . . . Their foot structure changed very rapidly to a three-toed sprung foot in which the pad disappeared and the two side toes became essentially functionless. Finally, in the Pliocene the line leading to the modern one-toed grazer went through a rapid loss of the two side toes on each foot.[33]

Note: When J.B.Birdsell, the author of the above two quotes, uses terms like "sudden," "rapid," or "abrupt" differences he is meaning that no transitional forms have been identified — that fossils of four, three, and then one-toed animals appeared suddenly, without evidence in the fossils of gradual transitions. It is worth noting that no discovery has been made of a possible two-toed horse "transition form" that would help to smooth out the proposed evolution between these animals.

 * The supposed pedigree of the *Equidae* (horses, asses, zebras) is a deceitful delusion, which . . . in no way enlightens us on the paleontological origin of the horse.[34]

 Some scientists believe that *Hyracotherium* was actually a species similar to the rhinoceros, and not at all related to horses.[35]

 * Soviet paleontologists have discovered the fossilized tracks of an unknown species of *perissodactyls* (odd-toed animals) in the spurs of the Gissar Mountains in southern Uzbekistan near the village of Baysun. . . . An analysis of the rocks, which were taken to Tashkent, indicated that their age was about 90 million years old!
 The paleontologists on the expedition immediately thought of comparing the 86 horseshoe-shaped tracks with equine imprints of hoofs. In any case, one could talk about animals very much resembling the horse.[36]

 * The recent discovery of an exquisitely preserved population of primitive *Dinohippus* from Ashfall Fossil Beds in northeastern Nebraska . . . suggests that some individuals were tridactyl (three-toed), whereas others were monodactyl (one-toed).[37]

 * The construction of the whole Cenozoic family tree of the horse is a very artificial one, since it was put together from non-equivalent parts, and cannot therefore be a continuous transformation series.[38]

 * The popularly told example of horse evolution, suggesting a gradual sequence of changes from four-toed fox-sized

creatures living nearly 50 million years ago to today's much larger one-toed horse, has long been known to be wrong. Instead of gradual change, fossils of each intermediate species appear fully distinct, persist unchanged, and then become extinct. Transitional forms are unknown.[39]

   * The uniform, continuous transformation of *Hyracotherium* into *Equus*, so dear to the heart of generations of textbook writers, never happened in nature.[40]

   * Those who in the past have contemplated the formation of the modern horse by gradual evolution, beginning with this early genus, must now contend with the fact that at least two species of *Hyracotherium* lasted for several million years without appreciable change.[41]

   * The horse is the most famous example — the classic story of one genus turning into another, turning into another. Now it's becoming apparent that there's an overlap of these genera, and that there were many species belonging to each one. It's a very bushy sort of pattern that is, I think, much more in line with the punctuational model; there isn't just a simple, gradual transition from one horse to another. This is now becoming fairly well known.[42]

CONCEPT 10-4: WHALE FOSSILS DO NOT DEMONSTRATE EVOLUTION.

RATIONALE

In biological circles, whale evolution is another commonly debated subject. Whales and dolphins are known by the scientific name *cetacean*, and though they live in water, they are actually mammals. The fact of their habitat prompted evolutionists to suggest that *cetaceans* must have evolved from land mammals. The magazine *National Geographic* described whale evolution in the following way:

   The whale's ascendancy to sovereign size apparently began sixty million years ago when hairy, four-legged mammals, in search of food or sanctuary, ventured into water. As eons passed, changes slowly occurred. Hind legs disappeared, front legs changed into flippers, hair gave way to a thick smooth blanket of blubber, nostrils moved to the top of the head, the tail broadened into flukes, and in the buoyant water world, the body became enormous.[43]

Agreeing with the above scenario, the National Academy of Science proposes in their book *Teaching about Evolution*, that modern whales evolved via four intermediate creatures, as follows:

- *Mesonychid* (55 million years ago)
- *Ambulocetus* (50 million years ago)
- *Rodhocetus* (46 million years ago)
- *Basilosaurus* — Also known as *Eocene* (40 million years ago)[44]

When investigating evolutionary claims, it is essential to realize the distinction between what is proposed and what is actually known from discoveries. Artists' interpretations of how ancient animals may have appeared is often based upon little more than a few bones; rarely even a fraction of an entire skeleton. Similarly, author's "conclusions" are at times supported by a few real facts, and instead demonstrate considerable imagination. In the case of proposed whale evolution, both types of errors are epidemic.

As investigators ourselves, we must minimize both our own bias and the author's bias. Instead, we must consider the evidence. Is it really possible for whales to have evolved from mammals? Several conflicts are immediately evident.

- Fossils do not exist to document whale evolution. The seven-foot-long *Ambulocetus natans* (the second transitional form) is a proposed

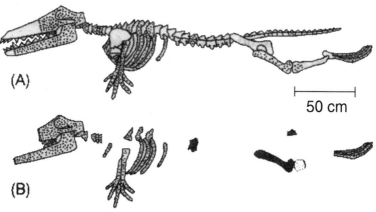

(A) Reconstruction of Ambulocetus, *"at the end of the power stroke during swimming."[45] The stippled bones were all that were found, and the shaded ones were found five meters above the rest. (B) With the "additions" removed, there really isn't much left of* Ambulocetus.

creature based upon only a few bones. It does not even include the more distal portion of the animal where the pelvis would be. But the pelvis must be examined to have any idea what kind of animal *Ambulocetus* really was, because for a land mammal to become a whale it must lose its entire pelvis. So little of the actual skeleton of *Ambulocetus* exists that it is impossible to identify it.

Basilosaurus, the fourth and last proposed whale transitional form, presents a similar challenge. This fantastic creature was actually a serpent-like sea mammal roughly 70 feet long, ten times longer than *Ambulocetus*. The animal dwelled only in the water, and shows no transitional features of land and water mammals. No fossil has ever been identified that could be a transition form between *Basilosaurus* and any other proposed whale ancestor.

• Insufficient time exists for such evolution to have occurred. Genetics calculations demonstrate that animals with 20 years between each generation (10 years in the case of whales) could transmit to their offspring no more than about 1,700 mutations during a 10-million-year period. However, almost all mutations are harmful to animals. They certainly rarely, if ever, produce improvements. Even if these 1,700 mutations were helpful, the new genetic code needed for a land animal to "become" a whale would be millions upon millions of beneficial mutations.

• Whales and land mammals are extremely contrasting creatures. Some of the distinct traits that make whales uniquely prepared for life in the sea include:

- Skin consisting of an unusual, fatty blubber to insulate the body
- A huge, forceful tail for locomotion in the water
- Eyes and ears appropriate for underwater vision and hearing, and able to withstand the enormous pressure of dives
- Nostrils (blowholes) on the top of the head to allow simultaneous swimming and breathing
- Efficient lungs for dives as long as 30 minutes
- Plankton filters in the mouth of some whales (Baleen) to filter food from the water
- Sonar capability for locating distant objects in water

Whales, and dolphins for that matter, are strikingly different from any other living thing. For them to have evolved via random mutations (putting just the right lipid, blubber, filter, sound sensor, blowhole, and tail muscle in just the right place) is mathematically so unlikely as to be absurd. What's more, gradual step-by-step evolution of these organs must overcome another huge obstacle: such features are almost useless until fully formed.

A whale with slightly thicker skin will become just as cold as one with normal skin. One whose eyes can withstand water pressure to a depth of 30 feet has no significant advantage of one that can only dive to 20 feet. But for natural selection to have "worked," even the smallest of these mutation-induced developments must lead to a clearly "superior" creature. Otherwise, there would be nothing to make that creature more likely to out-live the others. Yet partial developments like slightly thicker skin or slightly more pressure-resistant eyes offer the animal no clear survival advantage.

Whale evolution cannot possibly have occurred so quickly. Neither can it be explained through natural selection, nor proved from the fossil record.

EVIDENCE

* Presumably, various physiological mechanisms for handling oxygen debt and lactic acid buildup, as well as the development of blubber for fat storage and for temperature regulation, evolved early, though evidence of the evolutionary history is unavailable.[46]

* These mammals must have had an ancient origin, for no intermediate forms are apparent in the fossil record between the whales and the ancestral Cretaceous placentals. Like bats, the whales (using the term in a general and inclusive sense) appear suddenly in early Tertiary times, fully adapted by profound modifications of the basic mammalian structure for a highly specialized mode of life. Indeed, the whales are even more isolated with relation to other mammals than the bats; they stand quite alone.[47]

* We must suppose the existence of innumerable collateral branches leading to many unknown types. . . . One is inclined to think in terms of possibly hundreds, even thousands of transitional species on the most direct path between a hypothetical land ancestor and the common ancestor of modern whales. . . . We are forced to admit with Darwin that in terms of gradual evolution, considering all the collateral branches that must have existed in the crossing of such gaps, the number of transitional species must have been inconceivably great.[48]

* We do not yet know anything about the post-cranial anatomy of early Eocene whales.[49]

* The inferred posture and range of motion of the hind limb of *Basilosaurus* are unusual for a mammal. . . . [They] appear to have been too small relative to body size to have assisted in swimming, and they could not possibly have supported the body on land.[50]

* The problem for Darwinians is in trying to find an explanation for the immense number of adaptations and mutations needed to change a small and primitive earthbound mammal, living alongside and dominated by dinosaurs, into a huge animal with a body uniquely shaped so as to be able to swim deep in the oceans, a vast environment previously unknown to mammals. . . . All this had to evolve in at most five to ten million years — about the same time as the relatively trivial evolution of the first upright walking apes into ourselves.[51]

* Whale expert G.A. Mchedlidze also concluded that these proposed whale transition forms cannot be defended. Rather, it is more appropriate to consider them completely different animals.[52]

Most embarrassing to evolutionists is the fact that *coelacanth*, another proposed whale "missing link," was caught off the coast of Madagascar in 1938. *Coelacanth* allegedly disappeared seventy million years ago, according to evolutionary theory, and was replaced by more developed species![53]

Population genetics calculations show that animals with 20 years between each generation (ten years in the case of whales) could pass on no more than about 1,700 mutations in 10 million years. Almost all mutations are harmful to animals, not helpful. Even if these 1,700 mutations were helpful, this is not nearly enough new genetic code a land animal would need to "become" a whale.[54]

* The whale's ascendancy to sovereign size apparently began sixty million years ago when hairy, four-legged mammals, in search of food or sanctuary, ventured into water. As eons passed, changes slowly occurred. Hind legs disappeared, front legs changed into flippers, hair gave way to a thick smooth

blanket of blubber, nostrils moved to the top of the head, the tail broadened into flukes, and in the buoyant water world, the body became enormous.[55]

* We do not possess a single fossil of the transitional forms between the aforementioned land animals [i.e. carnivores and ungulates] and the whales.[56]

* The serpentine form of the body and the peculiar shape of the cheek teeth make it plain that these *archaeocetes* [like *Basilosaurus*] could not possibly have been the ancestor of modern whales.[57]

* Since the pelvic girdle is not preserved, there is no direct evidence in *Ambulocetus* for a connection between the hind limbs and the axial skeleton. This hinders interpretations of locomotion in this animal, since many of the muscles that support and move the hind limb originate on the pelvis.[58]

CHAPTER ELEVEN

HUMAN FOSSIL EVIDENCE: NO EVOLUTION

INTRODUCTION

In comparison to any other living creature, human beings are extremely unique. Evolutionists contend, however, that humans descended from apes through a series of transition forms. They use the term "hominoids" for extinct apes that may or may not have ever been related to humans. The term "hominids" is used for extinct somewhat man-like apes which evolutionists believe are more closely related to humans. *Ramapithecus* and *Australopithecus* are the two hominids most often cited.

For evidence, evolutionists point to several fossil discoveries that they allege show these transitions. These fossils are hardly full skeletons, though. Usually they consist of only a fragment of skull, pelvis, or long bone. What's more, there exists extreme disagreement among "experts" concerning what species name to attach to which fossils, and just how these creatures are related to humans.

It is now widely recognized that the structures of these extinct creatures are not similar to humans, but rather more on the order of the chimpanzee, orangutan, or gibbon. To the creationist, all these hominids are not in any way human, but rather extinct apes.

Neanderthal Man, whose contrived images are common in textbooks, we know today was actually a modern human who suffered from disease known to cause physical deformities. The thirst to find fossils of an ape-man has also lead to fraud and deception, best illustrated by the so-called Nebraska Man and Piltdown Man.

Additional challenges to the idea of human evolution come from evidence showing *Australopithecus, Homo habilis, Homo erectus,* and modern humans all living together at the same time. But this is impossible if they actually evolved from one another! The truth is, they did not.

CONCEPT 11-1: FOSSIL EVIDENCE DOES NOT SUPPORT HUMAN EVOLUTION.

RATIONALE

Humans possess some physical similarities with other primates, especially the apes. These include an opposing thumb and the ability to walk upright. These aside, however, human learning, reasoning, creative power, and communication abilities are completely unmatched in comparison to other animals.

Evolutionists argue that human beings and apes (including chimpanzees, orangutans, gorillas, and gibbons) all descended from some unknown ancestor. The ape-like ancestors, or missing links, that led to modern man are commonly alleged to have been:

> *Ramapithecus*
> *Australopithecus*
> *Homo habilis*
> *Homo erectus* (Java man, Peking man)
> *Homo sapiens* (modern man)

EVALUATING ALLEGED HUMAN FOSSILS

How do scientists determine whether or not a fossilized skeleton is related to *Homo sapiens?* This can be a very challenging undertaking. Some factors to be considered include:

• Features of the fossils. When evaluating proposed fossils, scientists consider many features, comparing them with modern apes, extinct apes, modern man, and other similar fossils. In particular, scientists pay attention to the size and shape of the skull, the form of the brow ridges above the eyes, and the way the cheekbones are swept back relative to the jaw. They also consider the length and shape of teeth, jaw configuration, length and shape of arms and legs, slant of the pelvis and lower back, form of the feet, and volume of the cranium, which reflects the size of the animal's brain.

Complicating this process is the fact that few skeletons are complete. Commonly, the only remains discovered are pieces of skull, pelvis, and perhaps extremity fragments. Doubtlessly, it may be difficult to be dogmatic about a creature's identity with so little evidence to consider.

• Age of the fossils. Assigning a date to a fossil may help to reveal its identity. If, for example, one argues that Animal A evolved into Animal B, dating methods should show that Animal A is indeed older than B. As we discussed in chapter 7, however, popular dating methods are unreliable, and evolutionists themselves have many disagreements over the ages of alleged human ancestors.

• Quantity of similar fossils. A tremendous challenge to human evolution is the fact that so few suspected ape-human transitional forms have ever been discovered. The dinosaur supposedly reigned from a period beginning 220 million years ago until 60 million years ago. We have discovered tens of thousands of near-perfect dinosaur fossils on all seven continents. By contrast, man is said to have existed for the last one million years. Yet the total number of hominid (ape-men) fossils ever found on earth wouldn't fill the top of a kitchen table. The small number of fossils makes the case for human evolution even more difficult to prove.

After reviewing the evidence, many scientists conclude that the alleged "ape-men" did not arise through a series of evolutionary stages. Instead, some were actually varieties of true humans, such as the Neanderthals. Others were entirely non-humans, like the australopithecine apes, which are now extinct. And nowhere do the fossils show transition from one creature into another. Instead, both humans and apes appear in the fossils as fully formed creatures, just as would be expected if both were created that way from the beginning.

EVIDENCE

* It must be significant that nearly all the evolutionary stories I learned as a student have now been debunked. . . .

Proposed human evolution

The point emerges that, if we examine the fossil record in detail, whether at the level of orders or of species, we find, over and over again, not gradual evolution, but the sudden explosion of one group at the expense of another.[1]

* This presents the public for the first time with the notion that there are no actual fossils directly antecedent to man [as] . . . the creationists have insisted on for years.[2]

* If man, or even his ape ancestor, or even the ape ancestor's early mammal ancestor, existed as far back as in the Carboniferous period in any shape, then the whole science of geology is so completely wrong that all geologists will resign their jobs and take up truck driving.[3]

* Paleoanthropologists seem to make up for a lack of fossils with an excess of fury, and this must now be the only science in which it is still possible to become famous just for having an opinion. As one cynic says, in human paleontology the consensus depends on who shouts loudest.[4]

* But anatomy and the fossil record cannot be relied on for defining evolutionary lineages. Yet paleontologists persist in doing just this. They rally under the banner of a methodology called cladistics, in which family trees of living and fossil primates are constructed on the basis of "primitive" and "derived" traits (mostly of teeth and bones), which are either shared or not shared. Shared primitive characteristics are shared because they come from a common ancestor, unshared derived characteristics reveal separate evolutionary paths. The subjective element in this approach to building evolutionary trees, which many paleontologists advocate with almost religious fervour, is demonstrated by the outcome: there is no single family tree on which they agree. On the contrary, almost every conceivable combination and permutation of living and extinct hominoids has been proposed by one cladist or another.[5]

* In fact, "virtually all our theories about human origins were relatively unconstrained by fossil data," observes David Pilbeam. "The theories are . . . fossil-free or in some cases even fossil-proof." This shocking statement simply means that there is and always has been far more fleshing out of the course and cause of human evolution than can fully be justified by the scrappy skeleton provided by the fossils. "As a result," he con-

tinues, "our theories have often said far more about the theorists than they have about what actually happened."[6]

* In recent years several authors have written popular books on human origins which were based more on fantasy and subjectivity than on fact and objectivity.[7]

* Biologists impressed by the inherent improbability of every single step that led to the evolution of man consider what Simpson called "the prevalence of humanoids" exceedingly improbable.[8]

* In each case, although initial studies suggest that the fossils are similar to humans, study of the complete evidence readily shows that the reality is otherwise.[9]

* On the fundamental level, it becomes a rigorously demonstrable fact that there are no transitional types, and that the so-called missing links are indeed non-existent.[10]

* All that paleoanthropologists have to show for more than 100 years of digging are remains from fewer than 2,000 of our ancestors. They have used this assortment of jawbones, teeth, and fossilized scraps, together with molecular evidence from living species, to piece together a line of human descent going back 5 to 8 million years of time when humans and chimpanzees diverged from a common ancestor.[11]

* The fossils that decorate our family tree are so scarce that there are still more scientists than specimens. The remarkable fact is that all the physical evidence we have for human evolution can still be placed, with room to spare, inside a single coffin.[12]

* Modern apes, for instance, seem to have sprung out of nowhere. They have no yesterday, no fossil record. And the true origin of modern humans — of upright, naked, toolmaking, big-brained beings — is, if we are to be honest with ourselves, an equally mysterious matter.[13]

* It is quite obvious that modern man could not have arisen from any ape, let alone a monkey, at all similar to those of today. . . . . It is ridiculous to describe man as a "naked" or any other kind of ape.[14]

* No scientist could logically dispute the proposition that man, without having been involved in any act of divine

creation, evolved from some ape-like creature in a very short space of time — speaking in geological terms — without leaving any fossil traces of the steps of the transformation. As I have already implied, students of the fossil primates have not been distinguished for caution. . . . The record is so astonishing that it is legitimate to ask whether much science is yet to be found in this field at all.[15]

CONCEPT 11-2: MODERN HUMANS LIVED ALONGSIDE PROPOSED HUMAN ANCESTORS.

RATIONALE

An essential principle of natural selection is that one species dies out in favor of another "superior" species. Therefore, we should never find two species living together that evolved from one another.

However, evidence exists that the proposed human ancestors all lived together at the same time. This is completely contrary to the theory of evolution. Consider the fact that the australopithecines are thought to have lived between one and four million years ago, and the first humans one million years ago. Yet a specimen thought to be 3.5 million years old was found containing both *Australopithecus* and human footprints, side by side. Now, if *Australopithecus* evolved into *Homo sapiens*, how could they have possibly been living together?

Equally puzzling: *Homo sapiens* bones were recently found in the Cretaceous stratum, a geologic rock layer in Moab, Utah, thought to be 100 million years old. This is far older that the one-million-year maximum age evolutionists assign to modern humans. Modern humans living 100–250 million years ago would mean that they were present earlier than even the dinosaurs!

Evidence such as this — modern humans living alongside alleged ape ancestors, and human remains dated as older than the dinosaurs — make the case for human evolution even more difficult to argue.

EVIDENCE

* As if this evidence were not enough contradiction against evolution, consider the age of other fossils of modern humans. *Homo sapiens* bones were recently found in the Cretaceous stratum — a geologic rock layer in Moab, Utah, thought to be 100 million years old, and far older than the one-million-year maximum age evolutionists assign to modern humans.[16]

* Make no mistake about it . . . they are like modern human footprints. If one were left in the sand of a California beach today, and a four year old were asked what it was, he would instantly say that somebody walked there.[17]

* There is evidence from East Africa for late-surviving small *Australopithecus* individuals that were contemporaneous first with *Homo habilis*, then *Homo erectus*.[18]

* Human footprints have been repeatedly discovered in the Upper Carboniferous period [supposedly 250 million years old].[19]

* The first bipedal trail, consisting of five footprints in sequence, was discovered in 1977 at Laetoli site A.[20]

* The humanness of the plantar (sole) anatomy exhibited by the G prints is underscored by observing the feet and footprints of habitually barefoot people. . . . The footprints of both the Machiguenga and the Laetoli G bipeds exhibit strong heel, ball, and first toe impressions and a well-developed medial longitudinal arch, which is the hallmark of human feet.[21]

* In sum, the 3.5-million-year-old footprint trails at Laetoli site G resemble those of habitually unshod modern humans. None of their features suggest that the Laetoli hominids were less capable bipeds than we are. If the G footprints were not known to be so old, we would readily conclude that they were made by a member of our genus, *Homo*. . . . In any case, we should shelve the loose assumptions that the Laetoli footprints were made by Lucy's kind, *Australopithecus afarensis*.[22]

* The uneroded footprints show a total morphological pattern like that seen in modern humans. . . . Preliminary observations and experiments suggest that the Laetoli hominid trails at site G do not differ substantially from modern human trails made on a similar substrate.[23]

CONCEPT 11-3: *RAMAPITHECUS* WAS NOT A HUMAN ANCESTOR.

RATIONALE

In 1932, fossil material was discovered in northwestern India by a Yale graduate student. It was given the name *Ramapithecus*. Similar fossilized skeletons were also found in Europe, Kenya, and Yunnan Province of China. In the beginning, *Ramapithecus* was identified as an early human ancestor. This hypothesis, however, was based only on similarities between a few *Ramapithecus* teeth and jaw fragments, and those of modern humans.

Ramapithecus, however, is structurally very different from humans. Today *Ramapithecus* is universally classified as an extinct ape. It represents just one of several creatures that were initially proposed as human ancestors. But the creature was ultimately relegated to the ape family when more complete evidence was available.

EVIDENCE

* *Ramapithecus*, an extinct group of primates that lived from about 12 to 14 million years ago, was for a time regarded as a possible ancestor of *Australopithecus* and, therefore, of modern humans. Fossils of *Ramapithecus* were discovered in N. India and in E. Africa, beginning in 1932. Although it was generally an apelike creature, *Ramapithecus* was considered a possible human ancestor on the basis of the reconstructed jaw and dental characteristics of fragmentary fossils. A complete jaw discovered in 1976 was clearly nonhominid, however, and *Ramapithecus* is now regarded by many as a member of *Sivapithecus*, a genus considered to be an ancestor of the orangutan.[24]

* On the basis of these tooth-size calculations, at least, there would appear to be little evidence to suggest that several different hominoid species are represented among the Old World dryopithecine fossils of late Miocene and early Pliocene times. Neither is there compelling evidence for the existence of any distinct hominid species during this interval, unless the designation "hominid" means simply any individual ape that happens to have small teeth and a correspondingly small face. Fossil hominoids such as *Ramapithecus* may well be ancestral to the hominid line in the sense that they were individual members of an evolving phyletic line from which the hominids later diverged. They themselves nevertheless seem to have been apes — morphologically, ecologically, and behaviorally.[25]

* The oldest human fossils are less than 4 million years old, and we do not know which branch on the copious bush of apes budded off the twig that led to our lineage. (In fact, except for the link of Asian *Sivapithecus* to the modern orangutan, we cannot trace any fossil ape to any living species. Paleontologists have abandoned the once popular notion that *Ramapithecus* might be a source of human ancestry.) Thus, sediments between 4 and 10 million years in age are potential

guardians of the Holy Grail of human evolution — the period when our lineage began its separate end run to later domination, and a time for which no fossil evidence exists at all.[26]

* The case for *Ramapithecus* as a hominid is not substantial and the fragmentary material leaves many questions open. . . . I am reluctant to anticipate further new discoveries, but I would expect that the genus *Homo* will eventually be traced into the Pliocene at an age of between 4 and 6 million years, together with *Australopithecus*.[27]

* Locomotion, like body size, cannot be inferred without some post-cranial bones. It would be unwise to speculate about *Ramapithecus'* locomotion from a knowledge solely of its jaws and teeth.[28]

* The pelvis is probably the most diagnostic bone of the human line. . . . Yet an entire *Ramapithecus*, walking upright, has been "reconstructed" from only jaws and teeth. . . .

The prince's ape latched onto the position by his teeth and has been hanging on ever since, his legitimacy sanctified by millions of textbooks and *Time-Life* volumes on human evolution.

There are still no skulls, no pelvic or limb bones unequivocally associated with the teeth to show whether *Ramapithecus* had a brain like a hominid, swung through trees like an ape, or walked upright like a human.[29]

* The case for *Ramapithecus* as an ancestral human has been weak from the start and has not strengthened with the passage of time. Now that the molecular data are in, the mythical prince's ape, who would be man, has faded until nothing is left but his smile.[30]

CONCEPT 11-4: *AUSTRALOPITHECUS* WAS NOT A HUMAN ANCESTOR.

RATIONALE

Following *Ramapithecus*, *Australopithecus* is the next creature, chronologically speaking, popularly alleged to be a human ancestor. The first fossil was discovered in 1924 by Raymond Dart, who admitted that the skull had ape-like features, but thought the teeth were more human-like. Evolutionists variously claim it lived between 1 and 4.5 million years ago. One particular *Australopithecus* was found in Ethiopia in 1974 and given the name "Lucy." It was three and one-half feet tall, with a brain size of 380 to 450 cc.

Several subtypes of *Australopithecus* were also identified and assigned names indicating their similarity:

Australopithecus africanus
Australopithecus robustus
Australopithecus afarensis

Fossils of *Australopithecus* have been studied in painstaking detail: their manner of walking, the structure of their ear, pattern of tooth development, their long and powerful forearms, short hind limbs, structure of their feet, small-sized brains, and very ape-like skulls, jaws, and faces.

In common between all australopithecines is the fact that they had large, ape-like jaws, with cheek teeth similar to modern gorillas. Their brains were small, occupying about 500 cc or less of space, about one-third the space occupied by human brains. Aside from the skull, however, only a few fragments of pelvis, limb, and foot bones were ever recovered from the *Australopithecus* species.

Australopithecus africanus *skull (left) is quite similar to a modern orangutan skull (right).*[31]

Today, most leading scientists view *Australopithecus* as being too different from humans to possibly represent a step in human evolution. They instead place *Australopithecus* in the family of extinct apes; not in the lineage of modern humans. Donald Johanson himself, the discoverer of Lucy, later admitted that *Australopithecus* could not have been related to humans after all.

EVIDENCE

* The present results lead to the conclusion that the bipedalism of the *Australopithecus* must have differed from that of *Homo*. Not only did *Australopithecus* have less ability to maintain hip and knee extension during the walk, but also probably moved the pelvis and lower limb differently. It seems that the australopithecine walk differed significantly from that of humans, involving a sort of waddling gait, with large rotary movements of the pelvis and shoulders around the vertebral column. Such a walk likely required a greater energetic cost than does human bipedalism. The stride length and frequency of australopithecines, and consequently their speed, should have differed from that of *Homo* in contrast to some recent hypotheses of dynamic similarity among hominids. A previous paper has suggested that the pelvic proportions of *Australopithecus* could provide some arguments for an arboreal locomotion. The results of the present study suggest amplification of this opinion.[32]

* I expected the australopithecine natural endocasts to appear like miniature replicas of human brains because that had been the prevalent view in the scientific literature since 1925. . . . My analysis of the seven known australopithecine endocasts shows Radinsky's hunch was right: all of the convolutions that they preserve were apelike.[33]

* Interestingly, despite almost a decade of technically sophisticated analyses of australopithecine remains, there is still considerable controversy over their functional and phylogenetic significance — in particular whether they are too divergently specialized to be considered suitable ancestors for *Homo*.[34]

* Fossils of *Australopithecus* have been studied in painstaking detail: their manner of walking, the structure of their ear, pattern of tooth development, their long and powerful forearms, short hind limbs, structure of their feet, small-sized

brains, and very ape-like skulls, jaws, and faces. These prove that *Australopithecus* was an ape and in no way related to man. Donald Johanson himself, the discoverer of Lucy, later concluded that *Australopithecus africanus* (Lucy) was not related to humans at all![35]

* Lucy's skull (*Australopithecus afarensis*) was so incomplete that most of it was imagination, made of plaster of Paris, thus making it impossible to draw any firm conclusion about what species she belonged to.[36]

* It is overwhelmingly likely that Lucy (*Australopithecus afarensis*) was no more than a variety of pygmy chimpanzee. The evidence for the alleged transformation from ape to man is extremely unconvincing.[37]

* Though the standard idea is that some of the australopithecines are implicated in a lineage of humanlike forms, the new possibility suggested in this book, a radiation separate from either humans or African apes, has received powerful corroboration. It is now being recognized widely that the australopithecines are not structurally closely similar to humans, that they must have been living at least in part in arboreal [tree] environments, and that many of the later specimens were contemporaneous [living at the same time] or almost so with the earliest members of the genus *Homo*.[38]

Notice the last phrase of this statement. He is saying that australopithecines was found living with humans. How then, could australopithecines possibly be a human ancestor?

Anatomist Charles Oxnard is one of the best-respected experts on this subject. His own analysis of the bones of *Australopithecus africanus* led him to conclude that this creature was very unlike either humans or chimpanzees.[39]

* The first impression given by all the skulls from the different populations of *Australopithecus* is of a distinctly ape-like creature. . . . The ape-like profile of *Australopithecus* is so pronounced that its outline can be superimposed on that of a female chimpanzee with a remarkable closeness of fit. In this respect and also in the lack of chin and in possession of strong supra-orbital ridges, *Australopithecus* stands in strong contrast to modern [man] *Homo sapiens*.[40]

* The australopithecine skull is in fact so overwhelmingly

simian (ape) as opposed to human that the contrary proposition could be equated to an assertion that black is white.[41]

CONCEPT 11-5: *HOMO HABILIS* WAS NOT A HUMAN ANCESTOR.

RATIONALE

Another well-known series of fossilized creatures is known as *Homo habilis*. These initially seemed more man-like than *Australopithecus*, the adults being about three and one-half feet tall, with brains about one-third the size of humans, and long heavily built arms.

A wide variety of fossils were actually designated as *Homo habilis*, leading to confusion in the research community; so much so that *Homo habilis* has become known as a "wastebasket" designation. Also challenging to the proposed evolution of *Australopithecus* to *Homo habilis* is evidence that they both lived together. Today, after painstaking study, most paleontologists agree that *Homo habilis* is not related to humans. Rather, it is a variety of an extinct *Australopithecus* ape, more similar to the chimpanzee or orangutan than to humans.

EVIDENCE

* What has become of our ladder if there are three coexisting lineages of hominids (*Australopithecus africanus*, *Australopithecus robustus*, and *Homo habilis*), none clearly derived from one another? Moreover, none of the three display any evolutionary trends during their tenure on earth: none became brainier or more erect as they approached the present day.[42]

After painstaking study, most paleontologists today believe *Homo habilis* is not related to humans, but is rather a variety of *Australopithecus* ape, more on the order of a chimpanzee or orangutan.[43]

* It is increasingly clear that *Homo habilis* has become a wastebasket taxon, little more than a convenient recipient for a motley assortment of hominid fossils from the latest Pliocene and earliest Pleistocene.[44]

* The small *Homo habilis* material, including KNM-ER 1805, 1813, O.H.24, and O.H.62, does not belong in the genus *Homo* and should never have been so classified. This material is best described as being australopithecine. . . .

We have strong evidence that the category known as *Homo habilis* is not a legitimate taxon but is composed of a mixture of material from at least two separate taxa.[45]

* What the organal balance tells us is that this creature was perhaps even less bipedal than the australopithecines.

What we found in the size of the semicircular canal and the whole structure of the inner ear wasn't intermediate at all between what we saw in *Homo erectus* and the australopithecines.

Interestingly enough, I got support from other findings in East Africa. They found that limb bones are less adapted for bipedalism, for walking on two legs and are more ape-like than australopithecines.[46]

* The obvious taxonomic alternative, which is to transfer one or both of the taxa to one of the existing early hominid genera, is not without problems, but we recommend that, for the time being, both *H. habilis* and *H. rudolfensis* should be transferred to the genus *Australopithecus*.[47]

CONCEPT 11-6: *HOMO ERECTUS* WAS A MODERN HUMAN.

RATIONALE

Enormous attention has been focused on *Homo erectus* — the "species" thought to just proceed evolutionary development of *Homo sapiens*. The skulls of *Homo erectus* had prominent brow ridges; their bodies were proportioned similar to those of modern humans, and the size of their brains was on par with people today. Research into the middle ear structures indicate that *Homo erectus* walked upright just like you and me. Analysis of the social and cultural behavior of *Homo erectus* suggests that they hunted, built dwellings, and lived in communities. In sum, both the physical and behavioral characteristics of *Homo erectus* indicate that it was fully human, and should instead be designed *Homo sapiens*.

Lending confusion to the designation *Homo erectus* are two special cases: Java man and Peking man. These two creatures were also designated *Homo erectus*, and generated tremendous media attention.

The tale of Java Man (*Pithecanthropus erectus*) began in 1887, when a Dutch physician, Eugene Dubois, came across the top portion of a skull, with a femur found about 50 feet away. Based upon only imagined facial characteristic and the human-like femur, Dubois announced that he had discovered a *Homo erectus*. His claim generated considerable doubt. It was not until 30 years later that Dubois confessed to what else he discovered at the same site: two skulls of modern humans. This explained the human likeness of the femur. It also led Dubois to retract the designation *Homo erectus*, and to declare that the Java Man skull was simply a giant gibbon.

The story of Peking Man (*Sinanthropus pekinensis*) started near Beijing, China, in the 1920s and 1930s, where a group of skulls, jaws, and teeth were found, and designated as *Homo erectus*. Dr. Davidson Black, a professor of anatomy at Union Medical College in Beijing, examined just one tooth, thought it to be human-like, and made the announcement. Other researchers who studied the findings, however, were unconvinced. They found, for example, that Peking Man's brain size was considerably smaller than that of humans, and that fossils of ten modern human individuals were also found together with the *Sinanthropus* skulls. Boule and Vallois concluded that *Sinanthropus* were actually macaques or baboons that were used by true humans as food. All the fossils for Peking Man mysteriously disappeared sometime between 1941 and 1945. At the very least, it appears that the identification of *Sinanthropus* as a *Homo erectus* was based upon preconceived ideas, desire for fame, and possibly even fraud.

Aside from the obscure cases of Java Man and Peking Man, most paleoanthropologists today do not classify *Homo erectus* as transitional forms, but rather as true humans.

EVIDENCE

* In its totality, the structure of the *Sinanthropus* skull is still very ape-like.[48]

Some paleoanthropologists (almost all of whom support evolution) now even classify all *Homo erectus* as true humans and not transitional forms at all.[49]

* *Sinanthropus* manifestly resembles the great apes closely.[50]

Dubois' announced discovery of Java Man generated both attention and doubt. German zoologists tended to think Java Man was actually an ape; the British considered it human, and the French, something between the two. It was not until thirty years later that Dubois confessed to what else he had discovered at the same site: two skulls of modern humans. This immediately explained the human likeness of the femur. It also assured the scientific community that Java Man was not a missing link at all, but actually a cover-up! Ultimately, Dubois himself declared that the Java Man skull was simply a giant gibbon of the ape family.[51]

* An interdisciplinary team of scientists suggests that one relative, *H. erectus*, was still alive in Java, Indonesia, as recently as 27,000 to 53,000 years ago — at least 250,000 years after it was thought to have gone extinct in Asia. If so, this remnant population of *H. erectus*, a species that first appeared in the fossil record about 2 million years ago, would have been alive when modern humans and Neanderthals roamed the earth.[52]

* At this time, it is our opinion that some specimens attributed to *Homo erectus*, such as Java Man and Peking Man, are definitely from the ape family with no link of any kind to man.[53]

* A geologist at the Berkeley Geochronology Center, [Carl] Swisher uses the most advanced techniques to date human fossils. Last spring he was re-evaluating *Homo erectus* skulls found in Java in the 1930s by testing the sediment found with them. A hominid species assumed to be an ancestor of *Homo sapiens*, *erectus* was thought to have vanished some 250,000 years ago. But even though he used two different dating methods, Swisher kept making the same startling find: the bones were 53,000 years old at most and possibly no more than 27,000 years — a stretch of time contemporaneous with modern humans.[54]

* *Homo erectus* — many remains of this type have been found around the world. This classification now includes Java man and Peking man, which were once promoted as "missing links." Their skulls have prominent brow ridges, similar to the Neanderthals; their bodies were just like those of people today, only more robust. The brain size is within the range of people today and studies of the middle ear have shown that *Homo erectus* walked just like us. Both morphology and associated archaeological/cultural findings in association suggest that *Homo erectus* was fully human and should be included in *Homo sapiens*.[55]

A frequently overlooked fact about Peking Man is that the fossils of ten modern human individuals were also found at the same site as the *Sinanthropus* skulls.[56]

* As I now realize, extinct hominoids were not particularly modern. They were not like either living apes or human beings, but instead were unique, distinct animal species.[57]

* Thus, Swisher and his colleagues have very recently reported dates for the Ngandong *H. erectus* site in Java that center on only about 40,000 years ago. These dates, though very carefully obtained, have aroused considerable skepticism, but, if accurate, they have considerable implications for the overall pattern of human evolution. For they are so recent as to sug-

gest that the long-lived *H. erectus* might even have suffered a fate similar to that experienced by the Neanderthals in Europe: extinction at the hands of late-arriving *H. sapiens*.[58]

CONCEPT 11-7: NEANDERTHAL MAN WAS A MODERN HUMAN.

RATIONALE

Neanderthal Man is one of the best known "prehuman" creatures. First discovered in a cave near Dusseldorf, Germany, he is often portrayed as a semi-erect figure, carrying a club, and with a brutish expression. Much has been learned, however, in the one hundred years since Neanderthal Man was discovered. Research has determined that Neanderthal Man suffered from the disease rickets. Caused by vitamin D deficiency in one's diet, rickets causes bones to become unusually soft and easily malformed. This fact helps to explain that often ruddy appearance of the Neanderthals.

Recent DNA analysis of a Neanderthal skeleton revealed its DNA to be very similar to that of modern humans, even when accounting for the fact that the DNA was thousands of years old. These facts lend credence to the conclusion that Neanderthal was fully human.

EVIDENCE

* Is Neanderthal man alive and living in outer Mongolia? Myra Shackley tentatively posed this question in 1980 in her

An early model of Neanderthal Man no longer considered valid (left). Modern-day model of Neanderthal Man (above).

(Courtesy of the Department of Library Services, American Museum of Natural History.)

semi-popular book *Neanderthal Man* (Duckworth). Probably to the surprise of many (but not all) archaeologists, she repeats it in the latest issue of the much-respected archaeology journal *Antiquity* (vol. LVI p 31).[59]

* The sightings of "wild men" with the physical appearance of Neanderthals together with the tool finds represent to Myra Shackley "an impressive body of material which it is difficult to disregard."[60]

* Now at long last, thanks to the investigations of Dr. Francis Ivanhoe of London, who published his findings in the August 8, 1970, issue of *Nature*, the Neanderthal puzzle may have been solved. His review of the currently available anthropological and medical evidence shows that Neanderthal man was evidently the victim of his decision to move too far north at the wrong time, the onset of a glacial age. In doing so, contends Dr. Ivanhoe, he lost sufficient contact with the ultra-violet rays of the sun and because his diet did not provide the missing nutrient, he contracted rickets, the vitamin D deficiency disease, which was to deform him for thousands of years to follow.[61]

* He had a brain with a capacity sometimes larger than that of modern man. He was a talented toolmaker and successful hunter, even dabbled in art and most importantly from a cultural standpoint, developed a rudimentary social and religious consciousness.[62]

* Amid stone implements typical of European Neanderthals excavated last year in a Slovenian cave, researchers found a piece of a juvenile bear's thighbone that contains four artificial holes and resembles a flute.[63]

* "This bone could have been used to make noise or, possibly, music," contends geologist Bonnie Blackwell of the City University of New York's Queens College in Flushing, N.Y. "It would not surprise me if this was a Neanderthal's musical instrument."[64]

* "Neanderthals were apparently quite similar to *Homo sapiens* in their behavior and cognitive capacities," Blackwell asserts. "In both groups, musical traditions probably extend back very far into prehistory."[65]

* Both Neanderthals and early modern humans buried

their dead, left behind similar types of tools and engaged in comparable animal-butchery practices, showing striking cultural parallels for different hominid species.[66]

* According to B. Arensberg and Yoel Rak of Tel Aviv University and their colleagues, the fossil hyoid, in size and shape, is just like a modern human's. The positions of the muscle attachments are also similar. The researchers believe that, despite their heavy jawbones, Neanderthals spoke a language.[67]

* But in 1989 a Neanderthal hyoid (throat) bone was found in Kebara cave near Mount Carmel in Israel in an excavation directed by Baruch Arensburg of Tel Aviv University. When the Arensburg group published their results in *Nature* in 1990, they argued that the hyoid was virtually indistinguishable from those of modern humans in size and shape. Neanderthals "appear to be as anatomically capable of speech as modern humans," the authors wrote.[68]

* Neanderthal man may have looked like he did, not because he was closely related to the great apes, but because he had rickets, an article in the British publication *Nature* suggests.[69]

* The diet of Neanderthal man was definitely lacking in vitamin D during the 35,000 years he spent on earth.[70]

Analysis of Neanderthal DNA failed to demonstrate any significant difference from DNA of modern humans.[71]

Today most scientists agree that Neanderthal Man stood fully upright, and that in the absence of disease, its features are no different than modern humans.[72]

CONCEPT 11-8: NEBRASKA MAN AND PILTDOWN MAN WERE FRAUDS.

RATIONALE

The instant fame associated with discovery of a human ancestor has incited some scientists to error and even fraud. In 1922 a simple tooth was discovered in western Nebraska, examined by renowned paleontologist Henry Fairfile Osborn, and declared to be that of another ape-man ancestor. Given the scientific name *Hesperopithecus*, it was publicly known as Nebraska Man. But within five years other studies were carried out by authorities who concluded the tooth from Nebraska Man was actually that of a wild pig extinct in North America, and currently living only in Paraguay.

Paleontology suffered another blow in 1912, when Arthur Smith Woodward, director of the Natural History Museum of London, along with Charles Dawson, a medical doctor, declared the discovery of another human ancestor. In a gravel pit near Piltdown, England, they discovered a jaw and part of a skull. The jaw seemed very ape-like, but the skull resembled that of a human. They named the famed creature *Eoanthropus dawsoni* — or Piltdown Man, and estimated him to be about 500,000 years old.

In the 1950s, though, a new technique was perfected to identify the age of bones — one based upon measuring the concentration of fluoride that the bones had absorbed from the surrounding soil. Piltdown Man's jaw was tested and found to contain no fluoride, proving that it was not a fossil at all and was only about a year old! The skull did contain fluoride, enough to date it at about 5,000 years old. The discrepancy prompted re-examination of the jaw and skull, and it was discovered the bones had been treated with a chemical to make them appear aged. The jaw was later found to be from an ape, and the skull from a modern-day human.

A lesser-known fraud was uncovered in 1983, when a group of European "experts" announced the discovery of the oldest human fossil ever found, "Orce Man" from southern Spain. Scientists determined that the skull involved was from a young donkey. Clearly, the haste to prove evolution's expectations at any cost exposes the bias of some in the scientific community.

EVIDENCE

* In 1983 a group of experts in Europe announced the discovery of a fossil declared to be oldest human even found, "Orce Man" from southern Spain. French scientists investigated the claim and declared that Orce Man was actually the skull of a four-month-old donkey![73]

* This remarkable discrepancy caused the jaw and skull to be carefully reexamined. Scientists discovered the bones had been soaked in a special chemical just to make them appear old! Ultimately, the jaw was identified from a recently died orangutan ape, and the skull that of a modern human. Piltdown Man was judged a complete sham![74]

Within five years other studies were carried out by authorities who declared that the tooth from Nebraska Man was actually that of a wild pig extinct in North America, and now living only in Paraguay.[75]

* Accepting this as inevitable and not necessarily damaging, it still comes as a shock to discover how often preconceived ideas have affected the investigation of human origins. There is, of course, nothing like a fake for exposing such weaknesses among the experts. For example, to look back over the bold claims and subtle anatomical distinctions made by some of our greatest authorities concerning the recent human skull and modern ape's jaw which together composed "Piltdown Man" rouses either joy or pain, according to one's feelings for the scientists.[76]

* This is a time-honored method [analyzing physical similarities] that can be extraordinarily powerful (for the eye and the mind are excellent computers of a kind). But we have merely to remember cases like Piltdown Man, which turned out to be a fraudulent composite of a genuine fossil skull cap and a modern ape jaw, or *Hesperopithecus*, the ape of the West, which eventually was discovered to be a peccary, or even of the completely different portraits that have been drawn for the facial features of a creature such as *Zinjanthropus* to realize that this method also has many difficulties.[77]

* [Frank] Spencer's cogent, fairminded, thorough and perceptive review of the evidence is presented in two companion volumes, *Piltdown: A Scientific Forgery* and the *Piltdown Papers 1908–1955*, just published by the Natural History Museum in London and Oxford University Press.
The Piltdown fossils, whose discovery was first announced in 1912, fooled many of the greatest minds in paleoanthropology until 1953, when the remains were revealed as planted, altered — a forgery.[78]

* New evidence has come to light that the hoax was a plot carried out by Sir Arthur Keith, one of the most eminent anatomists of the early 20th century, and Charles Dawson, the amateur antiquarian who found the remains.[79]

* The Piltdown man forgery of 1912 was one of the most successful and wicked of all scientific frauds.[80]

CHAPTER TWELVE

EVIDENCE FOR CREATION

INTRODUCTION

The origin of life can be explained by only two options: living beings either evolved from lifeless material, or were intentionally designed and created. The laws of probability demonstrate that our universe, and the life it contains, could not possibly have originated by random chance. Evolution — the mechanism of this chance event — is a hypothesis without evidence to lend support.

The evidence, instead, is in favor of intentional design and creation. Just how can we determine whether or not an object is created? Created objects are characterized by "specified complexity," that is, information arranged in a way that could not have happened by chance. Certainly, the complexity of living beings is very great, as is the order displayed by our universe; so great that the probability of appearance by chance is zero.

Creation is a "scientific" possibility. The most reliable scientific research can only be done on events in the present. Still, enormous evidence can be gathered from past events. Such evidence has caused many of the world's greatest scientists to affirm creation as the only reasonable explanation for life.

CONCEPT 12-1: CREATION IS A "SCIENTIFIC" EXPLANATION.

RATIONALE

The possibility of creation is automatically dismissed by some persons on the grounds that it is unscientific to consider such an alternative.

The National Academy of Sciences' authors of *Teaching about Evolution*, for example, dismiss creation as both "unscientific" and "religious." Their published reasoning is that the "basic proposals of creation science are not subject to test and verification."

This position should prompt us to reconsider just what is "science"? Simply put, science is the pursuit of knowledge about nature and the physical world. In this pursuit, any information from a reliable source (archaeology, statistics, or astronomy, to name a few) must be considered. Ideally, scientific facts can be monitored, repeated, and studied by multiple researchers, just to be certain they are correct. Scientific facts, however, have limits both on what can be studied and on the degree of certainty. Normally, science deals only with observable events in the present, not with unrepeatable events in the past. In the case of both creation and evolution, we're dealing with events that happened in the distant past. They can neither be observed nor repeated. Just like creation, evolution also "is not subject to test and verification."

Science can evaluate past events, but not with the absolute certainty available in the laboratory. Instead, science must gather the most reliable evidence available concerning past events.

When evaluating past events, two particular scientific principles are especially useful. The first is "causality," meaning that everything that has a beginning, including life and the universe, has a "cause." The second, "analogy," means that if intelligence is needed to generate information in the present, we can assume the same for the past.

Applying causality and analogy to explaining the world leads us to the conclusion that both life and the universe had a beginning, and therefore must have a "cause." Furthermore, intelligence is necessary to create complicated structures today, therefore we can also anticipate that enormous intelligent guidance was necessary to create complexity of life and the universe "in the beginning." The creation model fits perfectly with both principles of causality and analogy.

EVIDENCE

* It may seem paradoxical to say that Darwin was opposed to adaptationism, in that adaptation seems to be the keystone of natural selection. In fact, as Darwin recognized, a perfect Creator could manufacture perfect adaptations. Everything would fit because everything was designed to fit. It is in the imperfect adaptations that natural selection is revealed, because it is those imperfections that show us that a structure has a history. If there were no imperfections, there would be

no evidence of history, and, therefore, nothing to favor evolution by natural selection over creation.[1]

* The more statistically improbable a thing is, the less can we believe that it just happened by blind chance. Superficially the obvious alternative to chance is an intelligent designer.[2]

* The only competing explanation for the order we all see in the biological world is the notion of special creation.[3]

* Once we see that the probability of life originating at random is so utterly minuscule as to make it absurd, it becomes sensible to think that the favorable properties of physics, on which life depends, are in every respect deliberate. It is almost inevitable that our own measure of intelligence must reflect higher intelligence — even to the limit of God.[4]

* "Creation," in the ordinary sense of the word, is perfectly conceivable. I find no difficulty in conceiving that, at some former period, this universe was not in existence, and that it made its appearance in six days (or instantaneously, if that is preferred), in consequence of the volition of some preexisting Being. Then, as now, the so-called a priori arguments against theism, and, given a deity, against the possibility of creative acts, appeared to me to be devoid of reasonable foundation.[5]

* Perhaps the appearance of life on the earth is a miracle. Scientists are reluctant to accept that view, but their choices are limited. Either life was created on the earth by the will of a being outside the grasp of scientific understanding, or it evolved on our planet spontaneously, through chemical reactions occurring in nonliving matter lying on the surface of the planet.

The first theory places the question of the origin of life beyond the reach of scientific inquiry. It is a statement of faith in the power of a Supreme Being not subject to the laws of science. The second theory is also an act of faith. The act of faith consists in assuming that the scientific view of the origin of life is correct, without having concrete evidence to support that belief.[6]

* If living matter is not, then, caused by the interplay of atoms, natural forces and radiation, how has it come into being? . . . I think, however, that we must . . . admit that the only acceptable explanation is creation. I know that this is anathema to physicists, as indeed it is to me, but we must not reject

a theory that we do not like if the experimental evidence supports it.[7]

* We have not yet encountered any good in principle reason to exclude design from science. Design seems just as scientific (or unscientific) as its evolutionary competitors. . . .

An openness to empirical arguments for design is therefore a necessary condition of a fully rational historical biology. A rational historical biology must not only address the question, "Which materialistic or naturalistic evolutionary scenario provides the most adequate explanation of biological complexity?" but also the question "Does a strictly materialistic evolutionary scenario or one involving intelligent agency or some other theory best explain the origin of biological complexity, given all relevant evidence?" To insist otherwise is to insist that materialism holds a metaphysically privileged position. Since there seems no reason to concede that assumption, I see no reason to concede that origins theories must be strictly naturalistic.[8]

* Does the second law of thermodynamics apply to the universe as a whole? Are there processes unknown to us that occur somewhere in the universe, such as "continual creation," that have a decrease in entropy associated with them, and thus offset the continual increase in entropy that is associated with the natural processes that are known to us? If the second law is valid for the universe (we, of course, do not know if the universe can be considered as an isolated system) how did it get in the state of low entropy? On the other end of the scale, if all processes known to us have an increase in entropy associated with them, what is the future of the natural world as we know it?

Quite obviously, it is impossible to give conclusive answers to these questions on the basis of the second law of thermodynamics alone. However, we see the second law of thermodynamics as a description of the prior and continuing work of a creator, who also holds the answer to our future destiny and that of the universe.[9]

* From my earliest training as a scientist, I was very strongly brainwashed to believe that science cannot be consistent with any kind of deliberate creation. That notion has had to be painfully shed. . . .

Each found that the odds against the spark of life igniting accidentally on earth were . . . "10 to the power of 40,000. . . ."

They did calculations based on the size and age of the universe (15 billion years) and found that the odds against life beginning spontaneously anywhere in space were "10 to the power of 30. . . ."

At the moment, I can't find any rational argument to knock down the view which argues for conversion to God. . . . We used to have an open mind; now we realize that the only logical answer to life is creation and not accidental, random shuffling.[10]

CONCEPT 12-2: CREATION HAS RECOGNIZABLE CHARACTERISTICS.

RATIONALE

Does examining the world alone tell us whether or not it was created? Indeed, the arguments against evolution are impressive, and the possibility of creation is logical. But is there any empirical evidence of creation independent of these?

The quest for an answer begins with defining just what is meant by the word "created." In our daily lives we regularly encounter objects and decide, usually subconsciously, whether or not they were created. We find a published newspaper, a cellular phone, or a compact disc and realize immediately that these were intentionally designed and produced. But the mud on our car, dust in our house, and rocks in our garden we realize were neither intentionally planned nor built.

The music produced by the compact disc is completely different from the sound of the wind coming from an open car window. The print on the newspaper has no comparison with the pattern of dust on the fireplace mantel.

We distinguish the difference between created objects and those that are not created by the amount of information they contain. Created objects are characterized by "specified complexity." This means that they contain large quantities of organized information that could not possibly appear by chance. A published newspaper or a cellular phone contains just this kind of information, so they were obviously created.

One of the best examples of searching for specified complexity is the SETI program. The Search for Extraterrestrial Intelligence (SETI) program essentially listens to noise from outer space, trying to identify signals that are neither random nor a repetitive sequence (such as that produced by pulsars). Instead, they are seeking signals that contain complex information. Why is this the case? Because such signals containing such specified complexity could only be produced by another intelligent creature.

Living plants, animals, and microorganisms contain enormous

quantities of complex, organized information — exponentially greater than any printed or electronic device. This fact alone is de novo evidence that they were created.

EVIDENCE

* The assumption that the external world has systematic features that rational inquiry can uncover and incorporate into a coherent world view, probably owes its origin more to theology than science. The Judaic, Muslim and Christian traditions all propose a rational deity who is the creator of, but distinct from, the physical universe. This universe carries the imprint of a rational design in its detailed workings. This belief was implicit in the work of Isaac Newton and his contemporaries during the rise of modern science in the 17th century. Although the theistic dimension has long since faded, its implications for the natural order of the physical world remain little changed.[11]

> * Every painting has a painter
> Every watch has a watchmaker.
> Every book has a writer.
> Every design has a designer.
> Every computer has a programmer.[12]

* Indeed, the only competing explanation for the order we see in the biological world, this pattern of nested similarity that links up absolutely all known forms of life, is the notion of special creation: that a supernatural Creator, using a sort of blueprint, simply fashioned life with its intricate skein of resemblances passing through it. . . . And, of course, it was precisely this notion of divine creation that furnished the explanation for all life — its very existence, its exuberant diversity, and its apparent order — in Darwin's day.[13]

* Evolution may have scientific experts on its side, but it strains popular common sense. It is simply difficult to believe that the amazing order of life on earth arose spontaneously out of the original disorder of the universe.[14]

* Living things are distinguished by their specified complexity. Crystals such as granite fail to qualify as living because they lack complexity; mixtures of random polymers fail to qualify because they lack specificity.[15]

CONCEPT 12-3: LIVING BEINGS SHOW EVIDENCE OF CREATION.

RATIONALE

Living beings qualify as being created simply based on the fact that they house vast quantities of specified complexity. The DNA of virtually any cell contains more specific and organized information than that held in a typical public library. Above the cellular level, living tissues and organs demonstrate remarkable coordination and complex interdependency upon one another. Consider for a moment some of the more elaborate features of living creatures:

- Flight mechanics of a bird, as yet unduplicated
- Advanced communication skills of the dolphin
- Multiphasic metamorphosis of a butterfly
- Amazing genetics of tadpole-frog transformation
- Accurate navigation ability of the transcontinental migratory duck

Evolution is an inadequate explanation for the existence of these creatures. For one thing, random development of such advanced beings is entirely contrary to the forces of nature, particularly the law of entropy, which states: "Complex ordered arrangements and systems naturally become simpler and more disorderly (increased entropy or randomness) with time."

Evolution attempts to demonstrate that living beings became more complex and orderly on their own accord, without any external force. Yet the only way to counter the law of entropy is to bring in an external, purposeful, creative, and organizing force to impose order.

Some evolutionists admit that there are limits on what evolution could possibly accomplish. The now famous British evolutionist J.B.S. Haldane, for example, pronounced that evolution could never produce "various mechanisms, such as the wheel and magnet, which would be useless till fairly perfect."[16] In his judgment, the existence of such structures in living beings would prove evolution impossible, for evolution could never produce such advanced mechanisms.

More recent discoveries, however, now demonstrate that some living creatures actually have "wheels" within them. The rotary motor that turns the flagellum of some micro-organisms is a fine example of a living wheel. Magnetic sensors are also found within other creatures, such as turtles, monarch butterflies, and some bacteria. These use information from these sensors for self-navigation. In Haldane's own words, the very existence of these functional, physiologic wheels and magnets is proof that they were intentionally created and could never have self-evolved.

The specified complexity within living beings is in itself overwhelming evidence that they were created. No additional proof is essential.

EVIDENCE

* Lobster eyes, for example, are modeled on a perfect square with precise geometrical relationships. The lobster's eye design was copied by NASA in the construction of X-ray telescopes.[17]

* It is in biology that we find the most striking examples of self-organization. I need only cite the astonishing ability of an embryo to develop from a single strand of DNA, via an exquisitely well-orchestrated sequence of formative steps, into an exceedingly complex organism.[18]

* Perhaps in no other area of modern biology is the challenge posed by the extreme complexity and ingenuity of biological adaptations more apparent than in the fascinating new molecular world of the cell. . . . To grasp the reality of life as it has been revealed by molecular biology, we must magnify a cell a thousand million times until it is twenty kilometers in diameter and resembles a giant airship large enough to cover a great city like London or New York. What we would then see would be an object of unparalleled complexity and adaptive design. On the surface of the cell we would see millions of openings, like the portholes of a vast space ship, opening and closing to allow a continual stream of materials to flow in and out. If we were to enter one of these openings we would find ourselves in a world of supreme technology and bewildering complexity.

Is it really credible that random processes could have constructed a reality, the smallest element of which (a functional protein or gene) is complex beyond our own creative capacities, a reality which is the very antithesis of chance, which excels in every sense anything produced by the intelligence of man? Alongside the level of ingenuity and complexity exhibited by the molecular machinery of life, even our most advanced artifacts appear clumsy.[19]

* Altogether, a typical cell contains about ten million million atoms. Suppose we choose to build an exact replica to a scale one thousand million times that of the cell so that each atom of the model would be the size of a tennis ball. Constructing such a model at the rate of one atom per minute, it would take fifty million years to finish, and the object we would end up with would be the giant factory, described above, some twenty kilometres in diameter, with a volume thousands of times that of the Great Pyramid.[20]

* It would be an illusion to think that what we are aware of at present is any more than a fraction of the full extent of biological design. In practically every field of fundamental biological research ever-increasing levels of design and complexity are being revealed at an ever-accelerating rate.[21]

Realizing that evolution has limits on what it could possibly accomplish, the famous British evolutionist J.B.S. Haldane claimed in 1949 that evolution could never produce "various mechanisms, such as the wheel and magnet, which would be useless till fairly perfect."[22]

Some bacteria make use of an internal magnetic sensor as an aid in navigation.[23]

Research has discovered that the nervous system of leeches uses mathematical calculations to command the movement of its muscles.[24]

* When I make an incision with my scalpel, I see organs of such intricacy that there simply hasn't been enough time for natural evolutionary processes to have developed them.[25]

* In the realm of the senses, animals continue to amaze scientists. No longer impressed by a dog's ability to hear high-pitched whistles or a cat's ability to see in dim light, researchers have gone on to document far more unexpected animal perceptions in such animals as the platypus and praying mantis.

Take the bill of the duck-billed platypus. It serves as an antenna to pick up weak electrical signals, scientists report in the January 30 *Nature*. This is the first report of electroreception in mammals, say Henning Scheich of the Technical University of Darmstadt, West Germany, Anna Guppy of the Australian National University in Canberra City, and their colleagues.[26]

* The praying mantis provides another sensory surprise — a single "ear" that is a groove in the underside of its thorax. Long thought to be deaf, the insect possesses a "sensitive and specialized acoustic sense," David D. Yager and Ronald R. Hoy

of Cornell University report in the February 14 *Science*.

What the mantis hears is ultrasonic frequencies, perhaps wings rubbing abdomen during courtship or the sonar signals of insect-eating bats. The sensitivity to ultrasound is shared by some other insects that detect sound with more conventional organs. But all other insects that hear have two "ears," widely separated on the body.[27]

Monarch butterflies make use of an internal magnetic sensor as an aid in navigation.[28]

* The degree of fine-tuning of the 34 different characteristics of the universe that demand exquisite fine-tuning for physical life, measure at least ten trillion trillion trillion times greater than what the most brilliant and powerful and well-equipped humans can accomplish. Just this one characteristic of the universe suggests that the Creator is at least ten trillion trillion trillion times more intelligent, knowledgeable, creative, and powerful than human beings.[29]

Some living creatures have "wheels" within them. The rotary motor that turns the flagellum of some bacterium is a fine example of a living wheel.[30]

Turtles make use of an internal magnetic sensor to aid in navigation.[31]

Bats are endowed with a finely sensitive sonar system, able to detect an object as fine as a human hair from among its surroundings. To accomplish this, their sonar distinguishes ultra-sound echoes only 2 to 3 millionths of a second apart. Compare this with the fact that man-made sonar can distinguish echoes only 12 millionths of a second apart.[32]

* Insects include some of the most versatile and maneuverable of all flying machines. Although many show rather simple flight patterns, some insects, through a combination of low mass, sophisticated neurosensory systems and complex musculature, display astonishing aerobatic feats. Houseflies, for example, can decelerate from fast flight, hover, turn in their own length, fly upside down, loop, roll, and land on a ceiling — all in a fraction of a second.[33]

* The better we understand the functioning of insect wings, the more subtle and beautiful their designs appear. Earlier com-

parisons with sails now seem quite inadequate. The wings emerge as a family of flexible airfoils that are in a sense intermediate between structures and mechanisms, as these terms are understood by engineers. Structures are traditionally designed to deform as little as possible; mechanisms are designed to move component parts in predictable ways. Insect wings combine both in one, using components with a wide range of elastic properties, elegantly assembled to allow appropriate deformations in response to appropriate forces and to make the best possible use of the air. They have few if any technological parallels — yet.[34]

CONCEPT 12-4: THE UNIVERSE SHOWS EVIDENCE OF CREATION.

RATIONALE

Our universe is a truly remarkable place. Most of us, however, spend our lives consumed with tasks of daily living. But when we pause, consider, and examine the cosmos, we gain an appreciation for just how incredible the objects are that lie just beyond the earth. Consider, for example, that:

- The universe has at least 100 billion galaxies.
- The Milky Way Galaxy alone has 100 billion stars.
- Our solar system hurls through space at 600,000 mph.
- The earth rotates on its axis at 1,000 mph.
- The earth moves around the sun at 70,000 mph.
- Earth is 93,000,000 miles from the sun. If it were 7 million miles closer or 7 million miles farther away, humans would instantly either burn to death or freeze to death.
- The moon is 240,000 miles from the earth. If it were only 50,000 miles closer to the earth, our ocean tides would cover almost all the landmasses by 35–50 feet, twice a day.

While remarkable in its structure, outer space also contains many hazards: lethal gases, enormous pressures, extreme temperatures, deadly cosmic radiation, meteors, asteroids, and tremendous gravity. These will cause instant death to any living thing.

But life on earth is protected from almost all of these hazards. Furthermore, we not only have protection, but also water, food, and material resources — everything needed for life and civilization to thrive. While astronomers have begun to identify other planets outside our solar system, nowhere in the universe have they observed another environment so ideal for life as is the earth.

Why the Earth Is Unique for Life

All life depends on water. If the solid material of the earth were completely smooth, it would be covered by water 8,500 feet deep.

The gravity of the moon pulling on the earth causes the oceans to rise and fall forming the tides.

The earth is the perfect distance from the sun to keep it the right temperature, and the tilt of the earth causes the seasons.

The atmosphere not only provides air for breathing, but also deflects harmful space radiation and refracts solar radiation.

The environment must be almost perfect for living beings to exist. Much difference in temperature, gravity, atmospheric pressure, or radiation, to name just a few factors, would make life impossible, whether on earth, or anywhere else in the universe. Observation of the universe and the earth causes many scientists to agree that the very laws of physics seem precisely tailored to help life abound. This "life-supporting" character of the universe is called the "anthropic principle."

What is the possibility that our ideal, life-supporting universe came into existence through random chance? Or, is there a Designer and Creator behind it all? The question is similar to the probability of life arising spontaneously. The calculated statistical chance of our ideal planet forming at random is greater than 10^{1000}. And, as Dr. Emil Borel explains, anything with a chance of more than 1 in 10^{50} would never happen no matter how much time there is.

Why is it so improbable that our planet, along with the structures of the universe, would ever form? Because they both contain vast, enormous, specified complexity — complexity that can only result from an intentional, intelligent Creator.

Isaac Newton is recognized as one of the greatest, if not the single greatest, scientist who ever lived. His breadth of knowledge, his ability to analyze and synthesize the physical world, his development and use of the calculus, his formulation of the laws of motion, and the expression of the law of gravitation have been unequaled by any other scientist, before or since. Newton was clearly convinced, as are many scientists today, that the universe was created and sustained by God. No other possible explanation exists for the order and complexity it displays.

EVIDENCE

* The temptation to believe that the universe is the product of some sort of design is overwhelming. The belief that there is "something behind it all" is one that I personally share with, I suspect, a majority of physicists.[35]

* The very fact that the universe is creative, and that the laws have permitted complex structures to emerge and develop to the point of consciousness — in other words, that the universe has organized its own self-awareness — is for me powerful evidence that there is "something going on" behind it all. The impression of design is overwhelming. Science may explain all the processes whereby the universe evolves its own destiny, but that still leaves room for there to be a meaning behind existence.[36]

* This is the "anthropic principle" which recognizes that the heavens, the earth, and the things on the earth look very much as though they were made for man, to make the world a liveable place for humankind. [37]

* The universe must have known we were coming.[38]

* At least the anthropic principle suggests connections between the existence of man and aspects of physics that one might have thought would have little bearing on biology. In its strongest form the principle might reveal that the universe we live in is the only conceivable universe in which intelligent life could exist.[39]

* Our universe seems to be tailor-made for us.[40]

* Given the facts, our existence seems quite improbable — more miraculous, perhaps, than the seven-day wonder of Genesis. As physicist Freeman Dyson of the Institute for Advanced Study in Princeton, New Jersey, once remarked, "The universe in some sense must have known we were coming.[41]

* The anthropic principle is the most theistic (God-supporting) result ever to come out of science.[42]

* This most beautiful system of the sun, planets, and comets could only proceed from the counsel and dominion of an intelligent and powerful Being. This Being governs all things, not as the soul of the world, but as Lord over all, and on account of His dominion He is wont to be called Lord God, Universal Ruler.[43]

The calculated statistical chance of our ideal planet forming at random is greater than 10^{1000}. And as Dr. Emil Borel explains, anything with a chance of more than 1 in 10^{50} would never happen no matter how much time there is.[44]

* The degree of fine-tuning of the 34 different characteristics of the universe that demand exquisite fine-tuning for physical life, measure at least ten trillion trillion trillion times greater than what the most brilliant and powerful and well-equipped humans can accomplish. Just this one characteristic of the universe suggests that the Creator is at least ten trillion trillion trillion times more intelligent, knowledgeable, creative, and powerful than human beings.[45]

* The entire universe was made for man[46]

* So we live in a universe where the fundamental constants of nature seem to be "fine-tuned" to permit the existence of life and, perhaps, intelligence. Change any of the fundamental constants of nature and you could well have a universe in which no life exists at all.[47]

* One cannot be exposed to the law and order of the universe without concluding that there must be design and purpose behind it all. . . . The better we understand the intricacies of the universe and all it harbors, the more reason we have found to marvel at the inherent design upon which it is based.[48]

PART THREE

—

RECOMMENDED ACTION

Note: All information in the "Evidence" section is quoted material.
Those entries preceded by an asterisk are direct quotes;
otherwise the information is a summary of the publication cited.

CHAPTER THIRTEEN

REJECT EVOLUTION

INTRODUCTION

W hat was the origin of life? Some of the most insight-
ful scientists and philosophers have devoted their lives
to finding the answers. In reality, only two alternatives exist. Either life began spontaneously and developed through multiple millions of years worth of random chemical accidents, or life was
intentionally designed and created.

At this junction, it is appropriate to review the facts covered in
chapter 3. The theory of evolution is based upon three assumptions:

- **Spontaneous generation** — life beginning through the
  chance encounter of highly complex chemicals

- **Random mutation and natural selection** — spontaneous
  mutations causing "improvements" in some creatures, making them more likely to survive than other creatures

- **Enormous time** — allowing for such mutations and competition for survival to occur

Evolution is a past event that cannot be studied directly. For proof
that evolution occurred we would expect to find the following evidence:

- Probability is high
- Earth age is very advanced
- Fossil record demonstrates evolution

When matching the above assumptions with the evidence, we actually find:

- **Spontaneous generation.**

   In chapter 5 we reviewed the laws of chemistry and probability which show that spontaneous generation is clearly impossible.

- **Random mutation and natural selection.**

   In chapter 6 we reviewed evidence that mutations are almost always lethal, or leave the creature sterile at best. And, that natural selection provides no benefit to the creature until the new feature is fully functional. Actually, natural selection serves to preserve a species, not to make it become more varied.

   What's more, if random mutation and natural selection actually took place over many millions of years, then there must have lived vast numbers of transitional creatures. Yet in chapters 9, 10, and 11 we saw that there are no fossils of transitional creatures — human or otherwise.

- **Enormous time.**

   The earth must have been inhabitable for hundreds of millions of years for random mutation and natural selection to have time to develop humans and other advanced living beings. In chapters 7 and 8 we found that the commonly used dating methods are flawed at best, and that considerable scientific evidence points to both a young earth and a young universe.

The theory of evolution is in reality a concept without adequate evidence. It does not qualify to be called a "theory." Rather, it should be degraded to only a "hypothesis." Why, then, is this insupportable concept so accepted? In a word, it is because evolution is the only explanation for life without giving credit to a Creator/God. It is their commitment to the philosophy of naturalism and bias against belief in God that causes evolutionists to ignore the evidence and hold on to evolution.

Aside from poor scientific conclusions, evolution and naturalism carry significant dangers. They create the basis for human disrespect; for an attitude that treats people as no different than other animals. They also alienate people from any knowledge of or relationship with God, cutting them off from enormous personal inspiration, guidance, and wisdom.

Action must be taken. We must demand honesty: that the actual evidence for and against evolution must be taught in our schools. Creation should also be presented, along with its arguments and evidence. No apology is necessary for the fact that creation implies a Creator, for this is what the evidence reveals. Failure to take a stand will only perpetuate the destructive results of evolutionary thought.

CONCEPT 13-1: MANY REPUTABLE SCIENTISTS REJECT EVOLUTION.

RATIONALE

Rational and systematic thought, based upon reliable evidence, is the foundation of science, and largely responsible for its outstanding discoveries. Science fiction, on the other hand, is the realm of imagination and fantasy. While entertaining, science fiction does not promote itself as truth. Wishful thinking aside, a vast difference exists between science (the subject of facts) and science fiction (the subject of fantasy).

Darwin solidified the concepts of evolution about the time of the Civil War. He worked without the benefit of a science education, without a laboratory to test his hypothesis, and in the beginning, without even scientific associates to critique his ideas.

Scientific understanding and dialogue has grown enormously since 1859, and largely disproved Darwin's claims. Many in today's scientific community realize that evolution is actually science fiction — far more imagination than actual truth. But unlike most science fiction, this non-truth is not at all entertaining, let alone scientific. In an effort to reinforce their position, evolutionists employ significant speculation, occasional fraud, and very little reliable evidence. But occasionally, almost apologetically, a growing number of evolutionists are admitting the fragility of their theory.

Biographers note that Darwin himself, as he became older, was more critical and less convinced of evolution. Many other scientists recognized its glaring flaws as early as 1930. But the popularity of evolution continues to be strong today, in spite of the growing evidence against it.

EVIDENCE

* It must be significant that nearly all the evolutionary stories I learned as a student . . . have now been debunked.[1]

* Origins survey published in *Industrial Chemist* . . . February 1988. . . . Most surprising to nearly everyone was the fact that 20.6 percent of the scientists responding completely reject evolution! The editors wrote, "Remember these respondents are scientists and do not represent a typical sample of the U.S. population." Further, the scientific community is quite split on the question of whether creationism is hurting scientific education. A surprising 37.9 percent don't think that creationism is hurting scientific education, while 46.7 think it is. Less than half the scientists polled believed that it is even possible for man to have evolved without supernatural intervention (48.3%)! A

number of the scientists polled, 22.8 percent, believed that humans could only have evolved with supernatural intervention, while another 22.8 percent feel that human evolution is impossible under any circumstances.[2]

* Evolution is a fairy tale for grown-ups. This theory has helped nothing in the progress of science. It is useless.[3]

* Clearly, both believers and unbelievers in natural selection agreed that Darwinism had succeeded as an orthodoxy, as a rallying point for innumerable scientific, philosophical, and social movements. Darwin had been the oracle and the *Origin of Species,* the "fixed point with which evolution moved the world.[4]

* Readers of *American Scientist* may not realize the extent to which a major part of the field of biology and almost all of paleontology has rejected Darwin's insights concerning organic evolution. Natural selection is dismissed as contributing nothing more than "fine-tuning," and adaptation is largely ignored in practice.[5]

* A myth, says my dictionary, is a real or fictional story that embodies the cultural ideals of a people or expresses deep, commonly felt emotions. By this definition, myths are generally good things — and the origin stories that paleoanthropologists tell are necessarily myths.[6]

* A major problem in proving the theory [of evolution] has been the fossil record; the imprints of vanished species preserved in the earth's geological formations. This record has never revealed traces of Darwin's hypothetical intermediate variants. Instead, species appear and disappear abruptly, and this anomaly has fueled the creationist argument that each species was created by God as described in the Bible.[7]

* The popular conception of a triumphant Darwin increasingly confident after 1859 in his views of evolution is a travesty. On the contrary, by the time the last edition of the *Origin* was published in 1872, he had become plagued with self-doubt and frustrated by his inability to meet the many objections which had been leveled at his theory.[8]

* It was the absence of factual evidence which was the primary source of their skepticism and not religious prejudice.[9]

* Why then does the scientific theory of evolution hold on to the concept of chance to the degree it does? I suspect it is the fact that there is no alternative whatsoever that could explain the fact of universal evolution at least in principle, and be formulated within the framework of natural science. If no alternative should be forthcoming, if chance remains overtaxed, then the conclusion seems inevitable that evolution and therefore living beings cannot be grasped by natural science to the same extent as non-living things — not because organisms are so complex, but because the explaining mechanism is fundamentally inadequate.[10]

* A close examination of the last edition of the *Origin* reveals that in attempting on scattered pages to meet the objections being launched against his theory the much labored-upon volume had become contradictory. . . . The last repairs to the *Origin* reveal . . . how very shaky Darwin's theoretical structure had become. His gracious ability to compromise had produced some striking inconsistencies. His book was already a classic, however, and these deviations for the most part passed unnoticed even by his enemies.[11]

* Scientists at the forefront of inquiry have put the knife to classical Darwinism. They have not gone public with this news, but have kept it in their technical papers and inner counsels.[12]

* Owen Chadwick, Regius professor of modern history at Cambridge, wrote after extensive research: "At first much of the opposition to Darwin's theory came from scientists on grounds of evidence, not from theologians on grounds of Scripture.[13]

* According to the stated assumptions of cladistics none of the fossil species can be ancestral by definition. This presents the public for the first time with the notion that there are no fossils directly antecedent to man. What the creationists have insisted on for years is now being openly advertised by the Natural History Museum.[14]

* The theories of evolution, with which our studious youth have been deceived, constitute actually a dogma that all the world continues to teach: but each, in his specialty, the zoologist or the botanist, ascertains that none of the explanations furnished is adequate. . . . It results from this summary, that the theory of evolution is impossible.[15]

* I have always been slightly suspicious of the theory of evolution because of its ability to account for any property of living beings (the long neck of the giraffe, for example). I have therefore tried to see whether biological discoveries over the last thirty years or so fit in with Darwin's theory. I do not think that they do. . . . To my mind, the theory does not stand up at all.[16]

* I believe that one day the Darwinian myth will be ranked the greatest deceit in the history of science. When this happens many people will pose the question, "How did this ever happen?"[17]

* Darwin's evolutionary explanation of the origins of man has been transformed into a modern myth, to the detriment of science and social progress. . . . The secular myths of evolution have had a damaging effect on scientific research, leading to distortion, to needless controversy, and to the gross misuse of science. . . . I mean the stories, the narratives about change over time. How the dinosaurs became extinct, how the mammals evolved, where man came from. These seem to me to be little more than story-telling.[18]

* One of the most frequent objections against the theory of natural selection is that it is a sophisticated tautology. Most evolutionary biologists seem unconcerned about the charge and only make a token effort to explain the tautology away. The remainder, such as Professors Waddington and Simpson, will simply concede the fact. For them, natural selection is a tautology which states a heretofore unrecognized relation: the fittest — defined as those who will leave the most offspring — will leave the most offspring.

What is most unsettling is that some evolutionary biologists have no qualms about proposing tautologies as explanations. One would immediately reject any lexicographer who tried to define a word by the same word, or a thinker who merely restated his proposition, or any other instance of gross redundancy, yet no one seems scandalized that men of science should be satisfied with a major principle which is no more than a tautology. Until there is a successful resolution to this problem, as well as most of the others already mentioned, the theory of natural selection can never be seriously scientific.[19]

* The entropy law says that evolution dissipates the overall available energy for life on this planet. Our concept of evo-

lution is the exact opposite. We believe that evolution some-how magically creates greater overall value and order on earth. Now that the environment we live in is becoming so dissi-pated and disordered that it is apparent to the naked eye, we are for the first time beginning to have second thoughts about our views on evolution, progress, and the creation of things of material value.

Evolution means the creation of larger and larger islands of order at the expense of ever greater seas of disorder in the world. There is not a single biologist or physicist who can deny this central truth. Yet, who is willing to stand up in a classroom or before a public forum and admit it?[20]

* We are told dogmatically that evolution is an established fact; but we are never told who has established it, and by what means. We are told, often enough, that the doctrine is founded upon evidence, and that indeed this evidence "is hencefor-ward above all verification, as well as being immune from any subsequent contradiction by experience"; but we are left en-tirely in the dark on the crucial question wherein, precisely, this evidence consists.[21]

* And the salient fact is this: if by evolution we mean mac-roevolution (as we henceforth shall) then it can be said with the utmost rigor that the doctrine is totally bereft of scientific sanction. Now, to be sure, given the multitude of extravagant claims about evolution promulgated by evolutionists with an air of scientific infallibility, this may indeed sound strange. And yet the fact remains that there exists to this day not a shred of bona fide scientific evidence in support of the thesis that macroevolutionary transformations have ever occurred.[22]

* A growing number of respectable scientists are defecting from the evolutionist camp. . . . Moreover, for the most part these "experts" have abandoned Darwinism, not on the basis of religious faith or biblical persuasions, but on strictly scien-tific grounds, and in some instances, regretfully.[23]

CONCEPT 13-2: EVOLUTION SHOULD BE DOWNGRADED TO A HYPOTHESIS.

RATIONALE

The objective of science is to discover accurate information about the universe. As scientists work, they assign three levels of confidence to the accuracy of such information:

• **Hypothesis**. A hypothesis is a proposition, a possibility that requires investigation. A hypothesis, for example, might be that blood and ketchup are made of the same substance because they are both red in color. The truth of this hypothesis can then be tested to determine whether or not it is true.

• **Theory**. A theory is a proposition that has been tested, and so far been found to be correct. But not all the information is in yet and further testing is needed. In the world of physics, the string theory is very useful in explaining the relationship between gravity, time, energy, and matter. So far, it appears to be correct, but further analysis is essential.

• **Law**. A law is a proposition that has been meticulously examined with every known method, and been found absolutely correct, every time, every place, by every investigator. The law of entropy, which objects progress from order to disorder, is one such law.

Scientists regularly propose hypotheses to explain what they observe. If they find significant supporting evidence, the proposition will progress from being simply a hypothesis, to being recognized by the scientific community as a theory. If the theory then stands up to scrupulous analysis by every known method, it may then be elevated to a law.

Obviously, the standard for recognition as a law is very, very high. Extremely few theories, and far fewer hypotheses, ever have enough evidence to become laws. The concept of relativity is one of these few. Einstein studied the relationships between time, speed, matter, and energy, and proposed a "hypothesis of relativity." As he and others researched this hypothesis, they found it to be correct in explaining physical relationships of the universe. Support for the hypothesis of relativity continued to grow until 1915, when it was upgraded to a theory — the theory of relativity. Since that time, the theory of relativity has been tested a multitude of times and found to be always correct, in every place, by every researcher. So today, instead of referring to a theory, we speak of the law of relativity.

By contrast, Darwin's proposition has been known for 140 years as the theory of evolution. In spite of the designation "theory," however, these years of research have uncovered little in the way of support for evolution. Instead, evidence to the contrary continues to mount. This designation is a crime against scientific reason. We can no longer justifiably call it a theory. Evolution is no more than a hypothesis, a hypothesis that is far from proven.

EVIDENCE

* Biologists often affirm that as members of the scientific community they positively welcome criticism. Nonsense. Like everyone else, biologists loathe criticism and arrange their lives so as to avoid it. Criticism has nonetheless seeped into their souls, the process of doubt a curiously Darwinian one in which individual biologists entertain minor reservations about their theory without ever recognizing the degree to which these doubts mount up to a substantial deficit. Creationism, so often the target of their indignation, is the least of their worries.

Unable to say what evolution has accomplished, biologists now find themselves unable to say whether evolution has accomplished it. This leaves evolutionary theory in the doubly damned position of having compromised the concepts needed to make sense of life — complexity, adaptation, design — while simultaneously conceding that the theory does little to explain them.[24]

* [Natural selection] is accused of being an unfalsifiable theory which, according to the influential philosopher of science, Karl Popper, removes it from the realm of the scientific. Darwinian theory, Popper now says, is a "metaphysical research program."[25]

* Micro-mutations do occur, but the theory that these alone can account for evolutionary change is either falsified or else it is an unfalsifiable, hence metaphysical, theory. I suppose that nobody will deny that it is a great misfortune if an entire branch of science becomes addicted to a false theory. But this is what happened in biology. . . . I believe that one day the Darwinian myth will be ranked the greatest deceit in the history of science. When this happens, many people will pose the question: "How did this ever happen?"[26]

* As evolution is the unifying theory for biology, so naturalism is the unifying theory for all of science.[27]

* Karl Popper in his autobiography, *Unended Quest,* writes: "I have come to the conclusion that Darwinism is not a testable scientific theory, but a metaphysical research program — a possible framework for testable scientific theories."[28]

* Peter Medawar: "I think Popper is incomparably the greatest philosopher of science that has ever been."[29]

* In the meantime, the educated public continues to believe that Darwin has provided all the relevant answers by the magic formula of random mutations plus natural selection — quite unaware of the fact that random mutations turned out to be irrelevant and natural selection a tautology.[30]

* There is the theory that all the living forms in the world have arisen from a single source which itself came from an inorganic form. This theory can be called the "general theory of evolution" and the evidence which supports this is not sufficiently strong to allow us to consider it as anything more than a working hypothesis.[31]

* Few paleontologists have, I think, ever supposed that fossils, by themselves, provide grounds for the conclusion that evolution has occurred. An examination of the work of those paleontologists who have been particularly concerned with the relationship between paleontology and evolutionary theory, for example that of G.G. Simpson and S.J. Gould, reveals a mindfulness of the fact that the record of evolution, like any other historical record, must be construed within a complex of particular and general preconceptions, not the least of which is the hypothesis that evolution has occurred.[32]

* Then I woke up and realized that all my life I had been duped into taking evolutionism as revealed truth in some way.
I feel that the effects of hypotheses of common ancestry in systematics has not been merely boring, not just a lack of knowledge; I think it has been positively anti-knowledge.[33]

* The explanation value of the evolutionary hypothesis of common origin is nil! Evolution not only conveys no knowledge, it seems to convey anti-knowledge. How could I work on evolution ten years and learn nothing from it? Most of you in this room will have to admit that in the last ten years we have seen the basis of evolution go from fact to faith! It does seem that the level of knowledge about evolution is remarkably shallow. We know it ought not be taught in high school, and that's all we know about it.[34]

* Evolutionary theory has been enshrined as the centerpiece of our educational system, and elaborate walls have been erected around it to protect it from unnecessary abuse.[35]

* What the "record" shows is nearly a century of fudging and finagling by scientists attempting to force various fossil morsels and fragments to conform with Darwin's notions, all to no avail. Today the millions of fossils stand as very visible, ever-present reminders of the paltriness of the arguments and the overall shabbiness of the theory that marches under the banner of evolution.[36]

* Evolution is a hypothesis based on no evidence and irreconcilable with the facts. These classical evolutionary theories are a gross over-simplification of an immensely complex and intricate mass of facts, and it amazes me that they are swallowed so uncritically and readily, and for such a long time, by so many scientists without a murmur of protest.[37]

* While many inferences about evolution are derived from living organisms, we must look to the fossil record for the ultimate documentation of large-scale change. In the absence of a fossil record, the credibility of evolutionists would be severely weakened. We might wonder whether the doctrine of evolution would qualify as anything more than an outrageous hypothesis.[38]

* MacBeth suggests that we try to look at evolution with new eyes, that we admit to the public, and, if needed, to ourselves, that we have misgivings about Darwinism, and the synthetic theory, that we open debate. I think these are excellent suggestions.[39]

CONCEPT 13-3: EVOLUTION IS BASED UPON THE PHILOSOPHY OF NATURALISM/HUMANISM.

RATIONALE

A bazaar phenomenon continues to unfold around the entire world, in classrooms, governments, scientific establishments, and even Christian churches. In all these institutions, evolution is being taught as a fact of life, in spite of compelling evidence to the contrary.

We must ask, what is it about evolution that is so attractive? Why do so many people hang on to a concept that is so unsubstantiated? The short answer to this profound question is straightforward: Evolution is the only way to explain life without giving credit to God.

The real core issues surround God, the supernatural Creator. If evolution's leaders were to admit that life was indeed created, they also must admit there exists a Creator. And if there is a Creator, the Creator is also the ultimate authority, both over the universe and over individual lives. But many humans are often extremely proud, arrogant, and unwilling to change their lives. Acknowledging the authority of the Creator is simply more than they are willing to do, even if it means flatly denying the facts about creation and evolution.

A recent survey helped to confirm this anti-God, anti-Creator bias. Published in the journal *Nature*, it documented the religious views of members of the National Academy of Sciences — an organization wholly committed to evolutionary ideas. Of NAS members in biological and physical sciences, 72.2% were overtly atheistic, 20.8% agnostic, and only 7.0% claimed belief in a personal God. Of particular note is the fact that belief in God was lowest among biologists.

Each individual possesses a world view, a package of presumptions they use to make sense of the world. The world view used by evolutionists is naturalism. They presume from the beginning that there is no God, neither any action of creation. Closely related to naturalism is the philosophy of humanism. The first two tenets of the Humanist Manifesto II, signed in 1973 by many well-known evolutionists, are especially revealing of their anti-God bias:

- Humanists regard the universe as self-existing and not created.
- Humanism believes that man is a part of nature and has emerged as a result of a continuous process (i.e., evolution).

Naturalism and humanism are enormously dependent upon evolution to justify their views. Similarly, evolution is popular, not because it meets high scientific standards, but because it fits the world view of humanists and naturalists. The greatest challenge to their God-excluding philosophy is explaining their own existence. Evolution helps them to do just that, and still be consistent with a godless universe. This commitment to naturalism and humanism is profound. Dean Kenyon, a professor of biology at San Francisco State University, confesses that many scholars refuse to examine challenges to evolution because they "would open the door to the possibility (or the necessity) of supernatural origins of life."

The very best science demands that researchers look beyond their personal bias. When objects demonstrate specified complexity, a Designer and Creator clearly must exist. Yet the naturalistic bias among many scientists causes them to immediately reject the only possible explanation — supernatural design and creation.

EVIDENCE

* Humanism is a philosophical, religious, and moral point of view as old as human civilization itself. It has its roots in classical China, Greece, and Rome; it is expressed in the Renaissance and the enlightenment, in the scientific revolution, and in the twentieth century.

We therefore affirm the following:

First: Religious humanists regard the universe as self-existing and not created.

Second: Humanism believes that man is a part of nature and that he has emerged as the result of a continuous process.

Third: Holding an organic view of life, humanists find that the traditional dualism of mind and body must be rejected. . . .

Fifth: Humanism asserts that the nature of the universe makes unacceptable any supernatural or cosmic guarantees of human values. . . .

Tenth: It follows that there will be no uniquely religious emotions and attitudes of the kind hitherto associated with belief in the supernatural.[40]

* What all this means is that Christianity cannot lose the Genesis account of creation like it could lose the doctrine of geocentrism and get along. The battle must be waged, for Christianity is fighting for its very life.[41]

* Atheism is science's natural ally. Atheism is the philosophy, both moral and ethical, most perfectly suited for a scientific civilization. If we work for the American atheists today, atheism will be ready to fill the void of Christianity's demise when science and evolution triumph.

Without a doubt humans and civilization are in sore need of the intellectual cleanness and mental health of atheism.[42]

* Christianity has fought, still fights, and will fight science to the desperate end over evolution, because evolution destroys utterly and finally the very reason Jesus' earthly life was supposedly made necessary. Destroy Adam and Eve and the original sin, and in the rubble you will find the sorry remains of the Son of God. Take away the meaning of His death. If Jesus was not the redeemer who died for our sins, and this is what evolution means, then Christianity is nothing![43]

* Much evidence can be adduced in favor of the theory of evolution from biology, biogeography, and paleontology, but I still think that to the unprejudiced, the fossil record of plants is in favor of special creation . . . yet mutations and natural selection are the bricks with which the taxonomist has built his temple of evolution, and where else have we to worship?[44]

* The Old Testament, from its manifestly false history of the earth, was no more to be trusted than the sacred books of the Hindus, or the beliefs of any barbarian. The New Testament is a damnable doctrine. (I can) hardly see how anyone ought to wish Christianity to be true.[45]

Evolution is a way to explain everything without God. It helps atheists defend their own existence, and still be consistent with their "religion" of a godless universe.[46]

* The deceit is sometimes unconscious, but not always, since some people, owing to their sectarianism, purposely overlook reality and refuse to acknowledge the inadequacies and the falsity of their beliefs.[47]

* When it comes to the origin of life on this earth, there are only two possibilities: creation or spontaneous generation (evolution). There is no third way. Spontaneous generation was disproved 100 years ago, but that leads us only to one other conclusion: that of supernatural creation. We cannot accept that on philosophical grounds (personal reasons). Therefore, we choose to believe the impossible: that life arose spontaneously by chance.[48]

* In the evolutionary pattern of thought there is no longer either need or room for the supernatural. The earth was not created, it evolved. So did all the animals and plants that inhabit it, including our human selves, mind and soul as well as brain and body. So did religion.[49]

* Perhaps the appearance of life on the earth is a miracle. Scientists are reluctant to accept that view, but their choices are limited. Either life was created on the earth by the will of a Being outside the grasp of scientific understanding, or it evolved on our planet spontaneously, through chemical reactions occurring in non-living matter lying on the surface of the planet.

The first theory places the question of the origin of life beyond the reach of scientific inquiry. It is a statement of faith in the power of a Supreme Being not subject to the laws of science. The second theory is also an act of faith. The act of faith consists in assuming that the scientific view of the origin of life is correct, without having concrete evidence to support that belief.[50]

* In the meantime, the educated public continues to believe that Darwin has provided all the relevant answers by the magic formula of random mutation plus natural selection, quite unaware of the fact that random mutations turned out to be irrelevant and natural selection a tautology.[51]

* A recent survey, for example, was published in the journal *Nature* documenting the religious make up of the National Academy of Sciences, an organization exclusively committed to propagating evolution. One-half of all 517 NAS members in biological and physical sciences responded: 72.2% were overtly atheistic, 20.8% agnostic, and only 7.0% believed in a personal God. In fact, belief in God was lowest among biologists.[52]

* The theory of life that undermined nineteenth-century religion has virtually become a religion itself and in its turn is being threatened by fresh ideas. . . . In the past ten years has emerged a new breed of biologists who are considered scientifically respectable, but who have their doubts about Darwinism.[53]

* We take the side of science in spite of the patent absurdity of some of its constructs, in spite of its failure to fulfill many of its extravagant promises of health and life, in spite of the tolerance of the scientific community for unsubstantiated just-so stories, because we have a prior commitment, a commitment to materialism. It is not that the methods and institutions of science somehow compel us to accept a material explanation of the phenomenal world, but, on the contrary, that we are forced by our a priori adherence to material causes to create an apparatus of investigation and a set of concepts that produce material explanations, no matter how counterintuitive, no matter how mystifying to the uninitiated. Moreover, that materialism is an absolute, for we cannot allow a Divine Foot in the door.[54]

* In fact, evolution became in a sense a scientific religion; almost all scientists have accepted it and many are prepared to "bend" their observations to fit in with it.[55]

* The scientific humanist holds that humans are natural creatures living in a natural universe. Evolved from stardust by cosmic processes, humans emerged from creatures that adapt themselves to nature into the self-directive agents who re-create that nature to serve the needs of their own progressive enlightenment. There are in this universe not gods and humans, masters and slaves, but human beings in various stages of development, all born of the earth-womb.[56]

* They see, however, that there are some things in this universe we must accept as basic, brute fact. An uncreated universe — the space-time-matter trinity, or the cosmic movement continuum — is one such brute fact.[57]

* Most modern biologists, having reviewed with satisfaction the downfall of the spontaneous generation hypothesis, yet unwilling to accept the alternative belief in special creation, are left with nothing.[58]

* My attempts to demonstrate evolution by an experiment carried on for more than 40 years have completely failed. . . . It is not even possible to make a caricature of an evolution out of paleo-biological facts. . . . The idea of an evolution rests on pure belief![59]

* Quite openly, one of the leading punctuated equilibrists, Stephen Jay Gould, admits to his Marxism, and lauds the way in which his science is informed by his beliefs, and how conversely his beliefs are bolstered by his science. Specifically, Gould identifies three points where his paleontology and his Marxism interact, and where he feels drawn toward punctuated equilibrium because he is a Marxist — and where, no doubt, his Marxism guided his paleontological theorizing.[60]

* In short, what I argue is that through and through Gould produces and endorses a view of paleontology which is molded by, and conversely supports and proclaims a view of the world he holds dear. We are offered the fossil record as seen through the lens of Marxism.[61]

"Evolution as a scientific theory makes a commitment to a kind of naturalism" but this "may not be a good thing to admit in a court of law."[62]

* I know geologists who regard the whole of Darwin's theory and the present-day synthetic theory of evolution (which do in fact have weak spots) as a type of religion, but we may readily imagine the chaos that would face us in geology were the evolutionary concept to become a myth.[63]

* All manner of liberal thinkers have appropriated Darwin to find, at last, a scientific foundation for the liberal belief in progress, democratic egalitarian socialism, and an altruistic ethic of human solidarity. Marx himself viewed Darwin's work as confirmation by the natural sciences of his own views, and even Mao Tse-Tung regarded Darwin, as presented by the German Darwinists, as the foundation of Chinese scientific socialism.[64]

* Dean Kenyon, a professor of biology at San Francisco State University, admits that many scientists refuse to study problems with evolution because it "would open the door to the possibility (or the necessity) of supernatural origins of life."[65]

* All of us who study the origin of life find that the more we look into it, the more we feel it is too complex to have evolved anywhere. We all believe as an article of faith that life evolved from dead matter on this planet. It is just that life's complexity is so great, it is hard for us to imagine that it did.[66]

* Evolution [is] a theory universally accepted not because it can be proven by logically coherent evidence to be true, but because the only alternative, special creation, is clearly incredible.[67]

* Aspects of evolutionism are perfectly consistent with Marxism. The explanation of the origins of humankind and of mind by purely natural forces was, and remains, as welcome to Marxists as to any other secularists. The sources of value and responsibility are not to be found in a separate mental realm or in an immortal soul, much less in the inspired words of the Bible.[68]

CONCEPT 13-4: EVOLUTIONISTS OFTEN RADICALLY PROMOTE THEIR PHILOSOPHY.

RATIONALE

The anti-God, anti-creation bias of some evolutionists is not simply a benign, armchair philosophy. For many, it is a revolutionary "call to arms," a rallying point in their crusade to literally change the world with their humanist ideas.

Evolutionists claimed a victory in their battle against creationism with the Scopes trial of 1925. This extremely well-publicized debate gave evolutionists an opportunity to broadcast their views to America like never before. Then in 1959 they celebrated the Darwin Centennial, yet another grand occasion for proclaiming their philosophy. By that time many evolutionists concluded that creationism was dead, and no longer a force to threaten their advance.

But they were entirely wrong. Since the 1970s, a steady stream of scientists, authors, and public figures have mounted a serious challenge to the tenets of evolution. Furthermore, survey after survey show that the majority of Americans still believe in supernatural creation of life and the universe. Today not only are many Christians and those of other faiths renouncing evolution, but so are many scholars on scientific grounds alone.

Alarmed by this growing resistance, evolutionists have often become frustrated, even bitter. Redoubling their efforts, evolutionary propaganda is perhaps more visible than ever before. This is particularly true of their efforts to control public school curricula, largely through legislation to eliminate the discussion of creation in classrooms, and to restrict critical debate about evolution.

EVIDENCE

* In the meantime, the educated public continues to believe that Darwin has provided all the relevant answers by the magic formula of random mutations plus natural selection — quite unaware of the fact that random mutations turned out to be irrelevant and natural selection a tautology.[69]

* Such action, coupled with a series of recent legal defeats for "scientific creationism," means that the AHA's participation in the creation-evolution controversy has borne fruit. For it was the AHA, before any other organization, that issued in 1977 its famous "Statement Affirming Evolution as a Principle of Science" and warned the public of the dangers posed by the creationist movement. It was the AHA, and no other organization that chose to publish *Creation/Evolution*, a journal that continues to provide scientific rebuttals to creationist nonsense, thereby aiding those fighting at the local level. The AHA has been in this battle from the beginning and will stay with it as long as necessary.[70]

* You and I and other scientifically minded citizens must

REJECT EVOLUTION · 233

help the ACLU fight this movement to force fundamentalist religious doctrine into the public schools. . . . We must be prepared for the long and costly battle of challenging every creationist statute in every state in which it is introduced. Unbelievable as it may seem, there are millions of Americans who call themselves "scientific creationists. . . ."

These religious zealots . . . are marching like an army of the night into our public schools with their Bibles held high.[71]

* But, as we all know, the fundamentalists don't give up easily. For example, after the Supreme Court voted 7-2 against creationism last June in the Louisiana creationism case, a case in which the AHA was a plaintiff, the various creationist organizations began shifting gears. What is their newest tack? Academic freedom, of all things!

The Institute for Creation Research has begun encouraging the many existing creationist teachers in the public schools to teach creationism on their own in their science classes. Meanwhile other creationist groups are preparing test cases so they can launch a "Scopes trial in reverse." These organizations want one of their creationist teachers to get fired for teaching creationism so they can take that case all the way to the Supreme Court using a free speech and academic freedom line of argument.[72]

* These "creation-science" textbooks, if allowed in our schools, can only serve to increase that mental anguish by teaching that the Genesis gibberish is a legitimate scientific theory.[73]

* Christianity is — must be! — totally committed to the special creation as described in Genesis, and Christianity must fight with its full might, fair or foul, against the theory of evolution.[74]

* It becomes clear now that the whole justification of Jesus' life and death is predicated on the existence of Adam and the forbidden fruit he and Eve ate. Without the original sin, who needs to be redeemed? Without Adam's fall into a life of constant sin terminated by death, what purpose is there to Christianity? None.[75]

* Creationism is not scientific; it is a purely religious view held by some religious sects and persons and strongly opposed by other religious sects and persons. . . . Evolution is . . .

therefore the only view that should be expounded in public-school courses on science.

We, the undersigned, call upon all local school boards . . . to do the following:

— Resist and oppose measures . . . that would require creationist views of origins be given equal treatment and emphasis. . . .

— Reject the concept, currently being put forth by certain religious and pressure groups, that alleges that evolution is itself a tenet of a religion of "secular humanism," and as such is unsuitable for inclusion in the public school science curriculum.[76]

* Religious bigotry is abroad again in the land. . . . It does not satisfy them that biblical creationism receives equal time with other religious accounts of origins in courses in comparative theology. They demand that creationism be presented as a "scientific" alternative to evolution in science textbooks that deal with the origin and subsequent development of life before such textbooks can be approved for use in the public schools.[77]

* Although the creationists may be irrational, they are not to be dismissed as a lunatic fringe that can best be treated by being ignored. In California . . . they have proven themselves to be skillful tacticians, good organizers, and uncompromising adversaries.[78]

* I am convinced that the battle for humankind's future must be waged and won in the public school classroom by teachers who correctly perceive their role as the proselytizers of a new faith: a religion of humanity that recognizes and respects the spark of what theologians call divinity in every human being. These teachers must embody the same selfless dedication as the most rabid fundamentalist preachers, for they will be ministers of another sort, utilizing a classroom instead of a pulpit to convey humanist values in whatever subject they teach, regardless of the educational level — preschool day care or large state university. The classroom must and will become an arena of conflict between the old and the new — the rotting corpse of Christianity, together with all its adjacent evils and misery, and the new faith of humanism, resplendent in its promise of a world in which the never-realized Christian ideal of "love thy neighbor" will finally be achieved.

It will undoubtedly be a long, arduous, painful struggle replete with much sorrow and many tears, but humanism will emerge triumphant. It must if the family of humankind is to survive.[79]

* [Hitler] stressed and singled out the idea of biological evolution as the most forceful weapon against traditional religion and he repeatedly condemned Christianity for its opposition to the teaching of evolution. . . . For Hitler, evolution was the hallmark of modern science and culture, and he defended its veracity as tenaciously as Haeckel.[80]

* John Paul states — and I can only say amen, and thanks for noticing — that the half century between Pius's surveying the ruins of World War II and his own pontificate heralding the dawn of a new millennium has witnessed such a growth of data, and such a refinement of theory, that evolution can no longer be doubted by people of good will.[81]

* In conclusion, Pius had grudgingly admitted evolution as a legitimate hypothesis that he regarded as only tentatively supported and potentially (as I suspect he hoped) untrue. John Paul, nearly fifty years later, reaffirms the legitimacy of evolution under the NOMA principle — no news here — but then adds that additional data and theory have placed the factuality of evolution beyond reasonable doubt. Sincere Christians must now accept evolution not merely as a plausible possibility but also as an effectively proven fact.[82]

* The most important responsibilities of the geologists involve the effect of their findings on the mental and spiritual lives of mankind. Early geologists fought to free people from the myths of biblical creation. Many millions still live in mental bondage controlled by ignorant ranters who accept the Bible as the last word in science, and accept Archbishop Ussher's claim that the earth was created 4004 B.C. Attempts to reconcile Genesis with geology lead to numerous contradictions. . . . Also, the theory of evolution greatly affects modern thinking. Man's rise from simple life forms even today causes much controversy among "fundamentalists" who cling to a literal belief in the Bible.[83]

* But modern, scientific, progressive America witnesses, at this very moment, a resurgence of biblical literalism, fundamentalism and evangelicalism that almost defies belief. . . .

But of all the recent manifestations of old-time religion, I can think of none more intellectually impertinent or socially and politically ominous than that of the Creation Research Society and its Institute of Creation Research, devoted to destroying the ideas of cosmic and organic evolution. The mischief that this organization is prepared to do to the life and earth sciences, particularly in elementary and secondary schools, staggers the scientific imagination.[84]

* Johnny learns many remarkable doctrines at his full-gospel school, including the recent creation of the earth and the impossibility of organic evolution due to God's curse (Gen. 3:17) from which entropy has resulted.[85]

* The ideas and subjects Johnny is led to avoid are as noteworthy as the doctrines he learns. Since he learns that the fear of the Lord is the beginning of wisdom (Job 28:28; Prov. 1:7) and that he should stultify his intellect that he may truly be wise (1 Cor. 1:20; 3:18–20), he does not miss at the time the critical thinking that he might have been taught.[86]

*How much income will he, unnecessarily, forfeit because of his educational retardation, and what of the continuing psychological trauma inflicted on him due to having been sold a bill of goods in his early schooling? How badly has his career already been blighted? In light of the foregoing, it now occurs to him that he may have been abused as a child. Has Johnny been abused and, if so, does he enjoy a remedy?

It might seem that he has suffered an actionable harm, i.e., one for which the law will offer a remedy.[87]

* Put differently, should children have a positive right to be taught the truth and nothing but the truth (in appropriate depth, of course) as it can be ascertained at any given time, or should parents have as much leeway as possible in indoctrinating their children as they please? Put in yet a third way, should it now become possible to succeed in court with wrongful education suits when the gravity of what is alleged is tantamount to child abuse?[88]

* Statements about creation . . . should not be regarded as reasonable alternatives to scientific explanations for the origin and evolution of life.[89]

* Whether called "creation science," "scientific creationism," "intelligent-design theory," "young-earth theory" or some other synonym, creation beliefs have no place in the science classroom. Explanations employing non-naturalistic or supernatural events, whether or not explicit reference is made to a supernatural being, are outside the realm of science and not part of a valid science curriculum. Evolutionary theory, indeed all of science, is necessarily silent on religion and neither refutes nor supports the existence of a deity or deities.[90]

* Evolution does not violate the second law of thermodynamics: producing order from disorder is possible with the addition of energy, such as from the sun.[91]

* Courts have thus restricted school districts from requiring creation science in the science curriculum and have restricted individual instructors from teaching it. All teachers and administrators should be mindful of these court cases, remembering that the law, science, and NABT support them as they appropriately include the teaching of evolution in the science curriculum.[92]

* Creationists often complain that their theories and their colleagues are discriminated against by educators. . . . As a matter of fact, creationism should be discriminated against. . . . No advocate of such propaganda should be trusted to teach science classes or administer science programs anywhere or under any circumstances. Moreover, if any are now doing so, they should be dismissed. . . . I am glad this kind of discrimination is finally catching on, and I hope the practice becomes much more vigorous and widespread in the future.[93]

* The bourgeoisie was in need of a "proper" justification for the new factory system with its dehumanizing process of division of labor. By claiming that a similar process was at work in nature, Darwin provided an ideal rationale for those capitalists hell-bent on holding the line against any fundamental challenge to the economic hierarchy they managed and profited from.[94]

* Today, the official philosophy is Marxist-Leninism (of a kind). But without the secular, materialist approach of Darwinism (meaning now the broad social philosophy), the ground would not have been tilled for Mao and his revolutionaries to sow their seed and reap their crop.[95]

* Then it suddenly flashed upon me that this self-acting process would necessarily improve the race, because in every generation the inferior would inevitably be killed off and the superior would remain — that is, the fittest would survive. Then at once I seemed to see the whole effect of this.[96]

* Marx and Engels accepted evolution almost immediately after Darwin published *The Origin of Species*. Within a month, Engels wrote to Marx (Dec. 12, 1859): "Darwin, whom I am just now reading, is splendid." Evolution, of course, was just what the founders of communism needed to explain how mankind could have come into being without the intervention of any supernatural force, and consequently it could be used to bolster the foundations of their materialistic philosophy. In addition, Darwin's interpretation of evolution — that evolution had come about through the operation of natural selection — gave them an alternative hypothesis to the prevailing teleological explanation of the observed fact that all forms of life are adapted to their conditions.[97]

CONCEPT 13-5: A BELIEF IN EVOLUTION RESULTS IN DISRESPECT FOR HUMAN LIFE.

RATIONALE

A reasonable question must be addressed. In day-to-day life, does it really matter where we really came from? Whether we evolved or were created? Whether God is our Creator, or we descended from some ape-like creature? The answer is both essential and profound: Yes, absolutely, it does matter!

From the standpoint of scientific research, the false assumption that evolution is true has lead to many other false assumptions about paleontology, biology, astronomy, and world history. This has greatly deceived researchers who continue probing for answers consistent with evolution. In truth, few will ever be found.

But beyond the laboratory, evolution has particularly devastating personal and social implications. In both the first and the final analysis, evolution insists that humans are no more than random accidents of nature, no more unique or valuable that any other animal, or microorganism for that matter. Humans deserve no special treatment.

History is full of examples of governments and individuals who embraced evolution and devalued the lives of their people. Germicide, euthanasia, child abuse, abortion, racism, theft, and certainly murder are but a few consequences of such thinking. Darwin himself expressed through his personal life the inevitable results of evolutionary thinking. His writings are filled with statements of deep prejudice against blacks, native islanders, and women.

A dramatic example of evolutionary thought is the life of Adolph Hitler. He embraced evolution as the most powerful weapon available against Christian and traditional social values. In their place, Hitler worked to plunge the German people into a struggle for world domination wherein they would be the "fittest who survived." *Mein Kampf*, which literally means "my struggle," is a book authored by Hitler on this very subject. While not all the wickedness of Hitler's reign can be blamed on evolutionary concepts, it is certain that these profoundly influenced him, and many other depraved leaders, including Marx, Mussolini, Mao, and Stalin.

Adolf Hitler

These men were the fathers of modern Communist, Nazi, and Fascist dictatorships. But before we become too smug about their extremism, we must also realize that capitalism in the West has applied the philosophy of evolution in the world of business. The "survival of the fittest" has been used to justify immoral and unlawful corporate practices, including monopolism and child labor. In the evolution-permeated business world, justice is irrelevant. All that matters is squelching the competition and getting ahead of the rest. Such capitalists as Rockefeller and Carnegie often invoked the name of Darwin as they justified their business decisions.

Far from being an "innocent" abstract idea about events long ago, evolution brings with it a value system, or rather, lack of value system, that catalyzes disrespect for human beings wherever its philosophy takes hold.

Evidence

* Spencer coined the phrase "survival of the fittest," and Darwin adopted the parlance in later editions of his *Origin of Species*. Spencer used this principle — where competition for limited resources results in the survival of the inherently "better" candidate — to explain past, present, and future social conditions. . . .

What, then, is this idea? According to Spencer and his American disciples, business entrepreneurs like John D. Rockefeller and Andrew Carnegie, social hierarchy reflects the unwavering, universal laws of nature. Nature unfolds in such a way that the strong survive and the weak perish. Thus, the economic and social structures that survive are "stronger" and better, and those structures that don't were obviously meant to founder. . . . How do we know that capitalism is better than communism and that the mammal is better than the dinosaur? Because they survived, of course.[98]

* It is commonplace that Marx felt his own work to be the exact parallel of Darwin's. He even wished to dedicate a portion of *Das Kapital* to the author of *The Origin of Species*.[99]

* It is that, like Darwin, Marx thought he had discovered the law of development. He saw history in stages, as the Darwinists saw geological strata and successive forms of life.[100]

* Abstract. A central government policy of the Hitler administration was the breeding of a "superior race." This required, at the very least, preventing the "inferior races" from mixing with "superior" ones in order to reduce contamination of the latter's gene pool. The "superior race" belief is based on the theory of group inequality within each species, a major presumption and requirement of Darwin's original "survival of the fittest" theory. A review of the writings of Hitler and contemporary German biologists finds that Darwin's theory and writings had a major influence upon Nazi policies. Hitler believed that the human gene pool could be improved by selective breeding, using the same techniques that farmers used to breed a superior strain of cattle. In the formulation of his racial policies, he relied heavily upon the Darwinian evolution model, especially the elaborations by Spencer and Haeckel. They culminated in the "final solution," the extermination of approximately six million Jews and four million other people who belonged to what German scientists judged were "inferior races."[101]

* Among some animal species, then, infant killing appears to be a natural practice. Could it be natural for humans too, a trait inherited from our primate ancestors. . . .

Charles Darwin noted in *The Descent of Man* that infanticide has been "probably the most important of all" checks on population growth throughout most of human history.[102]

* Before 1859 many scientists had questioned whether blacks were of the same species as whites. After 1859, the evolutionary schema raised additional questions, particularly whether or not Afro-Americans could survive competition with their white near-relatives. The momentous answer was a resounding no.[103]

* Adolf Hitler's mind was captivated by evolutionary thinking — probably since the time he was a boy. Evolutionary ideas — quite undisguised — lie at the basis of all that is worst in *Mein Kampf*. A few quotations, taken at random, will show how Hitler reasoned. . . . "He who would live must fight, he who does not wish to fight in the world where permanent struggle is the law of life, has not the right to exist."[104]

* Evolution is a hard, inescapable mistress. There is just no room for compassion or good sportsmanship. Too many organisms are born, so, quite simply, a lot of them are going to have to die because there isn't enough food and space to go around. You can be beautiful, fat, strong, but it might not matter. The only thing that does matter is whether you leave more children carrying your genes than the next person leaves. It's true whether you're a prince, a frog, or an American elm. Evolution is a future phenomenon. Are your genes going to be in the next generation? That is all that counts.[105]

* I could show fight on natural selection having done and doing more for the progress of civilization than you seem inclined to admit. . . . The more civilized so-called Caucasian races have beaten the Turkish hollow in the struggle for existence. Looking to the world at no very distant date, what an endless number of the lower races will have been eliminated by the higher civilized races throughout the world.[106]

* At some future period, not very distant as measured by centuries, the civilized races of man will almost certainly exterminate, and replace, the savage races throughout the world. At the same time, the anthropomorphous apes . . . will no doubt be exterminated. The break between man and his nearest allies will then be wider, for it will intervene between man in a more civilized state, as we may hope, even than the Caucasian, and some ape as low as a baboon, instead of as now between the Negro [sic] or Australian and the gorilla.[107]

* It is generally admitted that with woman the powers of intuition, of rapid perception, and perhaps of imitation, are more strongly marked than in man; but some, at least, of these faculties are characteristic of the lower races, and therefore of a past and lower state of civilization. The chief distinction in the intellectual powers of the two sexes is shown by man's attaining to a higher eminence, in whatever he takes up, than can woman; whether requiring deep thought, reason, or imagination, or merely the use of the senses and hands. . . . The average of mental power in man must be above that of woman.[108]

* It is, indeed, fortunate that the law of the equal transmission of characters to both sexes has commonly prevailed throughout the whole class of mammals; otherwise it is probable that man would have become as superior in mental endowment to woman as the peacock is in ornamental plumage to the peahen. Thus man has ultimately become superior to woman, poetry, strength, voice, etc.[109]

Lanier: "There's a large group of people who simply are uncomfortable with accepting evolution because it leads to what they perceive as a moral vacuum, in which their best impulses have no basis in nature."

Dawkins: "All I can say is, That's just tough. We have to face up to the truth."[110]

* Evolutionary theory emphasizes the "survival of the fittest," and the idea that progress comes through elimination of less-fit organisms. This idea has been used to justify an ethic of selfishness by saying that selfish behavior has produced great evolutionary progress. Evolutionists generally hold that instances of cooperation and even altruism seen in nature are only the principle of the wolf pack — organisms banding to-

gether temporarily for mutual benefit in the struggle for individual survival.[111]

* In turn, biological evolutionism exerted ever-widening influences on the natural and social sciences, as well as on philosophy and even on politics. Not all of these extrabiological repercussions were either sound or commendable. Suffice it to mention the so-called Social Darwinism, which often sought to justify the inhumanity of man to man, and the biological racism which furnished a fraudulent scientific sanction for the atrocities committed in Hitler's Germany and elsewhere.[112]

* The creationists have portrayed Darwinism as a cornerstone of "secular humanism," a term they use to describe the belief that man, not God is the source of right and wrong. They blame humanist teaching for all sorts of modern ills — from juvenile delinquency to the high rate of abortions — and want to replace it with the teaching of Christian morality. . . .

As the creationists' goals become clear, many scientists, realizing that they have been secular humanists all along, are beginning to marshal their forces. . . . Evolutionists are beginning to realize that, for the first time in half a century, they may have to defend themselves in court.[113]

* From the *Preservation of Favoured Races in the Struggle for Life* [i.e., Darwin's subtitle to *Origin of Species*], it was a short step to the preservation of favoured individuals, classes or nations, and from their preservation to their glorification. Social Darwinism has often been understood in this sense: as a philosophy, exalting competition, power and violence over convention, ethics, and religion. Thus it has become a portmanteau of nationalism, imperialism, militarism, and dictatorship, of the cults of the hero, the superman, and the master race.[114]

* Hitler believed in struggle as a Darwinian principle of human life that forced every people to try to dominate all others; without struggle they would rot and perish. . . . Even in his own defeat in April 1945, Hitler expressed his faith in the survival of the stronger and declared the Slavic peoples to have proven themselves the stronger.[115]

* Orthodox Marxian socialists in the early years of the 20th century felt quite at home in Darwinian surroundings. Karl Marx himself, with his belief in universal "dialectical"

principles, had been as much a monist as Comte or Spencer. Reading *The Origin of Species* in 1860, he reported to Friedrich Engels, and later declared to Ferdinand LaSalle, that "Darwin's book is very important, and serves me as a basis in natural science for the class struggle in history." On the shelves of the socialist bookstores in Germany the words of Darwin and Marx stood side by side.[116]

* Yes, we are all animals, descendants of a vast lineage of replicators sprung from primordial pond scum.[117]

* Though both of us survived the war, we were victims of a cruel social ideology that assumes that competition among individuals, classes, nations, or races is the natural condition of life, and that it is also natural for the superior to dispossess the inferior. For the last century and more this ideology has been thought to be a natural law of science, the mechanism of evolution which was formulated most powerfully by Charles Darwin in 1859 in his *On the Origin of Species by Means of Natural Selection.*[118]

* The law of natural selection is not, I will maintain, science. It is an ideology, and a wicked one, and it has as much interfered with our ability to perceive the history of life with clarity as it has interfered with our ability to see one another with tolerance.[119]

* [Darwin's] aim was "to show that there is no fundamental difference between man and the higher mammals (monkeys) in their mental faculties." [In his *Voyage of the Beagle*, describing "the miserable inhabitants of Tierra del Fuego."]

Darwin hardly saw an Indian at all and could not speak one word of their language, yet his description of the Fuegians is still quoted as authoritative over a century later in countless so-called scientific works. . . . But these superficial comments of a passing tourist in 1832 were entirely without foundation. They were completely demolished by the findings of two missionary priests, both highly qualified scientists . . . on the staffs of American and European universities. . . . Darwin had no scientific qualifications at all.[120]

Two Roman Catholic scientists, both on the staff of American and European universities, also visited the same Indians and stated: "The Fuegian Indians were not cannibals; they believed in one Supreme Being, to whom they prayed with confidence; they had 'high principles of morality' and they rightly regarded the white people who exploited them as morally inferior to themselves."[121]

* His friend Lyell, after reading *Origin*, suggested that in a future edition he should "here and there insert an actual case to relieve the vast number of abstract propositions." It is, of course, the absence of actual cases that has always been the main difficulty with Darwin's evolution. There are no actual cases.[122]

* It is apparent that Darwin lost his faith in the years 1836–39, much of it clearly prior to the reading of Malthus. In order not to hurt the feelings of his friends and of his wife, Darwin often used deistic language in his publications, but much in his notebooks indicates that by this time he had become a "materialist" [more or less = atheist].[123]

* One of these shifts has been rather consistently side-stepped by all those who have occupied themselves with the history of the theory of natural selection. It is the question of the extent that Darwin's loss of Christian faith affected the conceptual framework on which the theory of natural selection rests. . . . Adopting natural selection rather than the hand of God as the active factor responsible for all that was formerly considered evidence for design was, of course, the last step. However, even the acceptance of evolution was already a fatal undermining of natural theology.[124]

* Founded, as are most great fallacies, upon a half-truth, Darwinism spawned many offshoots. One of these was launched by Darwin's first cousin, Francis Galton.

Obsessed, as were many, by the implications of the "fittest," Galton set out in 1883 to study heredity from a mathematical viewpoint. He named his new "science" eugenics, from a Greek root meaning both "good in birth" and "noble in heredity." His stated goal was to improve the human race, by giving "the more suitable races or strains of blood a better chance of prevailing speedily over the less suitable." His unstated goal was to play God.[125]

* Through the years since then, the ideas of superior and inferior people and societal control inherent in eugenics have helped bring real-life horrors to the world.

The idiot-savants engaged in eugenics studies, programs, or promotion reads like a list of 20th century Who's Who. Hitler was, of course, a very eminent convert, though seldom claimed by the Movement. Margaret Sanger, a vicious and open racist, is . . . despite her horrifying writings, lectures, and activities, still publicly honored for her efforts in birth control. These led to the "family planning" and "birth control" clinics now rife on the landscape. And these in turn preceded and paved the way for modern abortion "clinics" and their apologists, lobbyists, protectors, and financiers.[126]

CONCEPT 13-6: A BELIEF IN EVOLUTION RESULTS IN ALIENATION FROM GOD.

RATIONALE

Evolution is based upon an atheistic world view; that is, a presumption that there is no God. It teaches that we are utterly alone in the world, struggling for survival in competition against every other man and woman. There exists no God, no absolute authority, no moral foundation, no universal criteria for true and false. What is right or wrong is relative only to the values of those people at that time. As a consequence, the concept of evolution has driven more people away from trusting God than any other force in recent history.

But God is reality. God is the Creator. But even more than this, God is the source of enormous strength, inspiration, encouragement, and kindness for those who trust Him. The statements of God are also the foundation of right and wrong, of ethics, justice, and law, superseding the authority of any human being. They promote harmony and relationship with the Creator and with one another.

These are exactly the truths and strengths that evolution and its proponents want to deny the world. Advocating naturalism with its inherent hopelessness, they are zealous for each person on earth to share in their isolation and alienation from God. Remarkably, many individuals elect to follow them!

Rejecting God, evolution is a core concept for most of today's popular philosophies, including witchcraft, astrology, Hinduism, Buddhism, Taoism, and New Age. But this is actually nothing new at all. Pantheistic evolution was an essential tenet of the religions of the ancient nations, including Greece, Babylon, and Rome. As diverse as all these philosophies are from one another, they all deny both the Creator and special creation; they are all entirely opposed to biblical Christianity, to the Genesis account, and to a personal relationship with Jesus, the Creator.

EVIDENCE

* It is forty years since Humanist Manifesto I (1933) appeared. . . .

As in 1933, humanists still believe that traditional theism, especially faith in the prayer-hearing God, assumed to love and care for persons, to hear and understand their prayers, and to be able to do something about them, is an unproved and outmoded faith.[127]

* As non-theists, we begin with humans, not God; nature, not deity.[128]

* But we discover no divine purpose or providence for the human species. While there is much that we do not know, humans are responsible for what we are or will become. No deity will save us; we must save ourselves. . . .

Promises of immortal salvation or fear of eternal damnation are both illusory and harmful.[129]

* On 7 March 1837 I took lodgings in Great Marlborough Street in London and remained there for nearly two years until I was married. . . .

During these two years I was led to think much about religion. . . . But I had gradually come, by this time, to see that the Old Testament, from its manifestly false history of the world . . . was no more to be trusted than the sacred books of the Hindus, or the beliefs of any barbarian.[130]

* Thus disbelief crept over me at a very slow rate, but was at last complete. The rate was so slow that I felt no distress, and have never since doubted even for a single second that my conclusion was correct. I can indeed hardly see how anyone ought to wish Christianity to be true, for if so the plain language of the text seems to show that the men who do not believe, and this would include my father, brother, and almost all my best friends, will be everlastingly punished. And this is a damnable doctrine.[131]

* As far as Christianity was concerned, the advent of the theory of evolution and the elimination of traditional teleological thinking was catastrophic. The suggestion that life and man are the result of chance is incompatible with the biblical assertion of their being the direct result of intelligent creative activity. Despite the attempt by liberal theology to disguise the point, the fact is that no biblically derived religion can really be compromised with the fundamental assertion of Darwinian theory. Chance and design are antithetical concepts, and the decline in religious belief can probably be attributed more to the propagation and advocacy by the intellectual and scientific community of the Darwinian version of evolution than to any other single factor.[132]

* Many paleontologists, myself included, now view *Homo sapiens* as a tiny and unpredictable twig on a richly ramifying tree of life — a happy accident of the last geological moment, unlikely ever to appear again if we could regrow the tree from seed.[133]

* Darwin pointed out that no supernatural designer was needed, since natural selection could account for any known form of life, there was no room for a supernatural agency in its evolution. . . . We can dismiss entirely all idea of a supernatural overriding mind being responsible for the evolutionary process.[134]

* I use the word "humanist" to mean someone who believes that man is just as much a natural phenomenon as an animal or plant; that his body, mind, and soul were not supernaturally created but are products of evolution, and that he is not under the control or guidance of any supernatural being or beings, but has to rely on himself and his own powers.[135]

* Human beings are the natural culmination of millions of years of evolution; the body and brain (or personality) are so intimately connected that, when the body dies so does the brain — and the personality dies with it. No educated man or woman can possibly believe in the Christian notion of bodily resurrection. For similar reasons, humanists cannot believe in reincarnation.[136]

* I've always believed that we were, each of us, put here for a reason. That there is a plan, somehow — a divine plan for all of us. I know now that whatever days are left of me belong to Him.

I also believe this blessed land was set apart in a very special way. A country created by men and women who came here not in search of gold, but in search of God. They would be free people, living under the law with faith in their Maker and their future. Sometimes, it seems we've strayed from that noble beginning, from our conviction that standards of right and wrong do exist and must be lived up to. God, the source of our knowledge, has been expelled from the classroom. He gives us His greatest blessing: life — and yet many would condone the taking of innocent life. We expect Him to protect us in a crisis, but turn away from Him too often in our day-to-day living. And I wonder if He isn't waiting for us to wake up.[137]

* Either humankind is in a state of original sin or it is not. If it is, then there was reason for Jesus to die on the cross. If it is not, Calvary has as much relevance as a gladiator's death in the Coliseum.[138]

* Either Jesus Christ was the Son of God or He was not. If he was, other religions are false. Missionaries — Jesuits past and Evangelicals present — are right about this. If he was not, Christianity is a fraud — no salvation, no heaven, no nothing. You cannot be a Christian on Sunday and a Hindu on Monday.

I am sorry to be so rude about this (not that sorry!) but perhaps my indignation is a good point on which to go out. Unlike George Williams, I really want to believe. I find the goodies offered by Christianity extremely attractive. But I am damned (again!) if I am going to sell my evolutionary birthright for a mess of religious pottage. We see through a glass darkly; but, thanks to Charles Darwin, it is no longer so dark as when Saint Paul was penning a few thoughts to the Corinthians.[139]

* What makes well-meaning people fight so hard to keep children from learning a basic scientific principle? From the beginning of the American anti-evolution movement, the driving force has been the same: a struggle for souls. Students who learn evolution, the creationists reason, will come to doubt the existence of God. Without the moral rudder that religion provides, they will become bad people doing bad things. Evolution is thus evil and a cause of evil. As Henry M. Morris, the most influential twentieth-century creationist, wrote in 1963, "Evolution is at the foundation of communism, Fascism, Freudianism, social Darwinism, behaviorism, Kinseyism, materialism, atheism, and, in the religious world, modernism and Neo-orthodoxy."[140]

* Avoid Debates. If your local campus Christian fellowship asks you to "defend evolution," please decline. Public debates rarely change many minds; creationists stage them mainly in the hope of drawing large sympathetic audiences. Have you ever watched the Harlem Globetrotters play the Washington Federals? The Federals get off some good shots, but who remembers them? The purpose of the game is to see the Globetrotters beat the other team. And you probably will get beaten.[141]

* One reason education undoes belief is its teaching of evolution; Darwin's own drift from orthodoxy to agnosticism was symptomatic. Martin Lings is probably right in saying that "more cases of loss of religious faith are to be traced to the theory of evolution . . . than to anything else.[142]

* Darwin saw his discovery as strongly resistant to admixture with belief in God, while Jacques Monod goes further. "The mechanism of evolution as now understood," he tells us, "rules out any claim that there are final causes, or purposes being realized. [This] disposes of any philosophy or religion that believes in cosmic . . . purpose." Realizing that this conclusion could be colored by Monod's personal philosophy, I turn to the entry on "Evolution" in the *New Encyclopaedia Britannica* for a statement that might reflect, as well as any, consensus in the field. It tells me that 'Darwin showed that evolution's cause, natural selection, was automatic with no room for divine guidance or design.[143]

* Religion is like the human appendix: although it was functional in our distant ancestors, it is of no use today. Just as the appendix today is a focus of physical disease, so too religion today is a focus of social disease. Although religion was a force accelerating human evolution during the Ice Age, it is now an atavism of negative value.[144]

CONCEPT 13-7: THE "THEORY" OF EVOLUTION MUST BE REJECTED.

RATIONALE

Evolution is a theory entirely lacking in objective evidence to defend itself. It is also a shameless philosophy with disastrous personal and social fallout. Nevertheless, the leaders of evolution and humanism are extremely dedicated and intent on indoctrinating our students and the public at large in their dangerous philosophy.

We have allowed such people to direct our scientific and educational institutions, and they will continue to use these platforms to exhort the world as long as the public voices little objection. When people do insist that creation be at least mentioned, humanists and evolutionists inevitably insist that to do so would be to teach "religion," since creation implies a supernatural creator. And "religion," they contend, cannot be taught in schools, so creation cannot be mentioned. Three points need to be understood about this common line of reasoning:

• Educators commonly agree that "philosophy" can be discussed in school, but not "religion." But the line between a "philosophy" like humanism, and a "religion" like Christianity is undefinable. Both promote a particular world view, a perspective on ethics, history, and human nature. A "religion" may or may not include reference to a supernatural being, but beyond this characteristic, a "philosophy" and a "religion" are largely indistinguishable. Buddhism is an excellent example. While universally recognized as a religion, it does not promote a "god," and its teachings are acknowledged as a "philosophy." Christianity is clearly a philosophy, too. Simply because it promotes God is no justification for excluding its discussion.

• Scientific rationale and evidence for creation, and the arguments and evidence against evolution can stand alone. They do not rely upon any particular philosophy, religion or even world view for adequate defense. The abstract scientific method itself generates enormous proof for creation.

• The American people themselves want creation taught in their schools. An Associated Press/NBC National Poll found that 86 percent of the public desires that creation be taught alongside evolution in our public schools. Only 8 percent wanted evolution taught exclusively. Another 6 percent could not decide.

Since so much support exists for teaching creation, why do education's leaders persist in teaching only evolution? Ultimately, it's because we (the students, parents, and public officials) are allowing them. Everyone who participates in education — the students, parents, teachers, administrators, and tax payers — must be extremely aware of evolutionists' true intent: indoctrination of our youth with the corrupt philosophies of naturalism and humanism.

We simply must insist on honesty in science and in education. Evolution must be presented as the unconfirmed hypothesis that it actually is. The evidence against it must be revealed and discussed, rather than trying to deceive youth by merely insisting that evolution is true.

Creation must also be presented, along with its arguments and the overwhelming evidence of design. No apology need be made for the fact that creation implies a Creator. It is simply the truth, and no amount of "political correctness" should ever be allowed to obscure this fact.

It we fail to demand these changes, we will continue to witness tragic consequences on the impressionable minds of our youth. If we allow educators to teach that students are no more than "replicators from the slime," will we be surprised if they become entangled in depression, drug abuse, violence, and even suicide? If we continue to allow the amorality of evolution to be taught, shall we be stunned to observe a generation scarred by abortion, sexually transmitted diseases, and teenage pregnancy? If we neglect our responsibility and allow our children to be taught that there is no God and no moral absolutes, should we be shocked if they choose a life of apathy, dishonesty, or selfishness?

The future of our children and our society need not fulfill this scenario. The choice is yours and mine. We must demand that the truth about evolution be declared in every home, in every school, in every university, and every church.

EVIDENCE

An Associated Press/NBC National Poll found that 86% of all Americans wanted the creation model taught alongside the evolution model in the public school. Only eight percent wanted only evolution taught. Six percent could not decide.[145]

* Readers of *American Scientist* may not realize the extent to which a major part of the field of biology and almost all of paleontology has rejected Darwin's insights concerning organic evolution. Natural selection is dismissed as contributing nothing more than "fine-tuning," and adaptation is largely ignored in practice.[146]

* The Darwinian theory of descent has not a single fact to confirm it in the realm of nature. It is not the result of scientific research but purely the product of imagination.[147]

* We have had enough of the Darwinian fallacy. It is time that we cry: "The emperor has no clothes."[148]

* My abhorrence of Darwinism is understandable, for what member of the "lower races" could remain indifferent to the statement attributed to the great master (Darwin, 1881, in a letter to W. Graham) that "at no very distant date, what an endless number of the races will have been eliminated by the higher civilized races throughout the world." If Kellogg had been a victim of social Darwinism, she would not have been blinded by hero worship. Charles Darwin was not a prophet, not a messiah, not a demigod. He was a gentleman scientist of the Victorian Era, and an establishment member of a society that sent

gunboats to forcibly import opium into China, all in the name of competition (in free trade) and survival of the fittest.[149]

* No one, then, has ever seen one species change into another either in the fossil record or in breeding experiments. Darwin himself was unable to come up with a single indisputable case of one animal changing into another via "natural selection." His case was entirely theoretical; it rested on a chain of suppositions rather than empirical observation; the "facts" that he mustered were either made to fit the theory or were explained away.[150]

* I wish I were younger. . . . What inclines me now to think you may be right in regarding [evolution] as the central and radical lie in the whole web of falsehood that now governs our lives is not so much your arguments against it as the fanatical and twisted attitudes of its defenders.[151]

* I suppose that nobody will deny that it is a great misfortune if an entire branch of science becomes addicted to a false theory. But this is what has happened in biology: for a long time now people discuss evolutionary problems in a peculiar "Darwinian" vocabulary — "adaptation," "selection pressure," "natural selection," etc. — thereby believing that they contribute to the explanation of natural events. They do not, and the sooner this is discovered, the sooner we shall be able to make real progress in our understanding of evolution.

I believe that one day the Darwinian myth will be ranked the greatest deceit in the history of science.[152]

* I myself am convinced that the theory of evolution, especially the extent to which it's been applied, will be one of the great jokes in the history books in the future. Posterity will marvel that so very flimsy and dubious a hypothesis could be accepted with the incredible credulity that it has. I think that I spoke to you before about this age as one of the most credulous in history, and I would include evolution as an example. I'm very happy to say I live near a place called Piltdown. I like to drive there because it gives me a special glow. You probably know that a skull was discovered there, and no less than five hundred doctoral theses were written on the subject, and then it was discovered that the skull was a practical joke by a worthy dentist in Hastings who'd hurriedly put a few bones together,

not even of the same animal, and buried them and stirred up all this business. So I'm not a great man for bones.[153]

* Then I woke up and realized that all my life I had been duped into taking evolutionism as revealed truth in some way.[154]

* Meanwhile, their [evolutionists] unproven theories will continue to be accepted by the learned and the illiterate alike as absolute truth, and will be defended with a fanatic intolerance that has a parallel only in the bigotry of the darkest Middle Ages. If one does not accept evolution as an infallible dogma, implicitly and without question, one is regarded as an unenlightened ignoramus or is merely ignored as an obscurantist or a naive, uncritical fundamentalist.[155]

* Philosophically, the dogma of evolution is a dream, a theory without a vestige of proof. Within fifty years, children in school will read of extraordinary popular delusions, and this will be mentioned as one of the most absurd. Many a merry jest will be uttered bearing upon the follies of nineteenth century science.[156]

* Scientists who go about teaching that evolution is a fact of life are great con-men, and the story they are telling may be the greatest hoax ever. In explaining evolution, we do not have one iota of fact.[157]

CHAPTER FOURTEEN

ADVOCATE CREATION

INTRODUCTION

Evolution is propagated as the only credible, proven, and scientific explanation for the existence of life. Yet the concept is indefensible, and it is the ground for serious scientific, behavioral, and spiritual dilemmas. All the while, the scientific evidence points directly toward intentional design and creation. The enormous complexities of the universe, and living creatures in particular, cannot be reasonably explained in any other way.

The Bible's account of creation is consistent with the observable facts of science. What's more, many other evidences point toward the reliability of the Bible's record, including historical events, miraculous events, prophecy fulfilled, individual lives transformed, and the extraordinary life of Jesus.

"Theistic evolution" is an attempt by some to try and blend together the Bible's creation account with the ideas of evolution. Some people welcome this approach as a way of conforming both to the mainstream scientific community and to their spiritual convictions. There exist, however, numerous problems with the entire concept of theistic evolution that make it both irreconcilable and impossible.

Emphasis upon the facts of creation engenders a sense of awe and respect for our self and for other human beings. Since we were indeed purposefully designed, each human literally "bears the mark of God." Just as we respect the possessions of a great person, how much more shall we respect the creations formed by the Creator of the entire universe? This justifiable perspective will inevitably result in higher value being placed upon each and every individual!

Once people understand the facts of creation, many will be prompted to seek out the Creator himself. Just who is He? What is His character? What does He have to say about us and the lives we lead? Since He is the originator of all that exists, surely He has the best possible advice to share!

CONCEPT 14-1: MANY REPUTABLE SCIENTISTS RECOGNIZE THAT LIFE AND THE UNIVERSE WERE INDEED CREATED.

RATIONALE

Creation is an absolute reality in the judgment of many scientists. Rejecting the entire notion of particles-to-people evolution, they are convinced that the orderly, highly complex universe can only be explained by intentional design and special creation.

Isaac Newton, like most early scientists, understood that the earth was created.

The originators of modern science — Newton, Boyle, Faraday, to name a few — were, almost without exception, Bible-believing creationists. They considered themselves to be "thinking God's thoughts after Him," to be discovering the physical laws that God created at the beginning of time. They viewed their professions as extremely high callings, as expressions of the personal faith in God that each of these founding scientists possessed.

Many of today's prominent researchers also uphold creation. In the midst of evolution-oriented scientific establishments, these men and women see intelligent design in our universe. They develop their unique fields of study, convinced while doing so there is a Creator behind it all.

EVIDENCE

* No teacher should be dismayed at efforts to present creation as an alternative to evolution in biology courses; indeed, at this moment creation is the only alternative to evolution. Not only is this worth mentioning, but a comparison of the two alternatives can be an excellent exercise in logic and reason. Our primary goals as educators should be to teach students to think, and such as comparison, particularly because it concerns an issue in which many have special interests or are even emotionally involved, may accomplish that purpose better than most others.[1]

* Origins survey published in *Industrial Chemist* . . . February 1988. . . . Most surprising to nearly everyone was the fact that 20.6 percent of the scientists responding completely reject evolution! The editors wrote, "Remember these respondents are scientists and do not represent a typical sample of the U.S. population." Further, the scientific community is quite split on the question of whether creationism is hurting scientific education. A surprising 37.9 percent don't think that creationism is hurting scientific education, while 46.7 percent think it is. Less than half the scientists polled believed that it is even possible for man to have evolved without supernatural intervention (48.3 percent)! A number of the scientists polled, 22.8 percent, believed that humans could only have evolved with supernatural intervention, while another 22.8 percent feel that human evolution is impossible under any circumstances.[2]

* However, Faraday's belief in an underlying unity is not so surprising. He was a devout member of the Sandemanian Church, a fundamentalist Christian order that demanded total faith and total commitment. Sandemanians organized their daily lives through their literal interpretation of the Bible. Both Faraday's father and grandfather had been Sandemanians and, when he married Sarah Bernard in 1821, he married into a leading Sandemanian family.

Faraday found no conflict between his religious beliefs and his activities as a scientist and philosopher. He viewed his discoveries of nature's laws as part of the continual process of "reading the book of nature," no different in principle from the process of reading the Bible to discover God's laws. A strong sense of the unity of God and nature pervaded Faraday's life and work.[3]

* But Faraday laid down the conceptual framework of modern physics, later to be expressed in elegant mathematical form by Maxwell and others. So let us respect his work and remember him, not only as an experimental physicist and chemist, but also as a philosopher and the grandfather of field theory.[4]

* The fact that so many of the founders of modern biology, those who discovered all the basic facts of comparative morphology upon which modern evolutionary biology is based, held nature to be fundamentally a discontinuum of isolated and unique types unbridged by transitional varieties. A position absolutely at odds with evolutionary ideas, is obviously very difficult to reconcile with the popular notion that all the facts of biology irrefutably support an evolutionary interpretation.[5]

* Indeed, the only competing explanation for the order we all see in the biological world, this pattern of nested similarity that links up absolutely all known forms of life, is the notion of special creation: that a supernatural Creator, using a sort of blueprint, simply fashioned life with its intricate skein of resemblances passing through it.

And, of course, it was precisely this notion of divine creation that furnished the explanation for all life — its very existence, its exuberant diversity and its apparent order — in Darwin's day.[6]

* Creation and evolution, between them, exhaust the possible explanations for the origin of living things. Organisms either appeared on the earth fully developed or they did not. If they did not, they must have developed from pre-existing species by some process of modification. If they did appear in a fully developed state, they must indeed have been created by some omnipotent intelligence.[7]

* Did the [DNA] code and the means of translating it appear simultaneously in evolution? It seems almost incredible that any such coincidence could have occurred, given the extraordinary complexities of both sides and the requirement that they be coordinated accurately for survival. By a pre-Darwinian (or a skeptic of evolution after Darwin) this puzzle would surely have been interpreted as the most powerful sort of evidence for special creation.[8]

* Once we see, however, that the probability of life originating at random is so utterly minuscule as to make it absurd, it becomes sensible to think that the favorable properties of physics, on which life depends, are in every respect deliberate. . . . It is, therefore, almost inevitable that our own measure of intelligence must reflect higher intelligence — even to the limit of God.[9]

* It is my conviction that if any professional biologist will take adequate time to examine carefully the assumptions upon which the macro-evolutionary doctrine rests, and the observational and laboratory evidence that bears on the problem of origins, he/she will conclude that there are substantial reasons for doubting the truth of this doctrine. Moreover, I believe that a scientifically sound creationist view of origins is not only possible, but is to be preferred over the evolutionary view.[10]

* I think that we must go further than this [natural selection and species evolution] and admit that the only acceptable explanation is creation.[11]

* We now know a great deal more about living matter than Darwin knew. We know how nerves work and I regard each nerve as a masterpiece of electrical engineering. And we have thousands of millions of them in our body. We know how the muscles expand and contract and we know how our hearts beat. But we do not yet know how we think. The brain has parts specifically designed for this purpose.
"Design" is the word that springs to mind, on this subject. My biologist colleagues do not like it. They say that I should not object to a theory unless I have a better scientific one to replace it, a scientific one being a theory that can be falsified. My unscientific theory is that we have been designed in a macromutational way by an external creator. All the evidence supports this view but, of course, it cannot be sustained scientifically.[12]

* The sect sought to follow the teaching of the Bible, interpreted with a simple literalism and used as the sole guide.[13]

* Almost all the great figures of British physical science in the 19th century, such as Clerk Maxwell, Kelvin, and Stokes, were men of deep religious conviction. They seemed untroubled by the evolutionary storms that raged around them.[14]

* Faraday was a man of modesty and integrity, a scientist of great distinction and a religious believer of deep conviction and surprising simple-mindedness.[15]

* I doubt if there is any single individual within the scientific community who could cope with the full range of [creationist] arguments without the help of an army of consultants in special fields.[16]

* The world is too complicated in all its parts and interconnections to be due to chance alone. I am convinced that the existence of life with all its order in each of its organisms is simply too well put together. Each part of a living thing depends on all its other parts to function. How does each part know? How is each part specified at conception? The more one learns of biochemistry the more unbelievable it becomes unless there is some type of organizing principle — an architect.[17]

* Since the 1960s "scientific creationism" or "creation science" has mushroomed in the U.S. Instead of relying on the Bible, scientific creationists cite geological and other physical evidence as the basis for their views. Spear-heading this approach is the Institute for Creation Research, an organization in El Cajon, California, staffed by card-carrying Ph.D's such as Steve Austin, who insists that geological data reveal that life on Earth came into being just three or four thousand years ago.[18]

Many well-known scientists uphold creation as the only logical, believable explanation for the universe and for life. For the more famous figures, please see the following two books: *21 Great Scientists Who Believed the Bible* by A. Lamont and *Men of Science, Men of God* by Henry Morris.

CONCEPT 14-2: THE BIBLE'S EXPLANATION OF HISTORY IS CREDIBLE.

RATIONALE

The great majority of objective evidence from many sources, including astronomy, physics, and biosciences, points toward intentional design. But just who is the Designer, the Creator? The Genesis account remains the single most clear and reputable report of special creation. When considering all the information available — the varieties of life, layout of the universe, dating methods, archaeological evidence, and demographic findings — many scientists conclude there is no conflict with the Genesis account. The Bible's explanation of history is consistent with objective scientific evidence.

The Bible makes clear the identity of the Creator. With power and intelligence beyond imagination, He conceived and formed the cosmos. He designed the cells and their DNA, planned the organ systems, and produced the first of each species of living being. John refers to Him as the "Word" in this introduction to his letter:

> In the beginning was the Word, and the Word was with God, and the Word was God. He was with God in the beginning. Through him all things were made; without him nothing was made that has been made (John 1:1–3).

Jesus and God are one and the same, and the Creator of all that exists. Later in the New Testament, Paul further describes Jesus' role in creation:

> For by him all things were created: things in heaven and things on earth, visible and invisible, whether thrones or powers or rulers or authorities; all things were created by him and for him. He is before all things and in him all things hold together (Col. 1:16–17).

Genesis contains an outline of the events surrounding creation and the first years on earth. While Genesis does not answer every question about the details of those events, it does give us a basic knowledge of our origins, and a glimpse into the incredible nature of God.

EVIDENCE

* A.G.W. Cameron, a Goddard Institute lecturer and professor at Yeshiva University in New York, suggests that the creation of the solar system might have occurred in a matter of a few thousand years. Indeed, he suggests, it might have taken place so rapidly that the earth and some of the planets could have formed shortly before the sun did — which, in view of traditional thought, is a revolutionary proposal.[19]

* Until now, comparative linguistics revolved around studying corresponding use of sounds in a few languages at a time. This approach traces language roots back some 8,000 years at most.[20]

* For myself, faith begins with a realization that a supreme intelligence brought the universe into being and created man. It is not difficult for me to have this faith, for it is incontrovertible

that where there is a plan, there is intelligence — an orderly, unfolding universe testifies to the truth of the most majestic statement ever uttered — "in the beginning God."[21]

* I suspect . . . that the sun is 4.5 billion years old. However . . . I suspect that we could live with Bishop Ussher's value for the age of the earth and sun [about 5,000 years based upon history as recorded in the Bible]. I don't think we have much in the way of observational evidence in astronomy to conflict with that.[22]

* The American public is almost entirely divided between those who believe that God created man in his present form at one time in the last 10,000 years and those who believe in evolution or an evolutionary process involving God.[23]

* Of the participants in the poll, 44 percent, nearly a quarter of whom were college graduates, said they accepted the statement that "God created man pretty much in his present form at one time within the last 10,000 years."[24]

* Nine percent agreed with the statement: "Man has developed over millions of years from less advanced forms of life. God had no part in this process." Thirty-eight percent said they agreed with the suggestion that "man has developed over millions of years from less-advanced forms of life, but God guided this process, including man's creation." Nine percent of those interviewed simply said they did not know.[25]

* As a matter of fact, however, it may be stated categorically that no archaeological discovery has ever controverted a biblical reference. Scores of archaeological findings have been made which confirm in clear outline or in exact detail historical statements in the Bible. And, by the same token, proper evaluation of biblical descriptions has often led to amazing discoveries. They form tesserae in the vast mosaic of the Bible's almost incredibly correct historical memory.[26]

* Ussher represented the best scholarship in his time. He was part of a substantial research tradition, a large community of intellectuals working toward a common goal under an acceptable methodology.

Moreover, within assumptions of the methodology, this research tradition had considerable success. Even the extreme values were not very discordant, ranging from a minimum, for the creation of the earth, of 3761 B.C. in the Jewish calendar (still in use) to a maximum of just over 5500 B.C. for the Septuagint. Most calculators had reached a figure very close to Ussher's 4004. The Venerable Bede had estimated 3952 B.C., several centuries before, while J.J. Scaliger, the greatest scholar of the generation just before Ussher, had placed creation at 3950 B.C. Thus, Ussher's 4004 was neither idiosyncratic nor at all unusual; it was, in fact, a fairly conventional estimate developed within a large and active community of scholars.

James Barr explains the problems and complexities in an excellent article, "Why the World was Created in 4004 B.C.: Archbishop Ussher and Biblical Chronology."[27]

* Most remarkable of all is the fact that in science, as in the Bible, the world begins with an act of creation. That view has not always been held by scientists. Only as a result of the most recent discoveries can we say with a fair degree of confidence that the world has not existed forever, that it began abruptly, without apparent cause, in a blinking event that defies scientific explanation. Now we see how the astronomical evidence leads to a biblical view of the origin of the world. The details differ but the essential elements in the astronomical evidence and the biblical account of Genesis are the same.

The chain of events leading to man began suddenly and sharply, in a definite amount of time — in a flash of light and energy. The astronomers are so embarrassed by this that for the scientist who has lived by his faith in the power of reason, the story ends like a bad dream. He has scaled the mountain of ignorance, he is about to conquer the highest peak when he finds himself face-to-face with a group of theologians who have been there for centuries![28]

* There are a number of indicators that seem to indicate an age of no more than 10,000 years, at the very most, for the solar system and the earth.[29]

* Indeed, the Judeo-Christian tradition describes the beginning of the world in a way that is surprisingly similar to the scientific model. Previously it seemed scientifically unsound to have light created before the sun. The present scientific view does indeed assume the early universe to be filled with various kinds of radiation long before the sun was created. The Bible

says about the beginning: "And God said, Let there be light, and there was light. And God saw the light, that it was good."[30]

* A 1991 Gallup Poll showed that fully 47 percent of Americans, including a quarter of college graduates, continued to believe that "God created man pretty much in his present form at one time within the last 10,000 years."[31]

CONCEPT 14-3: "THEISTIC EVOLUTION" IS ERRONEOUS.

RATIONALE

Not all evolutionists are atheists or humanists. Some of them hold sincere, Bible-oriented convictions. For them, "theistic evolution" is a popular attempt to find a compromise between evolution and the Bible's creation account. Promoted among some religious leaders and misguided Christians, theistic evolution attempts to sanitize evolution by asserting that both are compatible — that there exists a middle ground between the "evolutionary facts" and "spiritual" convictions.

Theistic evolution has various forms, but they all contain the same message: God was indeed the creator, but that He did so through the means of evolution. However attractive this concept may seem on the surface, there exist numerous irreconcilable problems with the entire notion of theistic evolution:

- Evolution itself remains wholly unjustified as a scientific theory. Instead, the evidence indicates supernatural design and intentional creation.
- Accidental mutation and survival of the fittest through competition (essential tenets of evolution) are ideas completely foreign to the Bible's description of God as being personal and nurturing.
- Evolution's proposed scenario for the development of life is grossly inconsistent to that documented in the Book of Genesis.

One major point of contention is the meaning of the word "day." Theistic evolution commonly claims that the six "days" of creation were actually six "ages" or very long periods of time that would be essential for evolution to occur.

How long is an actual "day" in Genesis? The word "day" is translated from the Hebrew world *yom*. Careful analysis of the Bible's use of this word shows that, when combined with a number (such as "first day" or "second day"), *yom* always refers to a normal-duration day; never to an age, era, or any other lengthy period of time. The "day" referred to in Genesis was no longer or shorter than any other day since. Mention of the "morning" and "evening" of these first days (see Gen. 1:5, 8, 17, 19, 23, 31) is additional evidence that *yom* was used to mean a normal-length day.

The plural word "days" is translated from the Hebrew word *yamim*, plural for *yom*. The use of *yamim* always refers to literal, normal-length days. For example, when clarifying the commandment to observe the Sabbath (the day of rest), Moses mentions the literal days of creation:

> For in six days [*yamim*] the LORD made the heavens and the earth, the sea and all that is in them, and rested on the seventh day [*yom*]; therefore the LORD blessed the Sabbath day [*yom*] and made it holy (Exod. 20:11; NASB).

Beyond the word definition discrepancies, interpreting "days" as "long periods of time" causes other irresolvable problems. Genesis explains, for example, that on the third day God created plants. Genesis explains that the sun was not created until the fourth day. Now, if a day was actually a "long period of time" (hundreds of millions of years in the evolution scenario) how did these new plants possibly exist without sunlight to sustain photosynthesis?

Another irresolvable conflict between Genesis and evolution: Plants require carbon dioxide to sustain their metabolism. Yet animals, the sole producers of carbon dioxide, were not created until the fifth day. And, how did all the flowers, created on the third day, pollinate without the role of insects and birds, created on the fifth day?

It is simply impossible to find a compromise that remains faithful to both the accounts of Genesis and of evolution. Beyond the technical problems, evolution is by definition an atheistic process, one beyond the input or control of God. A God who "created" by evolution is, for all practical purposes, indistinguishable from no God at all. This stands in stark contrast with the God of the Bible, who expresses His power and character through the very objects of creation, and who is clearly intent and active in the lives of His people.

God can do anything. It goes with the job description. He could have created the universe and life over five seconds or five trillion years. If we are going to be consistent with the Bible's record, creation was completed in six normal-length days, not ages, or any other vast time periods, and God created living beings in their fully developed, modern forms, not through any means of transition forms or evolution. While trying to please both camps, many people compromise both their "science" and their "faith." The result can only be a wholly incompatible version of the two.

EVIDENCE

* Probably, so far as I know, there is no professor of Hebrew or Old Testament at any world-class university who does not believe that the writer(s) of Gen. 1–11 intended to convey to their readers the ideas that (a) creation took place in a series of six days which were the same as the days of 24 hours we now experience, (b) the figures contained in the Genesis genealogies provided by simple addition a chronology from the beginning of the world up to later stages in the biblical story, (c) Noah's flood was understood to be worldwide and extinguish all human and animal life except for those in the ark. Or, to put it negatively, the apologetic arguments which suppose the "days" of creation to be long eras of time, the figures of years not to be chronological, and the flood to be a merely local Mesopotamian flood, are not taken seriously by any such professors, as far as I know.[32]

* The Hebrew word *yom* and its plural form *yamim*, are used over 1,900 times in the Old Testament. . . . Outside of the Genesis 1 case in question, the two-hundred-plus occurrences of *yom* preceded by ordinals all refer to a normal twenty-four-hour day. Furthermore, the seven-hundred-plus appearances of *yamim* always refer to a regular day. Thus, it is argued [by young-earth creationists] that the Exodus 20:11 reference to the six "yamim" of creation must also refer to six regular days.

These arguments have a common fallacy, however. There is no other place in the Old Testament where the intent is to describe events that involve multiple and/or sequential, indefinite periods of time.[33]

* Darwin was well aware that a satisfactory explanation for the origin of life was of crucial importance to his theory. Undoubtedly he recognized that this was the weakest link in his theory. On the other hand, his early opponents, rather than accept defeat, found that here was a position whereby they might compromise with evolution. They argued that if God created the first living cell to contain the instructions for evolution, then the Christian need not surrender his faith. The Genesis account of creation could be believed by interpreting

the days to be eons of time. Darwin, in fact, had himself real-ized that this might be a subtle way of getting acceptance for his theory. Thus, we find in the early editions of *Origin of Species* the concluding paragraph: "There is grandeur in this view of life, with its several powers, having been originally breathed by the Creator into a few forms or into one."

Darwin's dishonesty is apparent. He had long been an athe-ist and had inserted the above paragraph to lessen the tumult he knew his book would create. He no more believed in a Creator than he did in a flat earth.[34]

* As far as Christianity was concerned, the advent of the theory of evolution and the elimination of traditional theo-logical thinking was catastrophic. The suggestion that life and man are the result of chance is incompatible with the biblical assertion of their being the direct result of intelligent creative activity.

Despite the attempt by liberal theology to disguise the point, the fact is that no biblically derived religion can really be compromised with the fundamental assertion of Darwin-ian theory. Chance and design are antithetical concepts, and the decline in religious belief can probably be attributed more to the propagation and advocacy by the intellectual and scien-tific community of the Darwinian version of evolution than to any other single factor.[35]

* It is incumbent on the theologian proposing the exist-ence of souls to explain how they may have evolved. For more fundamentalist types who do not believe in evolution, this is not a problem. But for the majority of clergy who accept sci-entific discoveries, including evolution, there are serious in-consistencies to be explained. Few people bother to think about these matters, but the inquiring mind cannot ignore the in-compatibilities implicit in considering the phylogeny of the soul. Indeed, this is the main reason why religion and evolu-tion cannot be reconciled, even by those religious liberals who would have us believe that evolution was itself part of the di-vine handiwork of the creator.[36]

* In the context of this standard position, I was enormously puzzled by a statement issued by Pope John Paul II on Octo-ber 22, 1996, to the Pontifical Academy of Sciences, the same body that had sponsored my earlier trip to the Vatican. In this document, entitled "Truth Cannot Contradict Truth," the pope defended both the evidence for evolution and the consistency of the theory with Catholic religious doctrine.[37]

* The Catholic Church had never opposed evolution and had no reason to do so. Why had the pope issued such a statement at all? And why had the press responded with an orgy of worldwide, front-page coverage?[38]

* Whatever the god implied by evolutionary theory and the data of natural history may be like, he is not the protestant God of waste not, want not. He is also not a loving God who cares about his productions. He is not even the awful God portrayed in the Book of Job. The god of Galápagos is careless, wasteful, indifferent, almost diabolical. He is certainly not the sort of god to whom anyone would be inclined to pray.[39]

* Meantime let me say that the conclusion I have come to is this: the law of Christ is incompatible with the law of evolution . . . as far as the law of evolution has worked hitherto. Nay, the two laws are at war with each other; the law of Christ can never prevail until the law of evolution is destroyed.[40]

* If we believe in a Creator, it is basically for moral reasons, in order to see a goal for our own lives. And why would God have to have chosen this extremely complex and difficult mechanism? When, I would say by definition, He was at liberty to choose other mechanisms, why would He have to start with simple molecules? Why not create man right away, as of course classical religions believed.

[Natural] selection is the blindest and most cruel way of evolving new species, and more and more complex and refined organisms. . . . The struggle for life and elimination of the weakest is a horrible process, against which our whole modern ethics revolts. An ideal society is a non-selective society, one where the weak is protected; which is exactly the reverse of the so-called natural law. I am surprised that a Christian would defend the idea that this is the process which God more or less set up in order to have evolution.[41]

* God can do anything, including creation of life and the universe in an instant if so desired. If we are going to be consistent with the Bible's record, creation was completed in six, normal-length days — not ages, or any other vast time periods.[42]

* A widespread theological view now exists saying that God started off the world, props it up and works through laws of nature, very subtly, so subtly that its action is undetectable. But that kind of god is effectively no different to my mind than atheism. To anyone who adopts this view I say, "Great, we're in the same camp; now where do we get our morals if the universe just goes grinding on as it does?" This kind of god does nothing outside of the laws of nature, gives us no immortality, no foundation for morals, or any of the things that we want from a god and from religion.[43]

* The implications of modern science, however, are clearly inconsistent with most religious traditions. No purposive principles exist in nature. Organic evolution has occurred by various combinations of random genetic drift, natural selection, Mendelian heredity, and many other purposeless mechanisms. Humans are complex organic machines that die completely with no survival of soul or psyche.[44]

* No inherent moral or ethical laws exist, nor are there absolute guiding principles for human society. The universe cares nothing for us and we have no ultimate meaning in life.[45]

* Of course, it is still possible to believe in both modern evolutionary biology and a purposive force, even the Judeo-Christian God. One can suppose that God started the whole universe or works through the laws of nature (or both). There is no contradiction between this or similar views of God and natural selection. But this view of God is also worthless. . . . [Such a God] has nothing to do with human morals, answers no prayers, gives no life everlasting, in fact does nothing whatsoever that is detectable. In other words, religion is compatible with modern evolutionary biology (and, indeed, all of modern science) if the religion is effectively indistinguishable from atheism.[46]

* Suppose God is somehow involved in the process that evolutionary biologists since Darwin have been describing. This would mean that He has created a situation in which His own involvement is so totally hidden that the process gives every appearance of operating without any guiding hand at all. In other words, He has created a situation in which it is reasonable for us to believe that He is not involved. But if it is

reasonable for us to believe that, then it is reasonable for us to reject the theistic interpretation.[47]

* Trying to reconcile evolution and religion leads to doublethink. Orwell defined doublethink as "the power of holding two contradictory beliefs in one's mind simultaneously, and accepting both of them.[48]

* We have failed to find a single example of the use of the word "day" in the entire Scripture where it means other than a period of twenty-four hours when modified by the use of the numerical adjective.[49]

CONCEPT 14-4: ADVOCATING CREATION FOSTERS RESPECT FOR HUMAN LIFE.

RATIONALE

The knowledge that we ourselves were intricately designed and intentionally created is a cornerstone of self-respect. This truth is also a foundation for humane interaction with one another. Never competitors in the struggle for survival — accidental mutants obstructing each other's personal advance — we are in reality a family of precious, awe-inspiring beings.

The concept of evolution clearly undermines the value of self-respect, and respect toward others. It is a central principle of most every anti-human philosophy and social force, including racism, fascism, and germicide. But wherever people recognize the truth about creation, and especially when they also embrace the Creator, integrity, altruism, philanthropy, and goodwill can truly flourish toward one another.

EVIDENCE

* The nonscientific influence was the Holocaust. The military collapse of Germany and the unveiling of the death camps prompted a universal revulsion of the intelligentsia against the intellectual traditions that had contributed to Nazi ideology, foremost among them the notion of a hierarchical subordination of human populations. That notion, which had underlain most earlier thinking about human evolution, was extirpated from anthropological thought after World War II and replaced with a firm faith in the unity, continuity, and equality of the Family of Man.[50]

* At age 79, Sir John Eccles . . . has declared war on the past 300 years of scientific speculation about man's nature.

Winner of the 1963 Nobel Prize in Physiology or Medicine for his pioneering research on the synapse (the point at which nerve cells communicate with each other), Eccles strongly defends the ancient religious belief that human beings consist of a mysterious compound of physical matter and intangible spirit.[51]

* Eccles drives home his controversial conclusion: "If I say that the uniqueness of the human self is not derived from the genetic code, not derived from experience, then what is it derived from? My answer is this: from a divine creation. Each self is a divine creation."[52]

* Christianity makes no distinction of race or of color; it seeks to break down all racial barriers. In this respect, the hand of Christianity is against that of Nature, for are not the races of mankind the evolutionary harvest which Nature has toiled through long ages to produce? May we not say, then, that Christianity is anti-evolutionary in its aim? This may be a merit, but if so it is one which has not been openly acknowledged by Christian philosophers.[53]

* But I would guess that 95 percent of the social scientists in America's elite universities — or could it be 99 percent? — would not sign the Declaration of Independence if they were honest about it. They simply do not believe in the first paragraph. They do not believe that rights come from any Creator. And thus, they cannot believe in the fundamental tenet of American democracy: majority rule with minority rights. Because unless rights come from a higher authority, one with the capability to endow rights unconditionally, the majority can always attach conditions to rights or deny them to whichever minority group it chooses to victimize.[54]

* The vertical harmony between man and God is also the prelude to and necessary condition for the horizontal peace between men. A man who is still at war within himself is not likely to make true peace with his neighbor.[55]

* I don't claim that Darwin and his theory of evolution brought on the Holocaust; but I cannot deny that the theory of evolution, and the atheism it engendered, led to the moral climate that made a holocaust possible.

But there is another, equally sinister, side to this argument.

Consider, if life has evolved, by chance alone, then no creature is qualitatively different from any other. If it is morally reprehensible to kill a man, then it is equally odious to kill our "brother" the chimpanzee. By the same token, how can we kill cows for food, or dogs or mice for research? And mosquitoes? Well, let's not carry things too far.

The Torah teaches us a different approach. . . . Man was also given dominion over all animals on land, sea, and air, as well as a moral code to live by. Therefore, he cannot be compared to animals and treated as such, nor can the animals be compared to man and accorded his rights.[56]

* So the abortion debate has its roots in two alternative ways of imaging the unborn. Our civilization, until recently, agreed in imagining the unborn child on the pattern of the Incarnation, which maximizes his dignity; but many people now imagine him on the pattern of evolution, as popularly understood, which minimizes his dignity.[57]

* My guess is that the popular theory of evolution appeals precisely as an alternative to the Christian view of man, which not only demands faith but imposes moral obligations. People who adopt evolutionism are not driven to it by consideration of the evidence; they like it without respect to the evidence, because they are passionate creatures, and it offers no moral impediment to their passions.[58]

CONCEPT 14-5: ADVOCATING CREATION FOSTERS RELATIONSHIP WITH GOD.

RATIONALE

The truth of creation impacts upon our self-image and upon the insight with which we view one another. But the influence can be even more profound. Considering the evidence, many people become determined to seek out the Creator himself. What is His character? What does He value? What does the Creator have to say about us? As the originator of all that exists, surely He has some great advice!

Simply observing the world can give you and me greater insight into the awesome nature of God. When we stand on a mountain top, gaze at a roaring river, watch animals in nature, or look at night deep into outer space we gain an appreciation of the immenseness, intelligence, and power of God. We can experience some of the sentiments of King David when he wrote:

The heavens declare the glory of God: the skies proclaim the work of his hands (Ps. 19:1),

and

How many are your works, O Lord! In wisdom you made them all; the earth is full of your creatures (Ps. 104:24).

Clearly, advocating creation aids people's appreciation for the character of God. Advocating creation is also essential to fostering personal relationships with Him. The core message of the Bible is that God cares and desires to reach out, forgive, and empower His people. But if our world does not even recognize it was created — let alone created by God — then the message of the Bible becomes abstract and more difficult to appreciate.

Ours is a secular culture, indoctrinated with naturalism and other godless philosophies. When sharing the message of the Bible with secular people, we dare not assume that they understand, let alone trust in, the facts of creation or the person of God. For these reasons, advocating creation is an essential component of sharing the message in our culture today.

EVIDENCE

* And He made from one, every nation of mankind to live on all the face of the earth, having determined their appointed times, and the boundaries of their habitatation, that they should seek God, if perhaps they might grope for Him and find Him, though He is not far from each one of us (Acts 17:26–27; NASB).

* The countries of the Far East and of the Southern Hemisphere want our science and technology, but they have no doctrine of creation. They do not realize that science and technology rest upon, indeed arise from, Christian foundations. This is true both historically and epistemologically. We must show them that it is the Creator God himself who stands behind everything, and that He provides the rational ground upon which the various sciences rest, as well as the world those sciences unlock and help to tame.[59]

* What most distinguishes the Declaration of Independence from the Communist Manifesto is that the former affirms, while the latter denies . . . the power of reason to apprehend trans-historical truths or "the laws of nature and of nature's God."[60]

* This freedom of the intellect is itself a part of the laws of nature and of nature's God, or say of creation; which means that these laws are constitutive of man's very being; they distinguish human from sub-human creation.[61]

* Hence each individual belongs to himself (ultimately to his Creator). He is a center of purposes and cannot be used as a mere means for a purpose. In other words, he cannot be used as if he were an inferior species. . . . He is the creature of God, not of society or of men.[62]

* The doctrine of creation, in general and in all its detail, is intimately bound up with the mystery of salvation. That is why no Catholic may call into question any aspect of the doctrine of creation which in fact the Church believes related to the mystery of salvation without also doubting that latter mystery.[63]

* 1) The whole world was created by God ex nihilo in the beginning of time.

2) The essential structure or order of the world presupposed for any subsequent activity or development was established by God and admits of no exceptions, except those directly produced by divine intervention.

3) The first man and first woman were made directly by God, by forming the male body out of pre-existing matter, the female body out of the body of the first man, by creating out of nothing a soul for each and then uniting soul to body as its form.[64]

* Sin is the expression of man's struggle with the meaning of his existence while missing life from God. It is all the varieties of ways man deals with and expresses his alienation from his Creator.[65]

* The problem is that, by denying the possibility of a relationship between God and man, atheism also denies the possibility of a just relationship between men. . . . Human life is sacred only if there is a God to sanctify it. Otherwise, man is just another collection of atoms and can be treated as such.[66]

* For since the creation of the world God's invisible qualities — his eternal power and divine nature — have been clearly seen, being understood from what has been made, so that men are without excuse. For although they know God, they neither glorified him as God nor gave thanks to him, but their thinking became futile and their foolish hearts were darkened. Although they claimed to be wise, they became fools. . . . They exchanged the truth of God for a lie, and worshipped and served created things rather than the Creator — who is for ever praised. Amen (Rom. 1:20–25).

CONCEPT 14-6: RECOGNIZED LEADERS ADVOCATE CREATION.

RATIONALE

It is well recognized that the great majority of America's founders were Bible-believing, creation-advocating Christians. They held human dignity in high regard, and recognized this virtue as a commandment from God himself. The preamble of the Declaration of Independence is filled with references to God the Creator, and the innate character He has bestowed upon human beings.

In just two hundred years the Christian beliefs and Bible-based philosophy of our nation's leaders has eroded enormously. The concept of evolution, with its accompanying philosophies of naturalism, humanism, and occultism, is largely to blame for this disastrous shift in values. That our nation must concern itself with enormous problems of immorality is no surprise, given the selfish, survival-of-the-fittest philosophy that dominates our nation.

Yet the counter-culture, creation-advocating voices of some leaders continue to be heard. We must listen to them carefully; not simply for the sake of history or our "Christian heritage," but because these are voices of truth. They invite our people back to their senses, back to the evidence, back to creation, back to God.

EVIDENCE

* No sooner had the great Creator of the heavens and the earth finished His almighty work, and pronounced all very good, but He set apart (not an anniversary, or one day in a year, but) one day in seven, for the commemoration of His inimitable power in producing all things out of nothing.[67]

* Here is my creed. I believe in one God, the Creator of the universe. That He governs it by His Providence. That He ought to be worshiped. That the most acceptable Service we render to Him is in doing good to His other Children. That the soul of Man is immortal, and will be treated with Justice in another Life respecting its conduct in this. These I take to be the fundamental principles in all sound religion.[68]

* The attitudes of college students — even those taking basic science courses — differ from those of the general public when it comes to the controversy over evolution versus creation science. This was one of the conclusions surprising researchers who conducted a year-long survey of nearly 2,400 students at Ohio State University.[69]

* 1. "Do you believe in Darwin's theory of evolution?" 63% Yes.

2. "If Darwin's theory of evolution is taught in public schools, should other views (including the divine origin of life through special creation) be taught too?" 80% Yes.[70]

* We hold these truths to be self-evident: that all men are created equal, that they are endowed by their Creator with certain inalienable rights, among these are life, liberty, and the pursuit of happiness, that to secure these rights governments are instituted among men.

Almighty God hath created the mind free. All attempts to influence it by temporal punishments or burdens . . . are a departure from the plan of the Holy Author of our religion. . . .

God who gave us life gave us liberty. Can the liberties of a nation be secure when we have removed a conviction that these liberties are the gift of God? Indeed I tremble for my country when I reflect that God is just, that his justice cannot sleep forever.[71]

Meantime, let me say that the conclusion I have come to is this: the law of Christ is incompatible with the law of evolution — as far as the law of evolution has worked hitherto. Nay, the two laws are at war with each other; the law of Christ can never prevail until the law of evolution is destroyed.[72]

* I wish I were younger. What inclines me now to think you may be right in regarding [evolution] as the central and radical lie in the whole web of falsehood that now governs our lives is not so much your arguments against it as the fanatical and twisted attitudes of its defenders.[73]

* Cheer Number One goes to the creationists for serving rational religion by demonstrating beautifully that we must take the creation stories of Genesis at face value. . . . Creationists list twenty or more contradictions that arise between sci-

ence and Scripture if the days are taken as geological eras instead of ordinary days.[74]

* Many Christians have taken the dishonest way of lengthening the days into millions of years, but the creationists make it clear that such an approach is nothing but a makeshift that is unacceptable biblically and scientifically.[75]

* And the creationists have also shown irrefutably that those liberal and neo-orthodox Christians who regard the creation stories as myths or allegories are undermining the rest of Scripture, for if there was no Adam, there was no fall; and if there was no fall there was no hell; and if there was no hell, there was no need of Jesus as Second Adam and Incarnate Savior, crucified and risen. As a result, the whole biblical system of salvation collapses.[76]

* Evolution thus becomes the most potent weapon for destroying the Christian faith.[77]

* Creationists deserve Cheer Number Two for serving rational religion by effectively eliminating the idea of "theistic evolution. . . ." Creationists rightly insist that evolution is inconsistent with a God of love.[78]

* Three cheers then, for the creationists, for they have cleared the air of all dodges, escapes, and evasions made by Christians who adopt nonliteral interpretations of Genesis and who hold that evolution is God's method of creation.[79]

* The American nation had been founded by intellectuals who had accepted a world view that was based upon biblical authority as well as Newtonian science. They had assumed that God created the earth and all upon it at the time of creation and had continued without change thereafter.[80]

* I've always believed that we were, each of us, put here for a reason. That there is a plan, somehow, a divine plan for all of us. I know now that whatever days are left of me belong to Him.

I also believe this blessed land was set apart in a very special way. A country created by men and women who came here not in search of gold, but in search of God. They would be free people, living under the law with faith in their Maker and their future. Sometimes, it seems we've strayed from that noble beginning, from our conviction that standards of right and wrong do exist and must be lived up to. God, the source of our knowledge, has been expelled from the classroom. He gives us His greatest blessing: life, and yet many would condone the taking of innocent life. We expect Him to protect us in a crisis, but turn away from Him too often in our day-to-day living. And I wonder if He isn't waiting for us to wake up.[81]

* Philosophically, the dogma of evolution is a dream, a theory without a vestige of proof. Within fifty years, children in school will read of extraordinary popular delusions, and this will be mentioned as one of the most absurd. Many a merry jest will be uttered bearing upon the follies of nineteenth century science.[82]

* It is impossible to account for the creation of the universe, without the agency of a Supreme Being.

It is impossible to govern the universe without the aid of a Supreme Being. It is impossible to reason without arriving at a Supreme Being. Religion is as necessary to reason, as reason is to religion. The one cannot exist without the other. A reasoning being would lose his reason, in attempting to account for the great phenomena of nature, had he not a Supreme Being to refer to; and well has it been said, that if there had been no God, mankind would have been obliged to imagine one.[83]

MORE RESOURCES

Vast quantities of new information are generated each year on the subjects of origins, creation, and evolution. Keeping up to date is now possible, thanks to the work of several quality organizations. For the latest information, please visit these organizations' websites. Most have search features that allow instant access to the most useful resources.

Answers In Genesis
http://www.answersingenesis.org/

Center For Scientific Creation
http://www.creationscience.com/

Creation Research Society
http://www.creationresearch.org/

Creation Research Science Education Foundation
http://www.worldbydesign.org/

Creation Science Movement
http://www.creationsciencemovement.com/

Creation Science Research Center
http://www.parentcompany.com/csrc/

Creation Super Library
http://www.christiananswers.net/creation/home.html

Creationism.org
http://www.creationism.org/

Institute for Creation Research
http://www.icr.org/

Revolution Against Evolution
http://www.rae.org/

Young Earth Creation Club
http://www.creationists.org/

Helping people recognize the truth about creation and the Creator calls for persistent teamwork. Please feel free to contact the author with comments or suggestions at: www.creativeenergy.org.

280 · CREATIVE DEFENSE

ENDNOTES

Chapter 2

1 Douglas J. Futuyma, *Science on Trial* (New York, NY: Pantheon Books, 1983), p. 197.
2 George Sim Johnston, "The Genesis Controversy," *Crisis* (May 1989): p. 17.
3 Davis A. Young, *Christianity and the Age of the Earth* (Grand Rapids, MI: Zondervan, 1982), p. 25.
4 John F. Schroeder, editor, *Maxims of Washington* (Mt. Vernon, VA: Mt. Vernon Ladies Association, 1942), p. 275.
5 Charles Darwin, *The Origin of Species* (London: A.L. Burt, 1859).

Chapter 3

1 Ernest L. Abel, *Ancient Views on the Origin of Life* (Rutherford, NJ: Dickinson University Press, 1973), p. 15.
2 Michael Denton, *Evolution: A Theory in Crisis* (London: Burnett Books, Ltd., 1985), p. 37.
3 Henry Fairfield Osborn, *From the Greeks to Darwin* (New York, NY: Charles Scribner's Sons, 1929), p. 48.
4 Stanley D. Beck, "Natural Science and Creationist Theology," *Bioscience*, vol. 32 (October 1982): p. 738–742. Beck was in the department of entomology, Wisconsin University; Sigma Xi lecture at Virginia Tech.
5 Rene Dubos, "Humanistic Biology," *American Scientist*, 53 (March 1965): p. 6.

Chapter 4

1 Anonymous, "The Battery-operated Duck-Billed Platypus," *New Scientist*, vol. 109 (February 13, 1986): p. 25.
2 Isaac Asimov, "In the Game of Energy and Thermodynamics You Can't Even Break Even," *Smithsonian Institute Journal* (June 1970): p. 10.
3 Regina Avraham, *The Circulatory System* (New York, NY: Chelsea House, 1989), p. 41.
4 George F. Cahill, *Science Digest* (1981): 89[3]:105.
5 William Beck, *Human Design* (New York, NY: Harcourt, Brace, Jovanovich, 1971), p. 189.
6 Richard Dawkins, *The Blind Watchmaker* (New York, NY: W.W. Norton, 1986), p. 115.
7 Paul C. Davies, "The Creative Cosmos," *New Scientist*, vol. 116 (December 17, 1987): p. 42.
8 Fritjof Capra, *The Web of Life* (New York, NY: Anchor Books, 1996), p. 82. Dr. Capra is director of the Center for Ecoliteracy in Berkeley, California, and is one of the most influential "New-Age" scientists.
9 Michael Denton, *Evolution: A Theory in Crisis* (Chevy Chase, MD: Adler and Adler Publishers, Inc., 1986), p. 328–330, 334, 342. Michael Denton is a molecular biologist.
10 W. Gitt, "Dazzling Design in Miniature," *Creation Ex Nihilo*, 20(l):6 (December 1997–February 1998).
11 D.T. Gish, *Evolution: The Fossils Say No* (El Cajon, CA: Institute for Creation Research, 1995), p. 312.
12 Stephen Jay Gould, "Through a Lens, Darkly," *Natural History* (September 1989): p. 24.
13 Alma E. Guinness, *ABC's of the Human Body* (Pleasantville, NY: Reader's Digest Association, 1987), p. 196, 208.
14 R. Howlett, "Flipper's Secret," *New Scientist*, 154 (2088): 34-39 (June 28, 1997).
15 J.A. Miller, "Sensory Surprises in Platypus, Mantis," *Science News*, vol. 129 (February 15, 1986): p. 104.
16 Leslie Orgel, "Darwinism at the Very Beginning of Life," *New Scientist*, vol. 94 (April 15, 1982): p. 151.

17 Llya Prigogine, "Can Thermodynamics Explain Biological Order?" *Impact of Science on Society,* vol. 23, no. 3 (1973): p. 178.

18 Carl Sagan, *Broca's Brain* (New York, NY: Random House, 1979), p. 275.

19 Carl Sagan, *Encyclopedia Britannica* (1974), 10:894.

20 Lewis Thomas, M.D., "On Science and Uncertainty," *Discover*, vol. 1 (October 1980): p. 59. Dr. Thomas was chancellor, Memorial Sloan Kettering Cancer Center, Manhattan.

21 Bert Thompson, *Creation Compromises* (Montgomery, AL: Apologetics Press, Inc., 1995), p. 25, 35, 40.

22 Robin J. Wooton, "The Mechanical Design of Insect Wings," *Scientific American*, vol. 263 (November 1990): p. 114.

23 Michael Behe, *Darwin's Black Box: The Biochemical Challenge to Evolution* (New York, NY: The Free Press, 1996).

24 Michael Denton, *Evolution: A Theory in Crisis* (London: Burnett Books, Ltd., 1985), p. 342.

25 C. M. Fraser et al., "The Minimal Gene Complement of *Mycoplasma genitalium*," *Science*, 270(5235):397-403 (October 20, 1995).

26 Frank B. Salisbury, "Doubts About the Modern Synthetic Theory of Evolution," *American Biology Teacher*, vol. 33 (September 1971): p. 336.

27 W. Wells, "Taking Life to Bits," *New Scientist*, 155(2095):30-33 (1997).

28 Don Boys, *Evolution: Fact, Fraud, or Faith?* (Largo, FL: Freedom Publications, 1994), p. 112.

29 Mike Benton, "Is a Dog More Like a Lizard or a Chicken?" *New Scientist*, vol. 103 (August 16, 1984): p. 19. Benton was a research scientist at the time in the museum of the University of Oxford, England.

30 Michael Denton, *Evolution: A Theory in Crisis* (London: Burnett Books, Ltd., 1985).

31 Paul Erbrich, "On the Probability of the Emergence of a Protein with a Particular Function," *Acta Biotheoretica*, vol. 34 (1985): p. 53.

32 Edward E. Max, "Plagiarized Errors and Molecular Genetics: Another Argument in the Evolution-Creation Controversy," *Creation/Evolution*, vol. 19 (1986): p. 36.

33 Henry M. Morris and Gary E. Parker, *What Is Creation Science?* (Green Forest, AR: Master Books, 1987), p. 52–61.

34 National Academy of Sciences, "Proceedings of the National Academy of Sciences," 95:11, 804; cited in *New Scientist*, 160(2154):23 (October 3, 1998).

35 Colin Patterson, editor, *Molecules and Morphology in Evolution,* "New Issues for Phylogenetics," review by Timothy Rowe (New York, NY: Cambridge University Press, 1987), p. 1183–1184.

36 Christian Schwabe and Gregory W. Warr, "A Polyphylectic View of Evolution," *Perspectives in Biology and Medicine*, vol. 27 (Spring 1984): p. 473–474, 476.

37 Christian Schwabe, "On the Validity of Molecular Evolution," *Trends in Biochemical Sciences* (July 1986).

38 N. Takahata, "A Genetic Perspective on the Origin and History of Humans," *Annual Review of Ecology and Systematics*, vol. 26 (1995): p. 343–344.

Chapter 5

1 "Evolution," *Encyclopedia Britannica*, 1977.

2 Michael Denton, *Evolution: A Theory in Crisis* (Bethesda, MD: Adler & Adler Publishers, 1985), p. 261.

3 Francis Crick, *Life Itself: Its Origin and Nature* (New York, NY: Simon & Schuster, 1981), p. 88. Dr. Crick received the Nobel Prize for his pioneering work in identifying the structure of DNA.

4 Klaus Dose, "The Origin of Life: More Questions than Answers," *Interdisciplinary Science Reviews*, vol. 13, no. 4 (1988): p. 352, 348. Dose is the director of the Institute for Biochemistry, Johannes Gutenberg University, West Germany.

5 Freeman Dyson, "Honoring Dirac," *Science*, vol. 185 (September 27, 1974): p. 1161. Dyson was at the Institute for Advanced Study, Princeton, New Jersey.

6 Douglas R. Hofstadter, *An Eternal Golden Braid* (New York, NY: Vintage Books, 1980), p. 548.

7 John Horgan, "In the Beginning," *Scientific American*, vol. 264 (February 1991): p. 119.

8 Sir Fred Hoyle and Chandra Wickramasinghe, *Evolution from Space* (New York, NY: Simon & Schuster, 1984), p. 148.

9 Sir Fred Hoyle, "The Big Bang in Astronomy," *New Scientist*, vol. 92 (November 19, 1981): p. 526–527. Sir Fred Hoyle, FRS, was an honorary research professor at Manchester University and University College, Cardiff. Twenty-five years earlier he was a university lecturer in mathematics at Cambridge University. Sir Fred Hoyle is a great British astronomer; he originated the steady state theory, but later repudiated both the steady state and big-bang theories.

10 Sir Fred Hoyle, *The Intelligent Universe* (New York, NY: Holt, Rinehart & Winston, 1983), p. 20–21, 23.

11 John Maddox, "The Genesis Code by Numbers," *Nature*, vol. 367 (January 13, 1994): p. 111.

12 Leslie E. Orgel, "Darwinism at the Very Beginning of Life," *New Scientist*, vol. 94 (April 15, 1982): p. 151. Orgel is at UCSD, is one of the top biochemists in the world, and of special repute in origin-of-life studies.

13 Leslie E. Orgel, "The Origin of Life on the Earth," *Scientific American*, vol. 271 (October 1994): p. 78.

14 Andrew Scott, "Update on Genesis," *New Scientist*, vol. 106 (May 2, 1985): p. 30, 33.

15 Paul S. Taylor, *Origins Answer Book* (Mesa, AZ: Eden Productions, 1990), p. 76, quoting Wildersmith.

16 Taylor, *Origins Answer Book*, p. 50.

17 Edward P. Tryon, "What Made the World?" *New Scientist* (March 8, 1984): p. 14. Edward P. Tryon is a professor of physics at City University of New York.

18 George Wald, "Origin, Life and Evolution." *Scientific American* (1978). Dr. George Wald is a professor emeritus of biology at Harvard and the Nobel Prize winner in biology in 1971.

19 Hubert P. Yockey, "Self-Organization Origin of Life Scenarios and Information Theory," *Journal of Theoretical Biology*, vol. 91 (1981): p. 26.

20 Anonymous, "Hoyle on Evolution," *Nature*, vol. 29 (November 12, 1981): p. 105.

21 Emile Borel, *Probabilities and Life* (New York, NY: Dover Publications, 1962). Dr. Borel is credited with discovering many of the laws of probability. Note: Dr. Emile Borel explains, in essence, that anything with a chance of more than 1 in 10^{50} would never happen, no matter how much time there is. So how could an event with a probability of 1 in 10 to the two billionth power ever happen? It is absolutely, emphatically impossible!

22 John Billingham and Rudolf Pe, editors, *Communications With Extra-Terrestrial Intelligence* (New York, NY: Pergamon Press, 1973).

23 Wayne Jackson, *The Evolution Revolution* (Montgomery, AL: Apologetics Press, Inc., 1994), quoting Edwin Conklin, *Reader's Digest* (January 1963): p. 92.

24 Sir Francis Crick, *Life Itself* (New York, NY: Simon and Schuster, 1981), p. 51, 88. Francis Crick was one of the two scientists who discovered the molecular structure of DNA.

25 Michael Denton, *Evolution: A Theory in Crisis* (London: Burnett Books, Ltd., 1985), p. 324.
26 Paul S. Taylor, *Origins Answer Book* (Mesa, AZ: Eden Productions, 1990), p. 24, quoting Michal Denton.
27 Paul Erbrich, "On the Probability of the Emergence of a Protein with a Particular Function," *Acta Biotheoretica*, vol. 34 (1985): p. 77.
28 Taylor, *Origins Answer Book*, p. 23–24, quoting John Grebe.
29 Hubert P. Yockey, "A Calculation of the Probability of Spontaneous Biogenesis by Information Theory," *Journal of Theoretical Biology*, vol. 67 (1977): p. 398.
30 Fred Hoyle, "Hoyle on Evolution," *Nature*, vol. 294 (November 12, 1981): p. 148, 527.
31 Sir Fred Hoyle and Chandra Wickramasinghe, "Where Microbes Boldly Went," *New Scientist*, vol. 91 (August 13, 1991): p. 412.
32 Taylor, *Origins Answer Book*, p. 24, quoting Fred Hoyle.
33 Leslie E. Orgel, "The Origin of Life on the Earth," *Scientific American*, vol. 271 (October 1994): p. 78.
34 James Lovelock, *The Ages of Gaia* (New York, NY: W.W. Norton and Co., 1988), p 24.
35 J. Monod, *Chance and Necessity* (New York, NY: Knopf, 1972), p. 136. Monod is a Nobel Prize winner and biochemist at the University of Paris.
36 Harold Morowitz, *Energy Flow In Biology* (New York, NY: Academic Press, 1968). Note: The size of this figure is truly staggering, since there are only supposed to be approximately 10^{80} electrons in the whole universe! To further illustrate, this is approximately the same ridiculous probability that an entire high school gym filled with dice could instantly explode and every one of the dice would land on the number one!
37 Pierre-Paul Grassé, *Evolution of Living Organisms* (New York, NY: Academic Press, 1977). Pierre-Paul Grassé, of the University of Paris, is past-president of the French Academy of Science.
38 Ilya Prigogine et al., "Thermodynamics of Evolution," *Physics Today* (November 1972): p. 23. Ilya Prigogine is a Nobel Prize winner.
39 Hubert P. Yockey, "A Calculation of the Probability of Spontaneous Biogenesis by Information Theory," *Journal of Theoretical Biology*, vol. 67 (1977): p. 396.

Chapter 6
1 Isaac Asimov, "In the Game of Energy and Thermodynamics You Can't Even Break Even," *Smithsonian Institute Journal* (June 1970): p. 6, 10–11.
2 Brian Charlesworth, "Entropy: The Great Illusion," *Evolution*, vol. 40, no. 4 (1986): p. 880, review of *Evolution as Entropy* by Daniel R. Brooks and E.O. Wiley (Chicago, IL: University of Chicago Press, 1986), p. 335. Charlesworth is in the department of biology, University of Chicago.
3 Jeremy Rifkin, *Entropy: A New World View,* "Afterword," by Nicholas Georgescu-Roegen (New York, NY: Viking Press, 1980), p. 263, 265.
4 Frank Greco, "On the Second Law of Thermodynamics,"*American Laboratory Practice* (October 1982): p. 88.
5 Sydney Harris, "Second Law of Thermodynamics," *San Francisco Examiner*, Field Enterprise (January 27, 1984).
6 Ilya Prigogine and Isabelle Stengers, *Order Out Of Chaos* (New York, NY: Bantam Books, 1984), p. 129.
7 Martin J. Klein, "Thermodynamics in Einstein's Thought," *Science*, vol. 157 (August 4, 1967): p. 509.

8 R.B. Lindsay, "Physics — To What Extent Is It Deterministic?" *American Scientist*, vol. 56 (Summer 1968): p. 100.

9 Jeremy Rifkin, *Entropy: A New World View* (New York, NY: Viking Press, 1980), p. 55.

10 Francisco J. Ayala, "Genotype, Environment and Population Numbers," *Science*, vol. 162 (December 27, 1968): p. 1456.

11 Francisco Ayala, "Mechanisms of Evolution," *Scientific American*, vol. 239 (September 1978): p. 63. Ayala is a leading modern neo-Darwinian biologist.

12 Fritjof Capra, *The Web of Life* (New York, NY: Anchor Books, 1996), p. 228. Dr. Capra is director of the Center for Ecoliteracy, in Berkeley, California, and one of the most influential "New Age" scientists.

13 Brian Charlesworth, "Entropy: The Great Illusion," *Evolution*, vol. 40, no. 4 (1986): p. 880, review of *Evolution as Entropy*, by Daniel R. Brooks and E.O. Wiley (Chicago, IL: University of Chicago Press, 1985).

14 Richard Dawkins, "Creation and Natural Selection," *New Scientist*, vol. 111 (September 25, 1986): p. 37. Dawkins was in the zoology department, Oxford University.

15 Environmental Mutagenic Society, "Environmental Mutagenic Hazards," *Science*, vol. 187 (February 14, 1975): p. 512.

16 John J. Fried, *The Mystery of Heredity* (New York, NY: J. Day Co., 1971), p. 135–136.

17 Pierre-Paul Grassé, *Evolution of Living Organisms* (New York, NY: Academic Press, 1977), p. 103. Pierre-Paul Grassé is a professor at the University of Paris and past-president of the French Academy of Science.

18 Ibid., p. 170.

19 J. Knight, "Top Translator," *New Scientist*, 158(2130):15 (April 18, 1998).

20 C.P. Martin, *American Scientist*, 41:100 (1953).

21 P.S. Moorhead and M.M. Kaplan, editors, *Mathematical Challenges to the Neo-Darwinian Interpretation of Evolution* (Philadelphia, PA: Wistar Institute Press, 1967), p. 50.

22 H.J. Muller, "How Radiation Changes the Genetic Constitution," *Bulletin of the Atomic Scientists,* vol. 11, no. 9 (November 1955): p. 331. Dr. H.J. Muller is a radiation and mutation expert.

23 J.D. Sarfati, "Decoding and Editing Design: Double Sieve Enzymes," *Creation Ex Nihilo Technical Journal*, 13(l):5-7 (1999).

24 Lee Spetner, *Not by Chance* (Brooklyn, NY: The Judaica Press, Inc., 1999), p. 131–132, 138, 143. See also review in *Creation Ex Nihilo*, 20(l):50-51 (December 1997/February 1998). Dr. Spetner is a biophysicist at Johns Hopkins University.

25 Christopher Wills, "Genetic Load," *Scientific American*, vol. 222 (March 1970): p. 98.

26 Richard Dawkins, "What Was All the Fuss About?" *Nature*, vol. 316 (August 22, 1985): p. 683.

27 Pierre-Paul Grassé, *Evolution of Living Organisms* (New York, NY: Academic Press, 1977), p. 87. Dr. Pierre-Paul Grassé is the scientist who held the Chair of Evolution at the Sorbonne in Paris for 20 years.

28 Ibid., p. 88.

29 Kevin Padian, "The Whole Real Guts of Evolution," *Paleobiology*, vol. 15 (Winter 1989): p. 77, review of *Genetics, Paleontology and Macroevolution* by Jeffrey S. Levinton (Cambridge, MA: Cambridge University Press, 1988).

30 W.J. ReMine, *The Biotic Message* (St. Paul, MN: St. Paul Science, 1993), chapter 8.

31 Wayne Jackson, *Creation, Evolution, and the Age of the Earth* (Stockton, CA: Courier Publications, 1989), p. 2, quoting George G. Simpson, *The Major Features of Evolution* (New York, NY: Columbia University Press, 1953), p. 96.

32 Huston Smith, "Evolution and Evolutionism," *The Christian Century*, vol. 99 (July 7–14, 1982): p. 757. Smith was professor of religion, Syracuse University.

33 Steven M. Stanley, "Macroevolution and the Fossil Record," *Evolution*, vol. 36 (May 1982): p. 465.

34 Colin Patterson, *Evolution* (London: British Museum of Natural History, 1978) p. 142.

35 Charles Darwin, *The Origin of Species*, 6th edition, 1859 (London: J.M. Dent and Sons Ltd., 1971).

36 I.L. Cohen, *Darwin Was Wrong: A Study in Probabilities* (Greenvale, NY: New Research Publications, Inc., 1984), p. 81.

37 Charles Darwin, *The Origin of Species* (London: A.L. Burt, 1859), p. 170.

38 Michael Denton, *Evolution: A Theory in Crisis* (London: Burnett Books, Ltd., 1985), p. 62.

39 Stephen J. Gould, "Not Necessarily A Wing," *Natural History*, vol. 94, no. 10 (October 1985): p. 12–13. Dr. Stephen J. Gould is a Harvard professor of evolutionary paleontology.

40 Stephen J. Gould, *Natural History*, 86(6): 22-30 (1977).

41 Stephen J. Gould, "Through a Glass, Darkly," *Natural History* (September 1989): p. 24.

42 Garrett J. Hardin, *Nature and Man's Fate* (New York, NY: Rinehart, 1961), p. 72.

43 Scott Huse, *The Collapse of Evolution* (Grand Rapids, MI: Baker Book House, 1988), p. 71.

44 Janus Koestler, *A Summing Up* (New York, NY: Vintage Books, 1978), p. 170.

45 Colin Patterson, *Evolution* (London: British Museum of Natural History, 1978), p. 142. Dr. Colin Patterson is the chief paleontologist, British Museum of Natural History.

46 Colin Patterson, "Cladistics," interview by Brian Leek, interviewer Peter Franz, March 4, 1982, BBC.

47 Wayne Jackson, *The Evolution Revolution* (Montgomery, AL: Apologetics Press, Inc., 1994), quoting Colin Patterson in a radio interview with the British Broadcasting Corporation on March 4, 1982.

48 Michael Pitman, *Adam and Evolution* (London: Rider, 1984), p. 67–68. Michael Pitman is a former chemistry professor at Cambridge.

49 David M. Raup, "Conflicts Between Darwin and Paleontology," *Bulletin of the Field Museum of Natural History*, vol. 50 (January 1979): p. 23.

50 Brian J. Atlers and William F. McComas, "Punctuated Equilibrium: the Missing Link in Evolution Education," *American Biology Teacher*, vol. 56 (September 1994): p. 337.

51 Ibid.

52 Larry Azar, "Biologists, Help!" *Bioscience*, vol. 28 (November 1978): p. 714.

53 Sarah Boxer, editor, "On the Rescue Gene and the Origin of Species," *Discover*, vol. 8 (August 1987): p. 7.

54 Carlton E. Brett, "Stasis: Life in the Balance," *Geotimes*, vol. 40 (March 1995): p. 18.

55 Brian Charlesworth, "Entropy: The Great Illusion," *Evolution*, vol. 40, no. 4 (1986): p. 880, review of *Evolution as Entropy* by Daniel R. Brooks and E.O. Wiley (Chicago, IL: University of Chicago Press, 1986). Charlesworth is in the department of biology, University of Chicago.

56 Richard Dawkins, "What Was All the Fuss About?" *Nature*, vol. 316 (August 22, 1985): p. 683.

57 Wayne Jackson, *The Evolution Revolution* (Montgomery, AL: Apologetics Press, Inc., 1994), quoting Stephen J. Gould, "The Return of Hopeful Monsters," *Natural History* (June/July 1977): p. 24.

58 Jackson, *The Evolution Revolution*, quoting Robert Jastrow, "Evolution: Selection for Perfection," *Science Digest*, 89 (11):86. Dr. Robert Jastrow is NASA science director.

59 Eveleen Richards, "A Political Anatomy of Monsters, Hopeful and Otherwise," *Isis*, vol. 85 (September 1994): p. 379.

60 Robert E. Ricklefs "Paleontologists Confronting Macroevolution," *Science*, vol. 199 (January 6, 1978): p. 59, review of *Patterns of Evolution as Illustrated by the Fossil Record,* edited by A. Hallam (New York, NY: Elsevier, 1977).

61 Keith Stewart Thomson, "The Meanings of Evolution," *American Scientist*, vol. 70 (September/October 1982): p. 530. Thomson was professor of biology and dean of the graduate school, Yale University.

62 Sewall Wright, "Character Change, Speciation, and the Higher Taxa," *Evolution*, vol. 36 (May 1982): p. 440.

63 Rudolf A. Raff and Elizabeth C. Raff, editors, *Development as an Evolutionary Process,* "Interpreting Great Developmental Experiments: The Fossil Record," by James W. Valentine and Douglas H. Erwin (New York, NY: A. R. Liss, Inc., 1987), p. 96.

Chapter 7

1 Derek V. Ager, *The Nature of the Stratigraphical Record* (New York, NY: John Wiley & Sons, 1993), p. 65. Ager was professor and head of the department of geology and oceanography, University College of Swansea.

2 Derek V. Ager, *The New Catastrophism* (New York, NY: Cambridge University Press, 1993), p. 47, 49, and 52.

3 R.E. Walsh and R.S. Crowell, editors, *Proceedings of the First International Conference on Creationism,* "Mount St. Helens and Catastrophism," by S.A. Austin (Pittsburgh, PA: Creation Science Fellowship, 1986).

4 F.A. Barnes, "The Case of the Bones in Stone," *Desert* (February 1975): p. 38–39.

5 F.A. Barnes, "Mine Operation Uncovers Puzzling Remains of Ancient Man," *Times-Independent*, Moab, Utah, June 3, 1971.

6 Guy Berthault, "Experiments on Laminations of Sediments, Resulting from a Periodic Graded-bedding Subsequent to Deposit: A Contribution to the Explanation of Lamination of Various Sediments and Sedimentary Rocks," *C. R. Academic des Sciences Paris*, vol. 303, series 2, no. 17 (1986): p. 1574.

7 F.M. Broadhurst, "Some Aspects of the Paleoecology of Non-Marine Faunas and Rates of Sedimentation in the Lancashire Coal Measures," *American Journal of Science*, vol. 262 (Summer 1964): p. 865. Broadhurst was in the department of geology, University of Manchester.

8 Alan H. Cutler and Karl W. Plessa, "Fossils out of Sequence: Computer Simulations and Strategies for Dealing with Stratigraphic Disorder," *Palaios*, vol. 5 (June 1990): p. 227. Cutler is in the department of geoscience at the University of Arizona.

9 R.G. Kazmann, "It's About Time: 4.5 Billion Years," quoting John Eddy, report on Symposium at Louisiana State University, *Geotimes*, vol. 23 (September 1978): p. 18.

10 Stephen Jay Gould, "Is Uniformitarianism Necessary?" *American Journal of Science*, vol. 263 (March 1965): p 226.

11 Edgar B. Heylmun, "Should We Teach Uniformitarianism?" *Journal of Geological Education*, vol. 19, no. 1 (January 1971): p. 35.

12 Albert G. Ingalls, "The Carboniferous Mystery," *Scientific American*, vol. 162 (January 1940): p. 14.

13 H.A. Makse, S. Havlin, P.R. King, and H.E. Stanley, "Spontaneous Stratification in Granular Mixtures," *Nature*, 386 (6623):379-382 (March 27, 1997).

14 Wayne Jackson, *Creation, Evolution, and the Age of the Earth* (Stockton, CA: Courier Publications, 1989), p. 5, quoting Stephen Moorebath, *Scientific American* (March 1977): p. 92. Dr. Stephen Moorebath of the University of Oxford is an evolutionist himself.

15 Byron Nelson, *The Deluge Story in Stone* (Minneapolis, MN: Augsburg Publishing House, 1968), p. 40.

16 J.E. O'Rourke, "Pragmatism versus Materialism in Stratigraphy," *American Journal of Science*, vol. 276 (January 1976): p. 53.

17 F.H.T. Rhodes, H.S. Zim, and P.R. Shaffer, *Fossils* (New York, NY: Golden Press, 1962), p. 10.

18 Paul Mason Tilden, "Mountains that Moved," *Science Digest* (June 1959): p. 74–75.

19 Niles Eldredge, *Time Frames: The Rethinking of Darwinian Evolution and the Theory of Punctuated Equilibria* (New York, NY: Simon and Schuster, 1985), p. 51–52. Niles Eldredge represents the American Museum of Natural History, New York.

20 J.E. O'Rourke, *American Journal of Science*, vol. 276 (January 1976): p. 53.

21 R.H. Rastall, *Encyclopedia Britannica*, vol. 10, 1956, p. 168. (R.H. Rastall is a lecturer in economic geology at Cambridge University.)

22 Samuel Paul Welles, "Fossils," *World Book Encyclopedia*, vol. 7 (1978): p. 364. Welles was research associate, Museum of Paleontology, University of California, Berkeley.

23 Samuel Paul Welles, "Paleontology," *World Book Encyclopedia*, vol. 15 (1978): p. 85.

24 Carl Wieland, *Stones and Bones* (Green Forest, AR: Master Books, Inc., 1994).

25 E.S. Moore, *Coal* (New York, NY: Wiley, 1940), 2nd edition. E.S. Moore is a coal geologist.

26 Anonymous, "Basic Coal Studies Refute Current Theories of Formation," *Research and Development*, vol. 26 (February 1984): p. 92.

27 Anonymous, "Striking Oil in the Laboratory," *Science News*, vol. 125 (March 24, 1984): p. 187.

28 Argonne National Laboratory, "Basic Coal Studies Refute Current Theories of Formation," *Research and Development* (February 1984): p. 82.

29 Elizabeth Pennisi, "Water, Water Everywhere," *Science News*, vol. 143 (February 20, 1993): p. 124.

30 Ivan T. Sanderson, *Uninvited Visitors* (New York, NY: Cowles Education Corp., 1967), p. 195–196.

31 Otto Stutzer, *The Geology of Coal*, translated by A.C. Noé (Chicago, IL: University of Chicago Press: 1940), p. 271.

32 S.A. Austin, "Excess Argon within Mineral Concentrates from the New Dacite Lava Dome at Mount St. Helens Volcano," *CEN Technical Journal*, 10 (3):335-343 (1986).

33 Wayne Jackson, *Creation, Evolution, and the Age of the Earth* (Stockton, CA: Courier Publications, 1989), p. 10, quoting from *Rock Strata and the Biblical Record,* Paul Zimmerman, editor (St. Louis: Concordia, 1970), p.70, quoting Kenneth L. Currie. Dr. Kenneth L. Currie represents the Canadian Geological Survey.

34 Wakefield Dort Jr., "Mummified Seals of Southern Victoria Land," *Antarctic Journal,* Washington, vol. 6 (September–October 1971): p. 211. Wakefield Dort Jr. is part of the department of geology at the University of Kansas.

35 Wayne Jackson, *Creation, Evolution, and the Age of the Earth* (Stockton, CA: Courier Publications, 1989), p. 8–9.

36 Ibid., p. 13.

37 Frederic B. Jueneman, "Secular Catastrophism," *Industrial Research and Development* (June 1982): p. 21.

38 *Creation Research Society Quarterly*, vol. 19(2) (September 1982): p. 123, quoting from Robert E. Lee, "Radiocarbon: Ages in Error," *Anthropological Journal of Canada*, vol. 19(3) (1981): p. 9.

39 R.L. Mauger, "K-Ar Ages of Biotites from Tuffs in Eocene Rocks of the Green River, Washakie, and Uinta Basins, Utah, Wyoming, and Colorado," University of Wyoming, contributions to *Geology*, vol. 15, no. 1 (Winter 1977): p. 37.

40 Colin Renfrew, *Before Civilization* (New York, NY: Alfred A. Knopf, 1975), p. 52.

41 Alan C. Riggs, "Major Carbon-14 Deficiency in Modern Snail Shells from Southern Nevada Springs," *Science*, vol. 224 (April 6, 1984): p. 58. Dr. Alan C. Riggs, formerly of the U.S. Geological Survey, is now on the staff of the University of Washington, Seattle.

42 Ingred U. Olsson, editor, *Radiocarbon Variations and Absolute Chronology, Proceedings of the Twelfth Nobel Symposium*, "C-14 Dating and Egyptian Chronology," by T. Save-Soderbergh and I.U. Olsson (Stockholm: Almqvist & Wiksell, and New York: John Wiley & Sons, Inc., 1970), p. 35. T. Save-Soderbergh and I.U. Olsson are of the Institute of Egyptology and Institute of Physics respectively, University of Uppsala, Sweden.

43 William J.J. Glashouwer and Paul S. Taylor, "The Earth, a Young Planet," a film produced by Eden Communications, Gilbert, AZ, 1983, quoting Harold S. Slusher. Dr. Harold Slusher is an astrophysicist and geophysicist.

44 A.A. Snelling. "The Cause of Anomalous Potassium-Argon 'Ages' for Recent Andesite Flows at Mt. Ngauruhoe, New Zealand, and the Implications for Potassium-Argon 'Dating,' " *Proceedings of the Fourth International Conference on Creationism, Creation Science Fellowship, Pittsburgh*, edited by E. Walsh (1998): p. 503–525.

45 A.A. Snelling, "Radiometric Dating in Conflict," *Creation*, 20(l):24-27 (December 1997–February 1998).

46 A.A. Snelling, "Stumping Old-Age Dogma," *Creation*, 20(4) (September/November 1998): p. 48–50.

47 William D. Stansfield, *The Science of Evolution* (New York, NY: Macmillan, 1977), p. 80 and 84. William D. Stansfield, Ph.D., is an instructor of biology at the California Polytechnic State University.

48 R.E. Taylor et al., "Major Revisions in the Pleistocene Age Assignments for North American Human Skeletons by C-14 Accelerator Mass Spectrometry: None Older than 11,000 C-14 years B.P.," *American Antiquity*, vol. 50, no. 1 (January 1985): p. 136.

49 Charles Weaver and J.M. Wampler, "K, Ar, Illite Burial," *Bulletin*, Geological Society of America, vol. 81 (November 1979): p. 3423.

50 Henry M. Morris and John D. Morris, *Modern Creation Trilogy*, vol. 2 (Green Forest, AR: Master Books, 1996), p. 317–320.

51 Walter T. Brown Jr., *In The Beginning* (Phoenix, AZ: Center for Scientific Creation, 1989), p. 53.

52 J.D. Sarfati, "Salty Seas: Evidence for a Young Earth," *Creation*, 21(l):16-17 (December 1998–February 1999).

53 M. Schweitzer and T. Staedter, "The Real Jurassic Park," *Earth* (June 1997): p. 55–57.

54 J.D. Sarfati, "Blowing Old-Earth Belief Away: Helium Gives Evidence That the Earth Is Young," *Creation*, 20(3):19-21 (June–August 1998).

55 Edward Blick, *Correlation of the Bible and Science* (Oklahoma City, OK: Hearthstone Publishing, 1994), p. 28.

56 John Maddox, "Halley's Comet Is Quite Young," *Nature*, vol. 339 (May 11, 1989): p. 95.

57 Anonymous, "Magsat Down, Magnetic Field Declining," *Science News*, vol. 117 (June 28, 1980): p. 407.

58 William J.J. Glashouwer and Paul S. Taylor, "The Earth, a Young Planet," quoting Thomas Barnes. Dr. Thomas Barnes is one of the most respected magnetic field physicists.

59 Jeremy Bloxham and David Gubbins, "The Evolution of the Earth's Magnetic Field," *Scientific American*, vol. 261 (December 1989): p. 71.

60 Ken Games, "The Earth's Magnetism — in Bricks," *New Scientist*, vol. 90 (June 11, 1981): p. 678. Games was in the department of geophysics, University of Liverpool.

61 J.D. Sarfati, "The Earth's Magnetic Field: Evidence that the Earth Is Young," *Creation*, 20(2):15-19 (1998).

62 Nelson Glueck, *Rivers in the Desert* (New York, NY: Farrar, Straus and Cudahy, 1968), p. 31. Glueck was president of Hebrew Union College, Jewish Institute of Religion.

63 Stephen Jay Gould, "Fall in the House of Ussher," *Natural History*, vol. 100 (November 1991): p 16. The James Barr article is found in *Bulletin*, John Rylands University Library of Manchester, vol. 67, p. 575–608.

64 Colin Renfrew, *Before Civilization* (New York, NY: Alfred A. Knopf, 1975), p. 21, 25, 28, 74. Colin Renfrew is recognized at one of the world's leading students of ancient history.

65 Anonymous, "Bushmen's Paintings Baffling to Scientists," *Evening News* January 1, 1970, London Express Service, printed in *Los Angeles Herald-Examiner,* January 7, 1970.

66 Anonymous, "Living Dinosaurs," *Science–80*, vol. 1 (November 1980): p. 6–7.

67 Anonymous, *Los Angeles Herald Examiner,* January 7, 1970.

68 Stephen Battersby, "Prehistoric Monsters," *Nature*, vol. 387 (May 29, 1997): p. 451.

69 Carl E. Baugh and Clifford A. Wilson, *Dinosaur* (Orange, CA: Promise Pub., 1991), p. 11-12.

70 Michael J. Benton, "Large-scale Replacements in the History of Life," *Nature*, vol. 302 (March 3, 1983): p. 17. Benton was in the department of zoology, Oxford University.

71 "Dragons," *Encyclopedia Britannica*, 1965 edition.

72 Warren E. Leary, "Dinosaurs May Inhabit Remote Jungle," *San Diego Union Tribune*, October 18, 1980, Washington Date Line.

73 Michale J. Novacek, Mark Norell, Malcolm C. McKenna, and James Clark, "Fossils of the Flaming Cliffs," *Scientific American*, vol. 271 (December 1994): p. 60, 62, and 66.

74 Alexander Romashko, "Tracking Dinosaurs," *Moscow News Weekly: Science and Engineering News,* no. 24, 1983, p. 10.

75 M. Schweitzer and T. Staedter, "The Real Jurassic Park," *Earth* (June 1997): p. 55–57.

76 Paul Taylor, *The Great Dinosaur Mystery and the Bible* (Denver, CO: Accent Publications Inc., 1989).

77 Walter A. Philips, "Dragon," *Encyclopedia Britannica*, vol. 7 (1949): p. 569–570.

78 Derek V. Ager, *The Nature of the Stratigraphical Record* (New York, NY: John Wiley & Sons, 1993), p. 80. Ager was professor and head of the department of geology and oceanography, University College of Swansea. He also served as president of the British Geological Association.

79 W.J. Arkell, *Jurassic Geology of the World* (New York, NY: Hafner Publishing Co., 1956), p. 615.

80 Anna K. Behrensmeyer, "Taphonomy and the Fossil Record," *American Scientist*, vol. 72 (November/December 1984): p. 560.

81 Victor Clube and Bill Napier, "Close Encounters with a Million Comets," *New Scientist*, vol. 95 (July 15, 1982): p. 151. Cube and Napier are the authors of *The Cosmic Serpent: A Catastrophist View of Earth History* (New York, NY: Universe Books, 1982).

82 Gordon L.H. Davies, "Bangs Replace Whimpers," *Nature*, vol. 365 (September 9, 1993): p. 115, review of *The New Catastrophism* by Derek Ager (New York, NY: Cambridge University Press, 1993).

83 J. William Dawon, *The Historical Deluge in Relation to Scientific Discovery*, p. 4ff. Sir J. William Dawon is a famous Canadian geologist.

84 Sir Cyril S. Fox, *Water* (New York, NY: Philosophical Library, 1952), p. 30. Fox was director, Geological Surveyor of India.

85 J.E. Hoffmeister and H.G. Multer, "Growth-Rate Estimates of a Pleistocene Coral Reef of Florida," *Bulletin, Geological Society of America*, vol. 75 (April 1964): p. 354–356.

86 Richard A. Kerr, "Fossils Tell of Mild Winters in an Ancient Hothouse," *Science*, vol. 261 (August 6, 1993): p. 682.

87 R.A. Kerr, "Pathfinder Tells a Geologic Tale with One Starring Role," *Science*, 279(5348) (January 9, 1998): p. 175.

88 Harry S. Ladd, "Ecology, Paleontology, and Stratigraphy," *Science*, vol. 129, no. 3341 (January 9, 1959): p. 72.

89 Nelson, *The Deluge Story in Stone*, p. 66 and 85.

90 Chris Raymond, "Discovery of Leaves in Antarctica Sparks Debate over Whether Region Had Near-Temperate Climate," *Chronicle of Higher Education* (March 20, 1991): p. A9.

91 Chris Raymond, "Scientists Report Finding Fossils of Dinosaurs in Antarctica's Interior," *Chronicle of Higher Education* (March 20, 1991): p. A11.

92 Bert Thompson, *The Global Flood of Noah* (Montgomery, AL: Apologetics Press, 1986), p. 13–14, 34–35, 44–45. Dr. Bert Thompson is a Texas A&M microbiologist.

Chapter 8

1 William J.J. Glashouwer and Paul S. Taylor, "The Earth, a Young Planet," a film produced by Eden Communications, Gilbert, AZ, 1983, quoting Harold Slusher. Slusher is a professor of physics at the University of Texas, El Paso, Texas.

2 Margaret Bishop, *Focus on Earth Science*, teacher's edition (Columbia, OH: Merrill, 1981), p. 470.

3 H.C. Arp, G. Burbidge, F. Hoyle, J.V. Narlikar, and N.C. Wickramasinghe, "The Extragalactic Universe: An Alternative View," *Nature*, vol. 346 (August 30, 1990): p. 809, 812.

4 Geoffrey Burbidge, "Why Only One Big Bang?" *Scientific American* (February 1992): p. 120.

5 John Billingham and Rudolf Pe, editors, *Communications With Extra-Terrestrial Intelligence* (New York, NY: Pergamon Press, 1979).

6 Albert Einstein, *Letters à Maurice Solovine* (Paris: Gauthier-Villars, 1956), p. 115.

7 Jay Gallagher and Jean Keppel, "Seven Mysteries of Galaxies," *Astronomy*, vol. 22 (March 1994): p. 39, 41.

8 John Gribbin, "Cosmologists Move Beyond the Big Bang," *New Scientist*, vol. 110, p. 30.

9 Paul Davies, "Chance or Choice: Is the Universe an Accident?" *New Scientist*, vol. 80 (1978): p. 506. Paul Davies is a British astronomer.

10 Sir Fred Hoyle, "The Big Bang under Attack," *Science Digest*, vol. 92 (May 1984): p. 84.

11 Fredrick Hoyle, *The Intelligent Universe* (New York, NY: Rinehart and Winston, 1983), p. 185. Sir Fredrick Hoyle is a renowned British astronomer.

12 Eric J. Lerner, "COBE Confounds the Cosmologists," *Aerospace America*, vol. 28 (March 1990): p. 38.

13 Michael D. Lemonick and J. Madeleine Nash, "Unraveling Universe," *Time* (March 6, 1995): p. 78.

14 N. Rescher, editor, *Scientific Explanation and Understanding*, "Cosmology, Probability, and the Need to Explain Life," by Leslie (Lanham, MD: University Press of America, 1983), p. 54.

15 Jayant V. Narlikar, "What if the Big Bang Didn't Happen?" *New Scientist*, vol. 129 (March 2, 1991): p. 49.

16 Ibid., p. 50.

17 Robert L. Oldershaw, "The Continuing Case for a Hierarchical Cosmology," *Astrophysics and Space Science*, vol. 92 (May 1983): p. 347.

18 Robert L. Oldershaw, "What's Wrong with the New Physics?" *New Scientist*, vol. 128 (December 22/29, 1990): p. 59.

19 Anthony L. Peratt, "Not with a Bang," *The Sciences* (January/February 1990): p. 26–27. Peratt is a physicist at Los Alamos National Laboratory, New Mexico.

20 Don H. Page, "Inflation Does Not Explain Time Asymmetry," *Nature*, vol. 304 (July 7, 1983): p. 39.

21 Ben Patrusky, "Why is the Cosmos 'Lumpy'?" *Science–81* (June 1981): p. 96.

22 Anthony L. Peratt, "Not with a Bang," *The Sciences* (January/February 1990): p. 27.

23 Corey S. Powell and Madhusree Mukerjee, "Cosmic Puffery," *Scientific American*, vol. 275 (September 1996): p. 20, 22.

24 Bert Thompson, *Cosmic Evolution and the Origin of Life* (Montgomery, AL: Apologetics Press, Inc. 1989), p. 7.

25 Herman Bondi, "Letters Section," *New Scientist* (August 21, 1980): p. 611, reference to quote by Karl Popper.

26 David Darling, "On Creating Something from Nothing," *New Scientist*, vol. 151 (September 14, 1996): p. 49.

27 Paul Davies, "Universe in Reverse: Can Time Run Backwards?" *Second Look* (September 1979): p. 27. Dr. Davies is a British astronomer.

28 Alan H. Guth, "Cooking Up a Cosmos," *Astronomy*, vol. 25 (September 1997): p. 54.

29 Ibid.

30 Ibid.

31 Alan H. Guth and Paul J. Steinhardt, "The Inflationary Universe," *Scientific American*, vol. 250 (May 1984): p. 128.

32 Konrad B. Krauskopf and Arthur Beiser, *The Physical Universe* (New York, NY: McGraw-Hill, 1973), p. 645.

33 André Linde, "The Self-Reproducing Inflationary Universe," *Scientific American*, vol. 271 (November 1994): p. 48.

34 Don H. Page, "Inflation Does Not Explain Time Asymmetry," *Nature*, vol. 304 (July 7, 1983): p. 40.

35 Harold Puthoff, "Everything for Nothing," *New Scientist*, vol. 127 (July 28, 1990): p. 55. Puthoff is a theoretical physicist at the Institute for Advanced Studies in Austin, Texas.

36 Quentin Smith, "Did the Big Bang Have a Cause?" *British Journal for the Philosophy of Science*, vol. 45 (June 1994): p. 666.

37 J.D. Sarfati, "Exploding Stars Point to a Young Universe," *Creation*, 19(3):46-49 (June–August 1998).

38 Walter Brown, *In The Beginning* (Phoenix, AZ: Center for Scientific Creation, 1989), p. 53.

39 John Maddox, "Halley's Comet Is Quite Young," *Nature*, vol. 339 (May 11, 1989): p. 95.

40 Don DeYoung, *Creation Ex Nihilo*, 14(4)43 (September–November 1992). Dr. Don DeYoung is professor of physics at Grace College in Indiana.

41 R.G. Kazmann, "It's About Time: 4.5 Billion Years," report on symposium at Louisiana State University, *Geotimes*, vol. 23 (September 1978): p. 18, quoting John Eddy. Dr. John A. Eddy is an astrophysicist at the Harvard-Smithsonian High Altitude Observatory in Boulder, Colorado.

42 John Gribbin, "The Curious Case of the Shrinking Sun," *New Scientist*, vol. 97 (March 3, 1983): p. 592–595.

Chapter 9

1 D.J. Futuyma, *Science on Trial* (New York, NY: Pantheon Books, 1983), p. 197.

2 D.B. Wilson, editor, *Did the Devil Make Darwin Do It?* "Interpreting Earth History," by B.F. Glenister and B.J. Witzke (Ames, IA: Iowa State University Press, 1983), p. 58.

3 Pierre-Paul Grassé, *Evolution of Living Organisms* (New York, NY: Academic Press, 1977), p. 4. Grassé held the Chair of Evolution at the Sorbonne for 30 years, and was editor of the 12-volume *Traite de Zoologie*.

4 Norman D. Newell, "Paleobiology's Golden Age," *Palaios*, vol. 2, no. 3 (1987): p. 306.

5 Mark Ridley, "Who Doubts Evolution?" *New Scientist*, vol. 90 (June 25, 1981): p. 831.

6 Stefan Bengtson, "The Solution to a Jigsaw Puzzle," *Nature*, vol. 345 (June 28, 1990): p. 765. Bengtson is at the Institute of Paleontology, Uppsala University, Sweden.

7 Ibid.

8 Robert L. Carroll, *Vertebrate Paleontology and Evolution* (New York, NY: W. H. Freeman and Co., 1988), p. 138.

9 A.H. Clark, editor, *Zoogenesis*, "The New Evolution," by A. H. Clark (Baltimore, MD: Williams and Wilkins, 1930), p. 189, 196.

10 Edwin H. Colbert and M. Morales, *Evolution of the Vertebrates* (New York, NY: John Wiley and Sons, 1991), p. 99.

11 Charles Darwin, *The Origin of Species*, "On the Imperfection of the Geological Record," chapter X (London: J.M. Dent & Sons Ltd., 1971), p. 292–293.

12 Erwin Douglas, James W. Valentine, and David Jablonski, "The Origin of Animal Body Plans," *American Scientist*, vol. 85 (March/April 1997): p. 126.

13 Niles Eldredge, "Did Darwin Get It Wrong?" *Nova* (November 1, 1981): p. 6.

14 Niles Eldredge, "Progress in Evolution?" *New Scientist*, vol. 110 (June 5, 1986): p. 55.

15 Stephen Jay Gould, "Evolution's Erratic Pace," *Natural History*, vol. 86 (May 1977): p. 14. Stephen Jay Gould is a professor of geology and paleontology at Harvard University.

16 S.J. Gould, "Is a New and General Theory of Evolution Emerging?" *Paleobiology*, vol. 6(1) (January 1980): p. 127.

17 S.J. Gould, "The Return of Hopeful Monsters," *Natural History*, vol. 86, (6) (June–July 1977): p. 24.

18 Stephen Jay Gould, "A Short Way to Big Ends," *Natural History*, vol. 95 (January 1986): p. 18.

19 Herbert Wray, "Fossils Indicate Early Land Animals," *Science News*, vol. 123 (June 4, 1983): p. 356.

20 Ibid., p. 357.

21 Kenneth J. Hsü, "Sedimentary Petrology and Biologic Evolution," *Journal of Sedimentary Petrology*, vol. 56 (September 1986): p. 729.

22 Tom S. Kemp, *Mammal-like Reptiles and the Origin of Mammals* (New York, NY: American Press, 1982), p. 3.

23 Ibid., p. 319.

24 David B. Kitts, "Paleontology and Evolutionary Theory," *Evolution*, vol. 28 (September 1974): p. 467. Kitts was a professor of scientific history, University of Oklahoma.

25 David B. Kitts, "Search for the Holy Transformation, *Paleobiology*, vol. 5 (Summer 1979): p. 354, review of *Evolution of Living Organisms*, by Pierre-P. Grassé.

26 Wayne Jackson, *The Mythology of Modern Geology* (Stockton, CA: Apologetics Press, 1980), p. 15, quoting Walter Lammerts, "Growing Doubts: Is Evolution Theory Valid?" *Christianity Today*, vol. VI (September 14, 1962): p. 4.

27 Luther D. Sunderland, *Darwin's Enigma* (Green Forest, AR: Master Books, 1984), p. 89, quoting Colin Patterson. Dr. Patterson is senior paleontologist at the British Museum of National History, London; owner and proprietor of the most complete fossil collection in the world.

28 Mark Ridley, *The Problems of Evolution* (New York, NY: Oxford University Press, 1985), p. 11.

29 Mark Ridley, "Who Doubts Evolution?" *New Scientist*, vol. 90 (June 25, 1981): p. 831. Ridley was in the department of zoology at Oxford University.

30 George G. Simpson, *Tempo and Mode in Evolution* (New York, NY: Columbia University Press, 1944), p. 107.

31 George G. Simpson, "The Nonprevalence of Humanoids," *Science*, vol. 143 (February 21, 1964): p. 772.

32 Stephen Stanley, *Macroevolution: Pattern and Process* (San Francisco, CA: W.H. Freeman, 1979), p. 39. Stanley is a paleontologist at Johns Hopkins University.

33 Bert Thompson, *Biological Evolution* (Montgomery, AL: Apologetics Press, Inc., 1989), p. 16–17.

34 Ronald R. West, "Paleoecology and Uniformitarianism," *Compass*, vol. 45 (May 1968): p. 216. Ronald R. West is an assistant professor of paleobiology at Kansas State University.

35 British Geological Association, "The Nature of the Fossil Record," *Proceedings of the Geological Association*, vol. 87, no. 2 (1976): p. 132–133.

36 W.A. Criswell, *Did Man Just Happen?* (Grand Rapids, MI: Zondervan Pub. House, 1973), p. 120.

37 Charles Darwin, *The Origin of Species,* p. 344.

38 Richard Dawkins, *The Blind Watchmaker* (New York, NY: W.W. Norton, 1987), p. 229.

39 T.N. George. *Science Progress*, vol. 48 (1960): p. 1.

40 Stephen Jay Gould, "Evolution's Erratic Pace," *Natural History*, vol. 86 (May 1977): p. 14.

41 Stephen Jay Gould, "Opus 200," *Natural History* (August 1991): p. 14.

42 Tom S. Kemp, "A Fresh Look at the Fossil Record," *New Scientist*, vol. 108 (December 5, 1985): p. 66. Kemp is the curator of the University Museum, Oxford University.

43 Jeffrey S. Levinton, "The Big Bang of Animal Evolution," *Scientific American*, vol. 267 (November 1992): p. 84. Levinton is the chairman, department of ecology and evolution, State University of New York at Stony Brook.

44 R. Monastersky, "When Earth Tipped, Life Went Wild," *Science News*, vol. 152 (July 26, 1997): p. 52.

45 J. Madeleine Nash, "When Life Exploded," *Time* (December 4, 1995): p. 68.

46 David M. Raup, "Conflicts Between Darwin and Paleontology," *Bulletin, Field Museum of Natural History*, vol. 50 (January 1979): p. 23. Raup is the curator of geology at the Field Museum.

47 D.M. Raup, *Bulletin, Field Museum of Natural History*, vol. 50 (1979): p. 22.

48 Mark Ridley, "Who Doubts Evolution?" *New Scientist*, vol. 90 (June 25, 1981): p. 831. Ridley was in the department of zoology at Oxford University.

49 George Gaylord Simpson, *Tempo and Mode in Evolution* (New York, NY: Columbia University Press, 1984), p. 99.

50 Peter J. Smith, "Evolution's Most Worrisome Questions," *New Scientist* (November 19, 1987): p. 59, review of *Life Pulse: Episodes from the Story of the Fossil Record* by Niles Eldredge (New York, NY: Facts on File Publ., 1987).

51 Thompson, *Biological Evolution*, p. 16–17.

52 Gerald T. Todd, "Evolution of the Lung and the Origin of Bony Fishes: A Causal Relationship?" *American Zoologist*, vol. 20, no. 4 (1980): p. 757. Todd was at the University of California, Los Angeles.

53 Rudoff A. Raff and Elizabeth C. Raff, editors, *Development as an Evolutionary Process*, "Interpreting Great Developmental Experiments: The Fossil Record," by James W. Valentine and Douglas H. Erwin (New York, NY: A.R. Liss, Inc., 1987), p. 84. Valentine is in the department of geological sciences at the University of California, Santa Barbara, and Erwin is at Michigan State University.

54 Ibid., p. 96.

55 A.E. Wildersmith, *The Natural Sciences Know Nothing of Evolution* (Green Forest, AR: Master Books, Inc., 1981), p. 166.

56 D.V. Ager, "The Nature of the Fossil Record," *Proceedings of the Geological Association*, vol. 87, no. 2 (1976): p. 132, from the presidential address, March 5, 1976.

57 Ibid.

58 Charles Darwin, *The Origin of Species* (London: J.M. Dent & Sons Ltd., 1971).

59 Michael Denton, *Evolution: A Theory in Crisis* (London: Burnett Books, Ltd., 1985), p. 160–161.

60 T. Neville George, "Fossils in Evolutionary Perspective," *Science Progress*, vol. 48 (January 1960): p. 1. George was professor of geology at the University of Glasgow.

61 Stephen Jay Gould, "A Short Way To Big Ends," *Natural History*, vol. 95 (January 1986): p. 18.

62 Neil A. Campbell, "Resetting the Evolutionary Timetable," interview with Steven M. Stanley, *Bioscience*, vol. 36 (December 1986): p. 725.

Chapter 10

1 Anonymous, "Chemistry of Still-Green Fossil Leaves," *Science News*, vol. 111 (June 18, 1977): p. 39.

2 C.A. Arnold, *An Introduction to Paleobotany* (New York, NY: McGraw-Hill Publishing Company, 1947), p. 7.

3 C.B. Beck, editor, *Origin and Early Evolution of Angiosperms* (New York, NY: Columbia University Press, 1976).

4 A.M. MacLeod and L.S. Cobley, editors, *Contemporary Botanical Thought* (Chicago, IL: Quadrangle Books, 1961), p. 97, quoting E.J.H. Corner. Dr. Corner is a professor of tropical botany at Cambridge University.

5 Patricia G. Gensel and Henry N. Andrews, "The Evolution of Early Land Plants," *American Scientist*, vol.75 (September/October 1987): p. 481.

6 N.F. Hughes, *Paleobiology of Angiosperm Origins: Problems of Mesozoic Seed-Plant Evolution* (Cambridge, MA: Cambridge University Press, 1976), p. 1–2.

7 E.C. Olson, *The Evolution of Life* (New York, NY: The New American Library, 1965), p. 94.

8 Frank B. Salisbury, "Doubts About the Modern Synthetic Theory of Evolution," *American Biology Teacher*, vol. 33 (September 1971): p. 338.

9 Stanley W. Angrist and Loren G. Hepler, *Order and Chaos* (New York, NY: Basic Books, Inc., 1967), p. 203–204.

10 National Academy of Science, *Teaching About Evolution and the Nature of Science* (Washington, DC: National Academy Press, 1998).

11 Anonymous, *New Scientist*, 154(2077):13 (April 12, 1997).

12 Anonymous, "Jurassic Bird Challenges Origin Theories," *Geotimes*, vol. 41 (January 1996), p. 7.

13 Ibid.

14 A.H. Brush, "On the Origin of Feathers," *Journal of Evolutionary Biology*, vol. 9 (1996): p. 140.

15 Alan Feduccia, "Evidence from Claw Geometry Indicating Arboreal Habits of *Archaeopteryx*," *Science*, vol. 259 (February 5, 1993): p. 792. Feduccia is a paleo-ornithologist at the University of North Carolina.

16 Ibid.

17 Ann Gibbons, "New Feathered Fossil Brings Dinosaurs and Birds Closer," *Science*, vol. 274 (November 1, 1996): p. 720.

18 Ibid.

19 Ibid.

20 Ibid.

21 D. Menton and C. Wieland, "Bird Evolution Flies Out the Window," *Creation Ex Nihilo*, 16(4):16-19 (September–November 1994).

22 R. Monastersky, "A Clawed Wonder Unearthed in Mongolia," *Science News*, vol. 143 (April 17, 1993): p. 245.

23 Ibid.

24 R. Monastersky, "Paleontologists Deplume Feathery Dinosaur," *Science News*, vol. 151 (May 3, 1997): p. 271.

25 V. Morell, "*Archaeopteryx*: Early Bird Catches a Can of Worms," *Science*, 259(5096):764-65 (February 5, 1993).

26 National Academy of Science, *Teaching About Evolution and the Nature of Science*, p. 8.

27 Douglas Palmer, "Learning to Fly," *New Scientist*, vol. 153 (March 1, 1997): p. 44, review of *The Origin and Evolution of Birds*, by Alan Feduccia (New Haven, CT: Yale University Press, 1996). Palmer is a paleontologist based in Cambridge, and Feduccia is a paleo-ornithologist at the University of North Carolina.

28 Ibid.

29 A. Perle et al, "Flightless Bird from the Cretaceous of Mongolia," *Nature*, 362:623-626 (1993).

30 D.P. Prothero, R.M. Schoch, editors, *Major Features of Vertebrate Evolution,* "On the Origin of Birds and of Avian Flight," by J.H. Ostrom (Knoxville, TN: University of Tennessee Press, 1994), p. 160–177.

31 A.J. Marshall, editor, *Biology and Comparative Physiology of Birds,* "The Origin of Birds," by W.E. Swinton, chapter 1 in Vol. 1 (New York, NY: Academic Press, 1960), p. 1. Dr. Swinton represents the British Museum of Natural History in London.

32 J.B. Birdsell, *Human Evolution* (Chicago, IL: Rand McNally College Pub. Co., 1975), p. 169.

33 Ibid., p. 170.

34 C. Depere, *Transformation of the Animal World* (New York, NY: Arno Press, 1980), p. 105. Dr. Depere is a French paleontologist.

35 G.A. Kerkut, *Implications of Evolution* (New York, NY: Pergamon Press, 1960), p. 149.

36 Yu Kruzhilin and V. Ovcharov, "A Horse from the Dinosaur Epoch?" *Moskovskaya Pravda*, "Moscow Truth", trans. A. James Melnick (February 5, 1984).

37 B.J. Macfadden, *Fossil Horses* (Cambridge, MA: Cambridge University Press, 1992), p. 255.
38 N. Neribert Nilsson, *Synthetische Artbuilding* (Lund, Sweden: Verlag CWE Gleerup, 1954). Nilsson is a Swedish professor of evolution.
39 B. Rensberger, *Houston Chronicle*, November 5, 1980, sec. 4, p. 15. Rensberger was reporting on the 1980 meeting of 150 evolutionists at the Chicago Field Museum of Natural History.
40 George Gaylor Simpson, *Life of the Past* (New Haven, CT: Yale University Press, 1953), p. 125, 127.
41 Stephen M. Stanley, "Macroevolution and the Fossil Record," *Evolution*, vol. 36, no. 3 (1982): p. 464.
42 Neil A. Campbell, "Resetting the Evolutionary Timetable," *Bioscience*, vol. 36 (December 1986): p. 726, interview with Stephen M. Stanley.
43 "Whales of the World" fold-out, reference to "Exploring the Lives of Whales," by Victor B. Scheffer, *National Geographic*, vol. 50 (December 1976): p. 752–767 . Schaeffer was chairman of the U.S. Marine Mammal Committee.
44 National Academy of Science, *Teaching About Evolution and the Nature of Science,* p. 18.
45 J.G.M. Thewissen, S.T. Hussain, and M. Arif, "Fossil Evidence for the Origin of Aquatic Locomotion in Archeocete Whales," *Science,* 263(5144): 210–212 (January 14, 1994). Perspective by A. Berta, "What Is a Whale?" same issue, p. 180–181.
46 Anonymous, "Whales," *Compton's Interactive Encyclopedia*, 1996.
47 E.H. Colbert, *Evolution of the Vertebrates* (New York, NY: John Wiley and Sons, 1955), p. 303.
48 Michael Denton, *Evolution: A Theory in Crisis* (Bethesda, MD: Adler & Adler, 1985), p. 174.
49 Philip D. Gingerich et al, "Origin of Whales in Epicontinental Remnant Seas: New Evidence from the Early *Eocene* of Pakistan" *Science*, vol. 220 (April 22, 1983): p. 405.
50 Philip D. Gingerich, B. Holly Smith, and Elwyn L. Simons, "Hind Limbs of *Eocene Basilosaurus:* Evidence for Feet in Whales," *Science*, vol. 249 (July 13, 1990): p. 155.
51 F. Hitching, *The Neck of the Giraffe* (New Haven, CT and New York, NY: Ticknor & Fields, 1982), p. 90. Hitching is a British science writer and evolutionist.
52 G.A. Mchedlidze, *General Features of the Paleobiological Evolution of Cetacea*, translated from Russian (Rotterdam: A.A. Balkema, 1986), p. 91.
53 Michael Pitman, *Adam and Evolution* (London: Rider, 1987), p. 235–236.
54 W.J. ReMine, *The Biotic Message* (St. Paul, MN: St. Paul Science, 1993), chapter 8.
55 Victor B. Scheffer, "Exploring the Lives of Whales," *National Geographic*, vol. 50 (December 1976): fold-out display.
56 E.J. Slijper, *Dolphins and Whales* (Ann Arbor, MI: University of Michigan Press, 1962), p. 17. Slijper is recognized as an evolutionary whale expert.
57 B.J. Stahl, *Vertebrate History: Problems in Evolution* (New York, NY: McGraw-Hill, 1974), p. 489. Barbara Stahl is a paleontologist.
58 J.G.W. Thewissen, S.T. Hussain, and M. Arif, "Fossil Evidence for the Origin of Aquatic Locomotion in *Archeocete* Whales," *Science*, 263(5144):210–212 (January 14, 1994), also *Perspective* by A. Berta, "What Is a Whale?" same issue, p. 180–181.
Chapter 11
1 D.V. Ager, "The Nature of the Fossil Record," *Proceedings of the Geological Association,* vol. 87, no. 2 (1976): p. 132–133. Dr. D.V. Ager is president of the British Geological Association.
2 L.B. Halstead, "Museum of Errors," *Nature* (November 20, 1980): p. 280.

3 Albert C. Ingalls, "The Carboniferous Mystery," *Scientific American*, CLXII (January 1940): p. 14.

4 J.S. Jones, "A Thousand and One Eves," *Nature*, vol. 345 (May 31, 1990): p. 395.

5 Jerald M. Loewenstein and Adrienne L. Zihlman, "The Invisible Ape," *New Scientist*, vol. 120 (December3, 1988): p. 58.

6 Roger Lewin, *Bones of Contention* (New York, NY: Simon and Schuster, 1987), p. 43.

7 Robert Martin, "Man Is Not an Onion," *New Scientist* (August 4, 1977): p. 283 and 285. Dr. Robert Martin is a Senior Research Fellow at the Zoological Society of London.)

8 Ernst Mayr, "Evolution," *Scientific American*, vol. 239 (September 1978): p. 52.

9 Charles E. Oxnard, *Fossils, Teeth and Sex: New Perspectives on Human Evolution* (Seattle, WA and New York, NY: University of Washington Press, 1987), p. 227. Charles E.Oxnard is professor of anatomy and human biology, University of Western Australia.

10 Wolfgang Smith, *Teilhardism and the New Religion: A Thorough Analysis of the Teachings of Pierre Teilhard de Chardin* (Rockford, IL: Tan Books and Publishers, Inc., 1988), p. 8.

11 Colin Tudge, "Human Origins: A Family Feud," *New Scientist*, vol. 146 (May 20, 1995): p. 24.

12 Lyall Watson, "The Water People," *Science Digest*, vol. 90, no. 5 (May 1982): p. 44.

13 Ibid.

14 Joseph Weiner, *The Natural History of Man* (New York, NY: Universe Books, 1971), p. 33. Dr. Weiner is a recognized paleontologist.

15 Sir Solly Zuckerman, *Beyond the Ivory Tower* (London: Weidenfeld & Nicholson, 1970), p. 64.

16 F.A. Barnes, *Desert Magazine,* 38:36-39 (February 1975).

17 Donald C. Johanson and Maitland A. Edey, *Lucy, the Beginnings of Mankind* (New York, NY: Simon and Schuster, 1981) p. 245–252.

18 R.E.F. Leakey and Alan Walker, *Science* 207:1103 (1980).

19 A.E. Wildersmith, *Man's Origin, Man's Destiny* (Wheaton, IL: Harold Shaw Publishers, 1970), p. 300.

20 Russell H. Tuttle, "The Pitted Pattern of Laetoli Feet," *Natural History*, vol. 99 (March 1990): p. 61.

21 Ibid., p. 63.

22 Ibid., p. 64.

23 T.D. White, *Science,* 208:175 (1980).

24 Anonymous, "Ramapithecus," *Columbia Encyclopedia* (2001).

25 Robert B. Eckhardt, "Population Genetics and Human Origins," *Scientific American*, vol. 226 (January 1972): p. 101. Robert Eckhardt teaches in the anthropology department at Pennsylvania State University.

26 Stephen Jay Gould, "Empire of the Apes," *Natural History*, vol. 96 (May 1987): p. 24.

27 Richard E. Leakey, "Hominids in Africa," *American Scientist*, vol. 64 (March/April 1976): p. 174, 176.

28 D.R. Pilbean, *The Evolution of Man* (New York, NY: Funk and Wagnalls, 1970), p. 107.

29 Adrienne L. Zihlman and Jerold M. Loewenstein, "False Start of the Human Parade," *Natural History*, vol. 88 (August/September 1979): p. 89.

30 Ibid., p. 91.

31 Illustration from "Rusch's Human Fossils," in *Rock Strata and the Bible Record*, P.A. Zimmerman, editor (St. Louis, MO: Concordia Pub. House, 1970).

32 Christine Berg, "How Did the *Australopithecines* Walk? A Biomechanical Study of the Hip and Thigh of *Australopithecus Afarensis*," *Journal of Human Evolution*, vol. 26 (April 1994): p. 271. Christine Berg is a researcher at the Natural History Museum in Paris, France.

33 Dean Falk, "The Petrified Brain," *Natural History*, vol. 93 (September 1984): p. 38.

34 James A. Hopson and Leonard B. Radinsky, "Vertebrate Paleontology: New Approaches and New Insights," *Paleobiology*, vol. 6 (Summer 1980): p. 263–264. Hopson was in the anatomy department at the University of Chicago.

35 D. Johanson and T.D. White, *Science*, 203:321, 1979; 207:1104, 1980.

36 Richard Leakey, *The Weekly Australian*, May 7–8, 1983, p. 3. Richard Leakey is the director of the National Museum in Kenya, and son of the famous paleontologist Louis Leakey.

37 Richard Leakey, "Lucy — Evolution's Solitary Claim for an Ape/Man: Her Position is Slipping Away," *Creation Research Society Quarterly*, vol. 22, no. 3 (December, 1985): p. 144–145.

38 Charles E. Oxnard, *The Order of Man* (New Haven, CT: Yale University Press, 1984), p. 3–4.

39 C.E. Oxnard, *Nature*, 258:389-395 (1975).

40 Joseph Weiner, *The Natural History of Man* (New York, NY: Universe Books, 1971), p. 45–46.

41 Sir Solly Zuckerman, *Beyond the Ivory Tower* (London: Weidenfeld & Nicholson, 1970), p. 78. Sir Solly Zuckerman is secretary of the Zoological Society of London and chief scientist advisor to the British government.

42 S.J. Gould, *Natural History*, 85:30 (1976).

43 S. Hartwig-Scherer and R.D. Martin, *Journal of Human Evolution*, 21:439-449 (1991).

44 Ian Tattersall, *Evolutionary Anthroplogy*, 1(1):34-36 (1992).

45 Lubenow, *Bones of Contention*, p. 165.

46 Fred Spoor, *Image of God*, video produced by Keziah Productions, Florence, KY, 1997. Dr. Fred Spoor teaches at University College, London.

47 B. Wood and M. Collard, "The Human Genus," *Science*, 284(5411) (1999): p. 70.

48 Boule, Marcellin, and Vallois, *Fossil Men* (New York, NY: Dryden Press, 1957), p. 136.

49 David L. Phillips, *Thesis* (Northridge, CA: California State University, January 1991), p. 28.

50 Teilhard de Chardin, *L'Anthropologie* (Paris: 1931).

51 Niles Eldredge, *Fossils — The Evolution and Extinction of Species* (New York, NY: Harry N. Abrams, Inc., 1991), p. 56.

52 Ann Gibbons, "*Homo erectus* in Java: A 250,000 Year Anachronism," *Science*, vol. 274 (December13, 1996): p. 1841.

53 D.T. Gish, *Evolution: The Fossils Still Say No* (El Cajon, CA: Institute for Creation Research, 1995), p. 304.

54 Leslie Kaufman, "Did a Third Human Species Live Among Us?" *Newsweek* (December 23, 1996): p. 52.

55 Lubenow, *Bones of Contention*, p. 134–143.

56 Patrick O'Connell, *Science of Today and the Problems of Genesis, Book 1* (Hawthorne, CA: Christian Book Club of America, 1969).

57 David Pilbeam, "Rearranging Our Family Tree," *Human Nature* (June 1978): p. 42.

58 Ian Tattersall, "Out of Africa Again . . . and Again?" *Scientific American*, vol. 276 (April 1997): p. 63. Tattersall is chairman of the anthropology department, American Museum of Natural History.

59 Anonymous, "Living Human Fossils in Outer Mongolia?" *New Scientist*, vol. 93 (March 25, 1982): p. 778.

60 Ibid.

61 Anonymous, "Neanderthal Man, Victim of Malnutrition," *Prevention* (October 1971): p. 116.

62 Ibid., p. 117.

63 Anonymous, "Neanderthal Noisemaker," *Science News*, vol. 150 (November 23, 1996): p. 328.

64 Ibid.

65 Ibid.

66 Bruce Bower, "'Neanderthals' Disappearing Act," *Science News*, vol. 139 (June 8, 1991): p. 361.

67 Sarah Bunney, "Neanderthals Weren't So Dumb After All," *New Scientist*, vol. 123 (July 1, 1989): p. 43.

68 Ann Gibbons, "Neanderthal Language Debate: Tongues Wag Anew," *Science*, vol. 256 (April 3, 1992): p. 33.

69 Francis Ivanhoe, "Neanderthals Had Rickets," *Science Digest*, vol. 69 (February 1971): p. 35–36.

70 Ibid., p. 35.

71 Marvin Lubenow, "Recovery of Neanderthal mtDNA: An Evaluation," *Creation Ex Nihilo Technical Journal*, 12(l):87-97 (1998).

72 E. Trunkaus and W.W. Howells, *Scientific American,* 241(6):118 (1979).

73 Anonymous, *Moline* (Illinois) *Daily Dispatch*, May 14, 1984.

74 S.J. Gould, *Natural History*, 88(3): 96 (1979).

75 W.K. Gregory, *Science,* 66:579 (1927).

76 Jaquetta Hawkes, *Nature*, 204:952 (1964).

77 Charles E. Oxnard, "Human Fossils: New Views of Old Bones," *American Biology Teacher*, vol. 41 (May 5, 1979): p. 264–276. Oxnard was dean of the graduate school and university professor in biological sciences and anatomy, University of Southern California.

78 Pat Shipman, "On the Trail of the Piltdown Fraudsters," *New Scientist*, vol. 128 (October 6, 1990): p. 52.

79 Ibid., p. 52.

80 Keith Stewart Thomson, "Piltdown Man: The Great English Mystery Story," *American Scientist*, vol.79 (May/June 1991): p. 194.

Chapter 12

1 Jeremy Cherfas, "The Difficulties of Darwinism," *New Scientist*, vol. 102 (May 17, 1984): p. 29.

2 Richard Dawkins, "The Necessity of Darwinism," *New Scientist*, vol. 94 (April 15, 1982): p. 130. Dr. Richard Dawkins is in the department of zoology, Oxford University, UK.

3 Paul S. Taylor, *Origins Answer Book* (Mesa, AZ: Eden Productions, 1990), p. 49, quoting Niles Eldredge. Dr. Niles Eldredge is a paleontologist and evolutionist, of the American Museum of Natural History.

4 Fred Hoyle and Chandra Wickramasinghe, *Evolution from Space* (London: Dent, 1981). Wickramasinghe is professor of astronomy and applied mathematics at University College, Cardiff.

5 Leonard Huxley, editor, *Life and Letters of Thomas Henry Huxley* (New York, NY: D. Appleton, 1909), Vol. 1, p. 241, quoting Thomas Huxley. Thomas Huxley was a dedicated atheist. So strong were his evolutionary views that he was called "Darwin's Bulldog."

6 Robert Jastrow, "God's Creation," *Science Digest* (Special Spring Issue, 1980): p. 68. Dr. Robert Jastrow is director of the Goddard Institute for Space Research at NASA.

7 H.S. Lipson, "A Physicist Looks at Evolution," *Physics Bulletin*, vol. 31 (May 1980): p. 138.

8 J.P. Moreland, editor, *The Creation Hypothesis*, "The Methodological Equivalence of Design and Descent: Can There Be a 'Scientific Theory of Creation?'" by Stephen Meyer (Downers Grove, IL: InterVarsity Press, 1994), p. 98. Stephen Meyer is a philosopher of science.

9 Gordon J. Van Wylen and Richard E. Sonntag, *Fundamentals of Classical Thermodynamics* (New York, NY: Wiley, 1986), p. 236–237. Van Wylen was dean of engineering at the University of Michigan, but is now president of Hope College.

10 C. Wickramasinghe, interview in *London Daily Express*, August 14, 1981. Wickramasinghe is professor of applied math and astronomy, University College, Cardiff.

11 Paul C. Davies, "Law and Order in the Universe," *New Scientist*, vol. 120 (October 15, 1988): p. 58. Davies was professor of theoretical physics, University of Newcastle-on-Tyne.

12 Richard Dawkins, *The Blind Watchmaker* (New York, NY: W.W. Norton, 1986), p. 130.

13 Niles Eldredge, *Time Frames* (New York, NY: Simon and Schuster, 1985), p. 29.

14 George M. Marsden, "Creation versus Evolution: No Middle Way," *Nature*, vol. 305 (October 13, 1983): p. 572. Marsden was in the department of history, Calvin College.

15 L. Orgel, *The Origins of Life* (New York, NY: John Wiley, 1973), p. 189.

16 D. Dewar, L. M. Davies, and J.B.S. Haldane, *Is Evolution a Myth? A Debate between D. Dewar and L.M. Davies vs. J.B.S. Haldane* (London: Watts & Co. Ltd/Paternoster Press, 1949), p. 90.

17 M. Chown, "X-ray Lens Brings Finer Chips into Focus," *New Scientist*, 151(2037) (July 6, 1996): p. 18.

18 Paul C. Davies, "The Creative Cosmos," *New Scientist*, vol. 116 (December 17, 1987): p. 42.

19 Michael Denton, *Evolution: A Theory in Crisis* (London: Burnett Books, Ltd., 1985), p. 328. Michael Denton is a molecular biologist.

20 Ibid., p. 329–330.

21 Ibid., p. 342.

22 Dewar, Davies, and Haldane, *Is Evolution a Myth?* p. 90.

23 M. Helder, "The World's Smallest Compasses," *Creation Ex Nihilo*, 20(2):5253 (March–May 1998).

24 R. Howlett, "Simple Minds," *New Scientist*, 158(2139):28-32 (June 20, 1998).

25 Paul S. Taylor, *Origins Answer Book* (Mesa, AZ: Eden Productions, 1990), p. 18, quoting C. Everett Koop. C. Everett Koop was a former surgeon general.

26 J.A. Miller, "Sensory Surprises in Platypus, Mantis," *Science News*, vol. 129 (February 15, 1986): p. 104.

27 Ibid.

28 A.H. Poirier, "The Magnificent Migrating Monarch," *Creation Ex Nihilo*, 20(l):28-31 (December 1997–February 1998).

29 Hugh Ross, "Science and Faith," *New Man* (September/October 1999). Hugh Ross is an astronomer and former research fellow at Cal Tech University.

30 J.D. Sarfati, "Design in Living Organisms: Motors," *Creation Ex Nihilo Technical Journal*, 12(t):3-5 (1998).

31 J.D. Sarfati, "Turtles — Reading Magnetic Maps," *Creation Ex Nihilo*, 21(2):30 (March/May 1999).

32 P. Weston, "Bats: Sophistication in Miniature," *Creation Ex Nihilo*, 21(l):28-3 1 (December 1998–February 1999).

33 Robin J. Wootton, "The Mechanical Design of Insect Wings," *Scientific American*, vol. 263 (November 1990): p. 114. Wootton is senior lecturer in biological science, University of Exeter, England.

34 Ibid., p. 120.

35 Paul C. Davies, "The Christian Perspective of a Scientist," *New Scientist* (June 2, 1983): p. 638. Davies is an Australian physicist and philosopher of science.

36 Paul C. Davies, *The Cosmic Blueprint* (New York, NY: Simon and Schuster, 1988), p. 203.

37 David Demick, *IMPACT No. 325*, Institute for Creation Research. Dr. David Demick is a medical pathologist.

38 Freeman Dyson, *Scientific American* (September 1971): p. 50. Dr. Freeman Dyson teaches at Princeton University.

39 George Gale, "The Anthropic Principle," *Scientific American*, vol. 245 (December 1981): p. 154.

40 John Gribbin, *Genesis: The Origins of Man and the Universe* (New York, NY: Delacorte Press 1981), p. 309. Dr. John Gribbin is a world-renowned cosmologist.

41 Judith Hooper, "Perfect Timing," *New Age Journal*, vol. 11 (December 1985): p. 18.

42 Robert Jastrow, *The Astronomer and God, Intellectuals Speak out About God* (New York, NY: Regenery Gateway, 1984). Dr. Robert Jastrow is founder and director of NASA Space Studies.

43 Motte's translation from the Latin in 1729, *Mathematical Principles of Natural Philosophy* (Berkeley, CA: University of California Press, 1934), quoting Isaac Newton, 1686. Isaac Newton is recognized as one of the greatest scientists of all time.

44 Borel, *Probabilities and Life.*

45 Hugh Ross, "Science and Faith," *New Man* (September/October 1999). Hugh Ross is an astronomer and former research fellow at Cal Tech University.

46 Bert Thompson and Wayne Jackson, *The Case for the Existence of God* (Montgomery, AL: Apologetics Press, Inc. 1996), p. 19–20.

47 James Trefil, "Was the Universe Designed for Life?" *Astronomy*, vol. 25 (June 1997): p. 56.

48 Wernher von Braun, *Applied Christianity* (May 1974): p. 8. Dr. Wernher von Braun is one of America's leading space scientists.

Chapter 13

1 Derek W. Ager, "The Nature of the Fossil Record," *Proceedings of the British Geological Association*, vol. 87, no. 2 (1976): p. 133.

2 Anonymous, "One Fifth of All Scientists Reject Evolution," *Bible Science Newsletter* (June 1988): p. 17.

3 Louis Bounoure, *The Advocate*, Thursday, March 8, 1984, p. 17. Professor Louis Bounoure is former president of the biological society of Strasbourg and director of the Strasburg Zoological Museum, later director of research at the French National Centre of Scientific Research.

4 Jacques Barzun, *Darwin, Marx, Wagner* (Garden City, NY: Doubleday and Co., 1959), p. 69.

5 C. Loring Brace, *American Scientist*, vol. 82 (September/October 1994): p. 484, review of *Species, Species Concepts, and Primate Evolution*, edited by William H. Kimbel and Lawrence B. Martin (New York, NY: Plenum Press, 1993).

6 Matt Cartmill, "Four Legs Good, Two Legs Bad," *Natural History*, vol. 92 (November 1983): p. 77.

7 Mark Czarnecki, "The Revival of the Creationist Crusade," *MacLean's* (January 19, 1981): p. 56.

8 Michael Denton, *Evolution: A Theory In Crisis* (London: Burnett Books, Ltd., 1986), p. 69.

9 Ibid., p. 104.

10 Paul Erbich, "On the Probability of the Emergence of a Protein with a Particular Function," *Acta Biotheoretica*, vol. 34 (1985): p. 53.

11 Loren Eisley, *Darwin's Century* (Garden City, NY: Doubleday, 1959), p. 242.

12 William Fix, *The Bone Peddlers* (New York, NY: Macmillan, 1984), p. 179–180.

13 Francis Glasson, "Darwin and the Church," *New Scientist*, vol. 99 (September 1, 1983): p. 639.

14 L. Beverly Halstead, "Museum of Errors," *Nature*, vol. 288 (November 20, 1980): p. 208. Halstead is professor of zoology and geology, University of Reading, United Kingdom.

15 P. Lemoine, editor, *5 Encyclopedie Francaise*, "Introduction: De L'Evolution?" by Paul Lemoine, (1937). (Paul Lemoine was director of the Natural History Museum in Paris and the editor of the *Encyclopedie Francaise*.)

16 H.S. Lipson, "A Physicist Looks at Evolution," *Physics Bulletin*, vol. 31 (1980): p. 138. H.S. Lipson is a British physicist and fellow of the Royal Society.

17 S. Lovtrup, *Darwinism: The Refutation of a Myth* (London: Croom Helmm, 1987), p. 422.

18 Colin Patterson, in an interview on British Broadcasting Corporation (BBC) television, March 4, 1982. Dr. Colin Patterson was senior paleontologist, British Museum of Natural History, London.

19 Gregory Alan Pesely, "The Epistemological Status of Natural Selection," *Laval Theologique et Philosophique*, vol. 38 (February 1982): p. 74.

20 Jeremy Rifkin, *Entropy: A New World View* (New York, NY: Viking Press, 1980), p. 55.

21 Wolfgang Smith, *Teilhardism and the New Religion* (Rockford, IL: Tan Books & Publishers, Inc., 1988), p. 2.

22 Ibid., p. 5.

23 Paul S. Taylor, *Origins Answer Book* (Mesa, AZ: Eden Productions, 1990), p. 107, quoting Wolfgang Smith. Dr. Wolfgang Smith is a physicist and mathematician.

24 David Berlinski, "The Deniable Darwin," *Commentary*, vol. 101 (June 1996): p. 28.

25 Tom Bethell, "Burning Darwin to Save Marx," *Harper's Magazine* (December 1978): p. 92.

26 I.L. Cohen, *Darwinism: The Refutation of a Myth* (London: Croom Helmm, 1987), p. 422.

27 Norman K. Hall and Lucia K.B. Hall, "Is the War between Science and Religion Over?" *The Humanist*, vol. 46 (May/June 1986): p. 27.

28 L. Beverly Halstead, "Popper: Good Philosophy, Bad Science?" *New Scientist*, vol. 87 (July 17, 1980): p. 215.

29 Ibid.

30 Koestler Janus, *A Summing Up* (New York, NY: Vintage Books, 1978), p. 185.

31 G.A. Kerkut, *Implications of Evolution* (Oxford, UK: Pergamon, 1960), p. 157.

32 David B. Kitts, "Search for the Holy Transformation," *Paleobiology*, vol. 5 (Summer 1979): p. 353; review of *Evolution of Living Organisms* by Pierre-P. Grassé. Kitts was professor of history of science, University of Oklahoma.

33 Colin Patterson, "Evolution and Creationism," Speech at the American Museum of Natural History, New York, November 5, 1981, p. 2. The late Dr. Patterson was a senior paleontologist at the British Museum of Natural History, and editor of its journal, as well as author of the book *Evolution*. He was one of the world's leading evolutionists, and regarded as the world's foremost fossil scientist.

34 Ibid.

35 Jeremy Rifkin, *Algeny* (New York, NY: Viking Press, 1983), p. 112.

36 Ibid., p. 125.

37 D.T. Rosevear, "Scientists Critical of Evolution," *Evolution Protest Movement Pamphlet*, no. 224 (July 1980): p. 4.

38 Steven M. Stanley, *Macroevolution: Pattern and Process* (San Francisco, CA: W. H. Freeman, 1979), p. 2.

39 E.O. Wiley, "Review of Darwin Retried by MacBeth," *Systematic Zoology*, vol. 24 (June 1975): p. 270. Wiley was in the department of ichthyology, CUNY, American Museum of Natural History.

40 American Humanist Association, "Humanist Manifesto I," *The New Humanist*, vol. 6 (May/June 1933). Preface by Paul Kurtz to AHA republication of Humanist Manifestos I and II.

41 G. Richard Bozarth, "The Meaning of Evolution," *American Atheist* (February 1978): p. 30.

42 Ibid.

43 Ibid.

44 A.M. MacLeod and L.S. Cobley, *Evolution in Contemporary Botanical Thought* (Chicago, IL: Quadrangle Books, 1961), p. 97, quoting E.J.H. Corner. Dr. Corner is a professor of tropical botany at Cambridge University.

45 Charles Darwin, *The Origin of Species* (London: A.L. Burt, 1859).

46 Richard Dawkins, *The Blind Watchmaker: Why the Evidence of Evolution Reveals a Universe without Design* (New York, NY: W.W. Norton, 1986), p. 6.

47 Pierre-Paul Grassé, *Evolution of Living Organisms* (New York, NY: Academic Press, 1977), p. 8. Pierre-Paul Grassé is a professor at the University of Paris and past-president of the French Academy of Sciences.

48 Scott Huse, *The Collapse of Evolution* (Grand Rapids, MI: Baker Book House, 1988), p. 3.

49 Sol Tax, editor, *Issues in Evolution*, Vol. 3 of *Evolution After Darwin* (Chicago, IL: University of Chicago Press, 1960), p. 260, quoting Julian Huxley. Julian Huxley is one of the best known naturalist and humanist philosophers.

50 Robert Jastrow, "God's Creation," *Science Digest* (Special Spring Issue, 1980): p. 68.

51 Arthur Koestler, *Janus: A Summing Up* (New York, NY: Random House, 1978), p. 184–185. Arthur Koestler is a British novelist.

52 E.J. Larson and L. Witham, "Leading Scientists Still Reject God," *Nature*, 394(6691):313 (July 23, 1998).

53 Brian Leith, *The Descent of Darwin: A Handbook of Doubts about Darwinism* (London: Collins, 1982), p. 11.

54 Richard Lewontin, "Billions and Billions of Demons," *The New York Review*, January 9, 1997, p. 31. Professor Richard Lewontin is a geneticist.

55 H.S. Lipson, "A Physicist Looks at Evolution," *Physics Bulletin*, vol. 31 (1980): p. 138. H.S. Lipson is professor of physics at University of Manchester, UK.

56 Lloyd Morain and Oliver Reiser, "Scientific Humanism: A Formulation," *The Humanist*, vol. 48 (September/October 1988): p. 33. Reprinted from Spring 1943 issue. Morain was editor of *The Humanist*; Reiser was professor of philosophy at University of Pittsburgh.

57 Ibid.

58 George Wald, "The Origin of Life," *Scientific American*, vol. 191(2) (August 1954): p. 46. Dr. George Wald is a famous Nobel Prize-winning professor of biology at Harvard University.

59 Heribert Nilsson, *Synthetische Artbildung* (Lund, Sweden: C.W.K. Gleerup, 1953), p. 1185, 1212. Heribert Nilsson of Lund University is a well-known scientist who spent his entire career trying to artificially foster evolution between creatures.

60 E. Geisler and W. Scheler, editors, *Darwin Today*, "The Ideology of Darwinism," by Michael Ruse (Berlin: Akademie-Verlag, 1983), p. 246. Ruse is professor of philosophy at Guelph University, Ontario, Canada.

61 Ibid.

62 Michael Ruse, symposium titled "The New Anti-Evolutionism" during the 1993 annual meeting of the American Association for the Advancement of Science. Michael Ruse is a gnostic philosopher.

63 B.S. Sokolov, "The Current Problems of Paleontology and Some Aspects of Its Future," *Paleontological Journal*, vol. 9, no. 2 (1975): p. 137.

64 George J. Stein, "Biological Science and the Roots of Nazism," *American Scientist*, vol. 76 (January/February 1988): p. 52.

65 Charles Thaxton, Walter Bradley, and Roger Olsen, *The Mystery of Life's Origin: Reassessing Current Theories* (New York, NY: Philosophical Library, 1984), foreword by Dean Kenyon.

66 Harold Urey, *Christian Science Monitor*, January 4, 1962. Harold Urey is a Nobel Prize laureate.

67 D.M.S. Watson, "Adaptation," *Nature*, 124:233 (1929). Professor D.M.S. Watson was one of the leading biologists and science writers of his day.

68 Robert M. Young, "The Darwin Debate," *Marxism Today* (theoretical and discussion journal of the Communist Party, London), vol. 26 (April 1982): p. 21.

69 Arthur Koestler, *Janus: A Summing Up* (New York, NY: Vintage Books, 1978), p. 185.

70 Isaac Asimov, letter from the president, American Humanist Association, January 1986, p. 2.

71 Isaac Asimov, fund appeal letter for ACLU, March 1982, p. 1.

72 Isaac Asimov, fund raising letter for AHA, March 1988, p. 2.

73 G. Richard Bozarth, "The Meaning of Evolution," *American Atheist* (February 1978): p. 19.

74 Ibid.

75 Ibid.

76 Bette Chambers (president, ASA), Isaac Asimov, Hudson Hoagland, Chauncey D. Leake, Linus Pauling, and George Gaylord Simpson (sponsoring committee), "A Statement Affirming Evolution as a Principle of Science," *The Humanist*, vol. 37, no. 1 (January/February 1977): p. 4–6. (Signed by 163 others — Rogers, Skinner, LaMont, Tax, Cloud, Commoner, Mayr, etc.).

77 Preston Cloud, "Scientific Creationism — A New Inquisition Brewing?" *The Humanist*, vol. 37, no. 1 (January/February 1977): p. 6.

78 Ibid., p. 7.

79 John J. Dunphy, "A Religion for a New Age," *The Humanist*, vol. 43 (January/February 1983): p. 26.

80 Daniel Gasmann, *The Scientific Origins of National Socialism: Social Darwinism in Ernst Haeckel and the German Monist League* (New York, NY: American Elsevier, 1971), p. 168.

81 Stephen Jay Gould, "Nonoverlapping Magisteria," *Natural History*, vol. 106 (March 1997): p. 60.

82 Ibid., p. 61.
83 Dorsey Hager, "Fifty Years of Progress in Geology," *Geotimes*, vol. 1 (August 1957): p. 12–13.
84 Delos B. McKown, "Close Encounters of an Ominous Kind: Science and Religion in Contemporary America," *The Humanist*, vol. 39 (January/February 1979): p. 4. Dr. McKown was head of the philosophy department, Auburn University.
85 Delos B. McKown and Clifton B. Perry, "Religion Separation and Accommodation," *National Forum: Phi Kappa Phi Journal*, vol. 68 (Winter 1988): p. 6. McKown and Perry are professors of philosophy, Auburn University.
86 Ibid.
87 Ibid.
88 Ibid., p. 7.
89 National Academy of Science, *Teaching About Evolution and the Nature of Science* (Washington, DC: National Academy Press, 1998), p. 129.
90 National Association of Biology Teachers, "Statement on Teaching Evolution," (policy adopted by NABT board on March 15, 1995), p. 1.
91 Ibid., p. 2.
92 Ibid., p. 3.
93 John Patterson, "Do Scientists and Educators Discriminate Unfairly against Creationists?" *Journal of the National Center for Science Education* (Fall 1984): p. 19.
94 Jeremy Rifkin, *Algeny* (New York, NY: Viking Press, 1983), p. 89.
95 Michael Ruse, "The Long March of Darwin," *New Scientist*, vol. 103 (August 16, 1984): p. 35, review of *China and Charles Darwin* by James R. Pusey (Cambridge, MA: Harvard University Press, 1983).
96 Alfred Russel Wallace, *The Wonderful Century: Its Successes and Its Failures* (New York, NY: Dodd, Mead: 1898), p. 362.
97 Conway Zirkle, *Evolution, Marxian Biology and the Social Scene* (Philadelphia, PA: University of Pennsylvania Press, 1959), p. 85–86.
98 Stephen T. Asma, "The New Social Darwinism: Deserving Your Destitution," *The Humanist*, vol. 53 (September/October 1993): p. 11.
99 Jacques Barzun, *Darwin, Marx, Wagner* (Garden City, NY: Doubleday, 1958), p. 8. Barzun was dean of the graduate faculties at Columbia University and a prominent contemporary historian.
100 Ibid., p. 170.
101 Jerry Bergman, "Eugenics and the Development of Nazi Race Policy," *Perspectives on Science and Christian Faith*, vol. 44 (June 1992): p. 109. Bergman is a professor of science at Northwest Technical College in Archbold, Ohio. He holds two doctorates, in psychology and biology.
102 Barbara Burke, "Infanticide," *Science–84* (May 1984): p. 29.
103 John C. Burnham, "A Discarded Consensus," *Science*, vol. 175 (February 4, 1972): p. 506, review of *Outcasts from Evolution: Scientific Attitudes of Racial Inferiority, 1859–1900* by John S. Haller Jr. (Urbana, IL: University of Illinois Press, 1971).
104 Robert E.D. Clark, *Darwin: Before and After* (London: Paternoster Press, 1948), p. 115.
105 Lorraine Lee Larison Cudmore, "The Center of Life," *Science Digest*, vol. 82 (November 1977): p. 46.
106 Gertrude Himmelfarb, *Darwin and the Darwinian Revolution* (London: Chatto & Windus, 1959), p. 343, quoting Charles Darwin, *Life and Letters of Charles Darwin*, 1, letter to W. Graham, July 3, 1881 (New York, NY: D. Appleton and Co., 1891), p. 316.
107 Charles Darwin, *The Descent of Man* (New York, NY: D. Appleton, 1897), p. 241–242.

108 Ibid., p. 586.

109 Ibid., p. 588.

110 Richard Dawkins, "Evolution: The Dissent of Darwin," *Psychology Today* (January/ February 1997): p. 62. A conversation between Jaron Lanier, a computer scientist, and Richard Dawkins, an evolutionist and professor at Oxford.

111 David Demick, *IMPACT No. 325*, Institute for Creation Research. David Demick is a medical pathologist.

112 Theodosius Dobzhansky, "Evolution at Work," *Science* (May 9, 1958): p. 1091.

113 Joel Gurin, "The Creationist Revival," *The Sciences,* New York Academy of Science, vol. 23 (April 1981): p. 34.

114 Gertrude Himmelfarb, *Darwin and the Darwinian Revolution* (London: Chatto & Windus, 1959), p. 343–344.

115 Peter Hoffman, *Hitler's Personal Security* (London: Macmillan Press, 1979), p. 264.

116 Richard Hofstadter, *Social Darwinism in American Thought* (New York, NY: George Braziller, Inc., 1959), p. 115.

117 J. Horgan, "The New Social Darwinists," *Scientific American*, 273(4) (October 1995): p. 151.

118 Kenneth Hsü, "Is Darwinism Science?" *Earthwatch* (March 1989): p. 15. Hsü is chairman, department of earth sciences, Swiss Federal Institute of Technology.

119 Ibid., p. 17.

120 Paul Kildare, "Monkey Business," *Christian Order*, vol. 23 (December 1982): p. 591. This is a British Roman Catholic periodical.

121 Ibid., p. 592.

122 Ibid., p. 594.

123 Ernst Mayr, "Darwin and Natural Selection," *American Scientist*, vol. 65 (May/June, 1977): p. 323.

124 Ibid., p. 327.

125 Otto Scott, "Playing God," *Chalcedon Report*, no. 247, February 1986, p. 1.

126 Ibid.

127 American Humanist Association, "Humanist Manifesto II," *The Humanist*, vol. 33 (September/October 1973): p. 4.

128 Ibid., p. 5.

129 Ibid., p. 6.

130 "A Scientist's Thoughts on Religion." *New Scientist*, vol. 104 (December 20/27, 1984): p. 75, quoting Charles Darwin, "Autobiography," reprinted in *The Voyage of Charles Darwin*, edited by Christopher Ralling (London: BBC, 1978).

131 Ibid.

132 Michael Denton, *Evolution: A Theory in Crisis* (London: Burnett Books, Ltd., 1985), p. 66.

133 Stephen Jay Gould, "Modified Grandeur," *Natural History*, vol. 102 (March 1993): p. 20.

134 Julian Huxley, *Issues Evolution*, edited by Sol Tax (Chicago, IL: University of Chicago Press, 1960), p. 45. Sir Julian Huxley, in his keynote address at the 1959 Darwinian Centennial.

135 Julian Huxley, Quoted in American Humanist Association brochure.

136 Corliss Lamont, "Humanism and Civil Liberties," *The Humanist*, vol. 51 (January/ February 1991): p. 5. Lamont is former professor of philosophy, Columbia University. He was also named "Humanist of the Year" in 1977.

137 Ronald Reagan, address at National Prayer Breakfast, 1982.

138 Michael Ruse, "A Few Last Words — Until the Next Time," *Zygon*, vol. 29 (March 1994): p. 78. Ruse is professor of philosophy and zoology, University of Guelph, Guelph, Ontario, Canada.

139 Ibid., p. 79.

140 Eugenie C. Scott, "Monkey Business," *The Sciences* (January/February 1996): p. 20. Scott is executive director of the National Center for Science Education, Berkeley, California, and received her Ph.D. in anthropology from Missouri University in 1974.

141 Ibid., p. 25.

142 Huston Smith, "Evolution and Evolutionism," *The Christian Century*, vol. 99 (July 7–14, 1982): p. 755. Smith was professor of religion, Syracuse University.

143 Leroy S. Rouner, editor, *On Nature*, Vol. 6, *Boston University Studies in Philosophy and Religion,* "Two Evolutions" by Huston Smith (Notre Dame, IN: University of Notre Dame Press, 1984), p. 48.

144 Frank R. Zindler, "Religion, Hypnosis and Music: An Evolutionary Perspective," *American Atheist*, vol. 26 (October 1984): p. 24. Zindler is former chairman, division of science, nursing, and technology, Fulton-Montgomery College, SUNY.

145 Associated Press/National Broadcasting Corporation.

146 C. Loring Brace, *American Scientist*, vol. 82 (September/October 1994): p. 484, review of *Species, Species Concepts, and Primate Evolution*, edited by William H. Kimbel and Lawrence B. Martin (New York, NY: Plenum Press, 1993).

147 J.W.G. Johnson, *Evolution?* (Los Angeles, CA: Perpetual Eucharistic Adoration, 1986), p. 3, quoting Albert Fleishman. Albert Fleishman is a professor of zoology and comparative anatomy at Erlangen University, Germany.

148 Kenneth J. Hsü, "Darwin's Three Mistakes," *Geology*, vol. 14 (1986): p. 534. Hsü is a well-known geologist at the Geological Institute in Zurich.

149 Kenneth J. Hsü, reply to comment on "Darwin's Three Mistakes," *Geology*, vol. 15 (April 1987): p. 377.

150 George Sim Johnston, "The Genesis Controversy," *Crisis*, May 1989, p. 14. Johnston is a Catholic writer.

151 Ronald Numbers, *The Creationists* (New York, NY: Adolph Knopf Co., 1992), quoting a private letter from C.S. Lewis to B. Acworth (1951), father of Richard Acworth, of the creation science movement.

152 Søren Løvtrup, *Darwinism: The Refutation of a Myth* (New York, NY: Croom Helm, 1987), p. 422.

153 Malcolm Muggeridge, *The End of Christendom* (Grand Rapids, MI: Eerdmans, 1980), p. 59. Malcolm Muggeridge is a world-famous journalist and philosopher.

154 Colin Patterson, "Evolution and Creationism," speech at American Museum of Natural History, transcript, New York, November 5, 1981, p. 2.

155 Alfred Rehwinkel, *The Wonders of Creation* (Minneapolis, MN: Bethany Fellowship, 1974), p. 31.

156 *Treasury of the Bible, New Testament*, Vol. 1 (Grand Rapids, MI: Zondervan, 1968), p. 498, quoting Charles Haddon Spurgeon.

157 N.J. Mitchell, *Evolution and the Emperor's New Clothes* (UK: Roydon Publications, 1982), title page, quoting T.N. Tahmisian in the *Fresno Bee*, August 10,1959. Dr. T.N. Tahmisian represents the United States Atomic Energy Commission.

Chapter 14

1 J.P. Zetterberg, editor, *Evolution Versus Creationism: The Public Education Controversy* (Pheonix, AZ: Oryx Press, 1983), p. 91, quoting R.D. Alexander. R.D. Alexander is professor of zoology (and an evolutionist himself) at the University of Michigan.

2 Anonymous, "One Fifth of All Scientists Reject Evolution," *Bible Science Newsletter* (June 1988): p. 17.

3 Jim Baggott, "The Myth of Michael Faraday," *New Scientist*, vol. 131 (September 21, 1991): p. 44–45.

4 Ibid., p. 46.

5 Michael Denton, *Evolution: A Theory in Crisis* (London: Burnett Books, Ltd., 1985), p. 100.

6 Niles Eldredge *Time Frames: The Rethinking of Darwinian Evolution and the Theory of Punctuated Equilibria* (New York, NY: Simon and Schuster, 1985), p. 29.

7 Douglas J. Futuyma, *Science on Trial* (New York, NY: Pantheon Books, 1983), p. 197.

8 Carl P. Haskins, "Advances and Challenges in Science in 1970," *American Scientist*, vol. 59 (May/June 1971): p. 298.

9 Sir Fred Hoyle and Chandra Wickramasinghe, "Convergence to God," *Evolution from Space* (London: J.M. Dent & Sons, Ltd, 1981), p. 141 and 144. The late Sir Fred Hoyle was a professor of astronomy at Cambridge University, and Chandra Wickramasinghe is a professor of astronomy and applied mathematics at University College in Cardiff.

10 D.H. Kenyon, "The Creationist View of Biological Origins," *NEX4 Journal* (Spring 1984): p. 33. Dean H. Kenyon is professor of biology at San Francisco State University.

11 H.S. Lipson, "A Physicist Looks at Evolution," *Physics Bulletin*, vol. 31 (1980): p. 138. H.S. Lipson is professor of physics at the University of Manchester, UK.

12 H.S. Lipson, "A Physicist's View of Darwin's Theory," *Evolutionary Trends in Plants*, vol. 2, no. 1 (1988): p. 6.

13 John Polkinghorne, "Religion's Private Hold on Faraday," *New Scientist*, vol. 130 (June 1, 1991): p. 46, review of *Michael Faraday: Sandemanian and Scientist*, by Geoffrey Cantor (New York, NY: Macmillan, 1991).

14 Ibid.

15 Ibid.

16 David M. Raup, "Geology and Creationism," *Bulletin, Field Museum of Natural History*, vol. 54 (March 1983): p. 16.

17 Allan Sandage, "A Scientist Reflects on Religious Belief," *Truth*, vol. 1 (1985): p. 54.

18 Margaret Werthelm, "God in the Lab," *New Scientist* (December 23/30, 1995): p. 41.

19 Jerry E. Bishop, "New Theories of Creation," *Science Digest*, vol. 72 (October 1972): p. 41.

20 Bruce Brower, "Talking Back in Time" *Science News*, vol. 145 (June 11, 1994): p. 376.

21 Arthur Compton. Dr. Arthur Compton is a winner of the Nobel Prize in physics.

22 R.G. Kazmann, "It's About Time: 4.5 Billion Years," report on symposium at Louisiana State University, *Geotimes*, vol. 23 (September 1978): p. 18, quoting John Eddy. Dr. John A. Eddy is an astrophysicist at the Harvard-Smithsonian High Altitude Observatory in Boulder, Colorado.

23 Gallup Poll, "44% Believe God Created Mankind 10,000 Years Ago," *San Diego Union Tribune*, August 30, 1982, p. A-12, *New York Times* Service, p. A-12.

24 Ibid.

25 Ibid.

26 Nelson Glueck, *Rivers in the Desert* (New York, NY: Farrar, Straus and Cudahy, 1968), p. 31. Glueck was president of Hebrew Union College, Jewish Institute of Religion.

27 Stephen Jay Gould, "Fall in the House of Ussher," *Natural History*, vol. 100 (November 1991): p. 16.
    The James Barr article is "Why the World was Created in 4004 B.C.: Archbishop Ussher and Biblical Chronology," Bulletin, John Rylands University Library of Manchester, vol. 67, p. 575–608).

28 Robert Jastrow, *God and the Astronomer* (New York, NY: W.W. Norton, 1978), p. 15. Dr. Robert Jastrow is director of the Goddard Institute for Space Research at NASA.

29 William J.J. Glashouwer and Paul S. Taylor, "The Earth, a Young Planet," a film produced by Eden Communications, Gilbert, AZ, 1983, quoting Harold S. Slusher. Dr. Harold Slusher, an astrophysicist and geophysicist.

30 Victor F. Weisskopf, "The Origin of the Universe," *American Scientist*, vol. 71 (September/October 1983): p. 480. Weisskopf is professor emeritus and former head, physics, MIT.

31 Margaret Werthelm, "God in the Lab," *New Scientist* (December 23/30, 1995): p. 40.

32 James Barr, in a letter to David Watson, 1984. Barr is a professor of Hebrew Bible, Vanderbilt University, and former Regius professor of Hebrew, Oxford University, Oxford, England.

33 Earl D. Radmacher and Robert D. Preuss, editors, *Hermeneutics, Inerrancy and the Bible*, "The Trustworthiness of Scripture in Areas Relating to Natural Science," by Walter L. Bradley and Roger Olsen (Grand Rapids, MI: Zondervan Publishing House, 1984), p. 299.

34 L.R. Croft, *How Life Began* (Durham, England: Evangelical Press, 1988), p. 20–21. Croft was a lecturer in biological "sciences," University of Salford.

35 Michael Denton, *Evolution: A Theory in Crisis* (London: Burnett Books, 1985), p. 66.

36 Richard J. Goss, "Biology of the Soul," *The Humanist*, vol. 54 (November/December 1994): p. 23. Goss is professor emeritus of biology, Brown University.

37 Stephen Jay Gould, "Nonoverlapping Magisteria," *Natural History*, vol. 106 (March 1997): p. 18.

38 Ibid.

39 David L. Hull, "The God of the Galápagos," *Nature*, vol. 352 (August 8, 1991): p. 486, review of *Darwin on Trial* by Philip Johnson (Washington, DC: Regnery Gateway, 1991). Hull is in the department of philosophy, Northwestern University.

40 Sir Arthur Keith, *Evolution and Ethics* (New York, NY: G.P. Putnam's Sons, 1947), p. 15.

41 Jacques Monod, "The Secret of Life," interview with Laurie John, Australian Broadcasting Co., June 10, 1976. (Shortly before his death).

42 Henry M. Morris, *Scientific Creationism* (Green Forest, AR: Master Books, Inc., 1974), p. 223–224.

43 Matthew H. Nitecki, editor, *Evolutionary Progress*, "Progress in Evolution and Meaning in Life" by William B. Provine (Chicago, IL: University of Chicago Press, 1988), p. 70.

44 William B. Provine, "Scientists, Face It! Science and Religion are Incompatible," *The Scientist* (September 5, 1988): p. 10.

45 Ibid.

46 William B. Provine, *Academe*, vol. 73 (January/February 1987): p. 51–52, review of *Trial and Error: The American Controversy over Creation and Evolution* by Edward J. Larson (New York, NY: Oxford University Press, 1985). Provine was professor of history of biology, Cornell University.

47 James Rachels, *Created from Animals* (New York, NY: Oxford University Press, 1990), p. 125. Rachels is professor of philosophy, University of Alabama.

48 Gerrit J. van der Lingen, "Creationism," letter to the editor, *Geotimes*, vol. 29 (October 1984): p. 4. Van der Lingen is with the New Zealand Geological Survey, University of Canterbury, Christchurch.

49 Arthur F. Williams, *Creation Research Annual* (Ann Arbor, MI: Creation Research Society, 1965), p. 10.

50 Matt Cartmill, David R. Pilbeam, and Glynn Isaac, "One Hundred Years of Paleoanthropology," *American Scientist*, vol. 74 (July/August 1986): p. 418.

51 John Gliedman, "Scientists in Search of the Soul," *Science Digest*, vol. 90 (July 1982): p. 77.

52 Ibid.

53 Sir Arthur Keith, *Evolution and Ethics* (New York, NY: G.P. Putnam's Sons, 1947), p. 72.

54 John Lenczowski, "The Treason of the Intellectuals: Higher Education, the Culture War and the Threat to U.S. National Security," *Policy Counsel* (Fall 1996): p. 45. Lenczowski is former Director of European and Soviet Affairs, National Security Council, 1983–1987.

55 Robert R. Reilly, "Atheism and Arms Control: How Spiritual Pathology Afflicts Public Policy," *Intercollegiate Review*, vol. 24 (Fall 1988): p. 18.

56 Edward Simon, "Another Side to the Evolution Problem," *Jewish Press* (January 7, 1983): p. 24B. Simon is professor of biology, Purdue University.

57 Joseph Sobran, "The Averted Gaze, Liberalism and Fetal Pain," *Human Life Review* (Spring 1984): p. 6.

58 Ibid., p. 10.

59 Michael Bauman, *Roundtable: Conversations with European Theologies* (Grand Rapids, MI: Baker Book House, 1990), p. 115, from an interview with Thomas Torrance.

60 Paul Eidelberg, "Karl Marx and the Declaration of Independence: the Meaning of Marxism," *Intercollegiate Review*, vol. 20 (Spring/Summer 1984): p. 4. Eidelberg was professor of political science, Bar Ilan University, Ramat-Gan, Israel.

61 Ibid., p. 5.

62 Ibid.

63 Peter Damian Fehlner, "In the Beginning: The Church's Teaching on the Origin of Man," *Christ to the World*, vol. 33 (May/August 1988): p. 247. The author is a Conventional Franciscan and has a doctorate in sacred theology at the Seraphicum in Rome (Pontifical Theological Faculty of St. Bonaventure). These articles all carry the "Imprimatur" of the Catholic Church.

64 Ibid.

65 David Needham, *Birthright: Christian, Do You Know Who You Are?* (Portland, OR: Multnomah Press, 1979), p. 25.

66 Robert R. Reilly, "Atheism and Arms Control," *Intercollegiate Review*, vol. 24 (Fall 1988): p. 19. Reilly is president of Inter-Collegiate Studies Institute.

67 Dr. Elias Boudinot, Independence Day Address on July 4, 1783, New Jersey Society of the Cincinnati. Boudinot was president of the Continental Congress in 1783 and first president of the American Bible Society.

68 *The Writings of Benjamin Franklin*, Vol. 10 (New York, NY: Macmillan Co., 1907), p. 84.

69 Earle Holland, "Creation 'Science': A Survey of Student Attitudes," *Ohio State University Quest*, vol. 7 (Spring 1985): p. 16.

70 Ibid.

71 Thomas Jefferson, miscellaneous writings as inscribed on the walls of Jefferson Memorial, Washington, D.C.

72 Sir Arthur Keith, *Evolution and Ethics* (New York, NY: Putnam, 1947), p. 15.

73 Cited by Dr. Ronald Numbers in his book, *The Creationists* (New York, NY: Adolph Knopf Co., 1991), p. 153, quoting a private letter (1951) from C.S. Lewis to Captain Bernard Acworth, one of the founders of the Evolution Protest Movement (England).

74 A.J. Mattill Jr., "Three Cheers for the Creationists," *Free Inquiry*, vol. 2 (Spring 1982): p. 17.

75 Ibid.

76 Ibid.

77 Ibid.

78 Ibid., p. 18.

79 Ibid.

80 Gilman Ostrander, *The Evolutionary Outlook, 1875-1900* (Clio, MI: Marston Press, 1971), p. 1.

81 Ronald Reagan, address at National Prayer Breakfast, 1982.

82 *Treasury of the Bible, New Testament,* Vol. 1 (Grand Rapids, MI: Zondervan, 1968), p. 498, quoting Charles Haddon Spurgeon.

83 John F. Schroeder, editor, *Maxims of Washington* (Mt. Vernon, VA: Mt. Vernon Ladies Association, 1942), p. 275, quoting George Washington.

ABOUT THE AUTHOR

Dr. Nicholas Comninellis teaches public health and family medicine at the University of Missouri-Kansas City and Trinity Lutheran Hospital.

He has authored two other books, *Shanghai Doctor* and *Where Do I Go to Get a Life?* and co-authored *Darwin's Demise* with Joe White of Kanakuk Kamps in Branson, Missouri. Nicholas' credits include numerous medical publications in the journals *Family Medicine* and *Tropical Doctor*, among others. He is especially passionate about outreach to neglected people, and spent several years working in Africa and China. Nicholas' home base is in Liberty, Missouri, where he is part of Shoal Creek Community Church. For more information or to contact the author please go to http://www.creativeenergy.org